Orphan Boys

PHIL MEWS

Orphan Boys

It takes a village to raise a child

JOHN BLAKE

Published by John Blake Publishing,
2.25, The Plaza,
535 Kings Road,
Chelsea Harbour
London, SW10 0SZ

www.johnblakebooks.com

www.facebook.com/johnblakebooks f
twitter.com/jblakebooks t

First published in 2017
This edition published in 2018

ISBN: 978 1 78606 899 6

British Library Cataloguing-in-Publication Data:

A catalogue record for this book is available from the British Library.

Design by www.envydesign.co.uk

Printed and bound in Great Britain by Clays Ltd, Elcograf S.p.A.

1 3 5 7 9 10 8 6 4 2

Papers used by John Blake Publishing are natural, recyclable products made from
wood grown in sustainable forests. The manufacturing processes conform to the
environmental regulations of the country of origin.

Every attempt has been made to contact the relevant copyright-holders,
but some were unobtainable. We would be grateful if the appropriate
people could contact us.

John Blake Publishing is an imprint of Bonnier Publishing
www.bonnierpublishing.com

For Roger.
Also for our parents, Harry and Alma Mews
and our grandparents, Harry and Margaret Close.
Together they shine bright amongst the stars.

AUTHOR NOTE
I have written our story using a large proportion of my own memory and topped up with anecdotes and information from people who were there at the time. Some people's names have been changed.

'The day we fret about the future
is the day we leave our childhood behind.'
PATRICK ROTHFUSS

Contents

1. The First Hour   1
2. Farmer's Sons   5
3. The Caravanners   15
4. Weekends   23
5. Showtime   33
6. Red, White & Blue   43
7. Dark Days   57
8. Staring Death in the Face   63
9. Tea & Sympathy   71
10. Smiling in the Face of Adversity   79
11. Storm Clouds Looming   85
12. Darker Days   91
13. Jam Tarts & Buckaroo!   97
14. Knights in Shining Armour   105

15. Scrapbooks & Stories 113
16. Short Trousers 121
17. Twenty-One Brothers 139
18. School Life 147
19. Grease is the Word 165
20. Winter Marches On 169
21. TV Stars 187
22. Cemetery Photo Shoot 199
23. Croquet & Gooseberries 207
24. Buckets & Spades 217
25. Dumpling 223
26. Getting a Good Look 231
27. Big Mews, Little Mews 241
28. A Terrapin & A Pickled Snake 251
29. A New Normal 257
30. Always On Edge 263
31. Ending on the Right Foot 273
32. Boarding School Antics 283
33. Running Away 291
34. Comfort Food 299
35. The Strength of a Woman 309
36. Not Suitable for Younger Viewers 321
37. A Fresh Start 329
Epilogue 333
Acknowledgements 337
Author Note 341

CHAPTER I

The First Hour

1978

It was thirty minutes since they had broken the news to us.

The gold photo frame looked the same as it had done the last two months since it was placed on top of the piano by Mam in the weeks after Dad's death. It was a picture of the two of them taken at a wedding in Scotland only weeks before my father died and it was the last ever photo taken of him.

Their faces looked different, hers more so than his. I had started to get used to not seeing him but now she too was gone from our lives and I would have to go through all this again. Their faces didn't look as clear, almost blurred, and as I paced backwards and forwards past the picture, I was aware of their eyes following me. They continued to smile, yet I could not; I could not smile today of all days. Despite there only being one person next to me at that moment, I felt that there were still four of us in the room. The small boy standing beside me said nothing. He sniffed and I turned to him. I looked down towards his face, tears trickling from his heartbroken eyes on to his red cheeks. He sniffed again in an attempt to stop his nose from running and tilted his head up to me, giving me a look that asked, 'What should we do now?' Of course, he expected me to have the answers for him, me being his big brother. The truth was, I didn't know.

All I knew was that I needed to stay firmly in the present. At that moment the past was far too painful to think about and the future incomprehensible. I put my arm around him briefly, aware that it would bring him little comfort but knowing it was better than doing nothing.

I looked back up to the top of the piano; they were still smiling.

I walked across to the window and pulled back the net curtain. I craned my neck to see if they might walk up the front path and that this was still some awful mistake. Nobody was there. I screwed my eyes tightly shut in the same way that I did when I needed to escape a bad dream. It never failed to work. Any second now I would wake up in my bed, they would be back and this pain would all go away. I could still hear the occasional sniff, so I hung on a little longer. Eventually, I took a leap of faith and opened my eyes. I was still standing in the same spot. My brother was still there looking at me, sniffing back his tears.

Up on the piano, they were still smiling.

I was aware that there were others in the house at that moment as I picked up on the voices outside the door, some of them barely audible as they spoke in hushed whispers. The phone rang and it was quickly answered. I didn't know what to do. I could open the door and expose the two of us to the adult world or we could stay here, with the door firmly closed, safe in our sanctuary.

2

Poor little Roger. He was now sitting on the sofa. I walked over and sat down next to him. Neither of us said anything as we both stared at them on top of the piano.

They were still smiling.

He buried his face in my jumper. His sniffs had now transformed into sobs. Silent sobbing, his sadness on a scale so immense no sound came from his mouth. His eyes screwed up, now spewing a river of tears as he gently shook. I found the silence of his sobbing deafening. There we were, just the two of us. He was the only one who understood at that point in time exactly how I felt and as the realisation dawned on me, I began to share his pain. My eyes gave way and the tears came with such a force that I found myself short of breath. My body was so desperate to let the grief out that once I started, I feared it might never stop.

I didn't see Grandad open the door and walk over towards us. I could smell his pipe tobacco, though. 'Warhorse' they called it. Mam used to buy it for him as a present from Mr Renwick's shop in the village. I'm sure he had every intention of uttering some words of comfort, but they did not come. Instead, he too was engulfed by sadness. Now the three of us were crying. After a while I slowly sat up, wiped my face and looked over at the piano.

They were still smiling; they were the only ones who were.

A sympathetic voice approached the room. It was Hilda, Mam's friend.

'Them poor bairns, it's heartbreaking,' she said as she wiped a tear from her face with her duster. 'Poor little orphans.'

For a second I wondered who she was talking about and then it hit me. *Orphans? We were orphans.* I felt as if I'd been punched. I repeated the word to myself.

'Orphans…' I mouthed the word silently.

More people came into the room and suddenly all eyes were upon us. Caring eyes of concern, yet none of them knowing quite what to say or do. All I could do was repeat the word quietly to myself.

'Orphans.'

I looked at all the older sad eyes gazing sympathetically at me and my little brother. Then I looked at the other two up on the piano.

They were still smiling.

I had never felt so much love as at that moment, yet as I repeated that word, 'Orphans,' I'd never felt more alone.

CHAPTER 2

Farmer's Sons

1976

Needless to say, we weren't always orphans.

Wind the clock back several years and life was perfect. My family was perfect. To me, the whole world was perfect. I lived in a big old house that sat on the edge of our farm on the outskirts of Stanhope, Weardale's largest village, which was technically a small market town. Nestling in the heart of County Durham in the north of England, it was here that I lived with the most loving parents and my two brothers. Richard, my sixteen-year-old brother, took after Mam with shoulder-length blond hair that made him popular with the girls. Roger, who was almost four, had short blond hair and loved playing with the animals on the farm. He also doted on me and followed me everywhere.

As for myself, at the age of six I was a slim boy with fair skin, freckles and hair that Mam always insisted on describing as auburn. The rest of the kids in my class at school called

5

it ginger. I was the odd one out of the three brothers in that respect. With ginger hair comes a sensitivity to the sun, and so lashings of sun cream were a regular fixture upon my arms and legs throughout that long, hot summer. Rather unfortunately, I was also prone to squinting in photographs against the bright sunshine.

If I were to pinpoint the most perfect time in my childhood, it would have to be the long, hot, sweltering summer of 1976, with its blistering heat and hosepipe bans, which seemed to go on forever. At Stanhope Hall Farm, I shared a small room with Roger that contained what Mam always referred to as a 'three-quarter bed', along with a pile of books and toys. There was one poster on the wall, The Six Million Dollar Man, or as we called him, 'The Bionic Man'. Now that Roger was out of his baby bed, I had to share mine with him, something I wasn't happy about. I liked the covers pulled tightly over me, whereas he was accustomed to kicking them onto the floor. This was how I woke up every morning, lying on the bed, shivering with the top sheet and a copious amount of blankets strewn across the thick blue carpet, the bedroom door wide open exactly as Roger had left it when he woke up and ran along the passage to jump into bed with Mam and Dad. Not wanting to be left out, I too would run along to our parents' bedroom and climb into their bed, firmly inserting myself in the middle and shoving my little brother along to make room for me. As the four of us lay there, crammed in, Mam used to sing, 'There were four in the bed and the little one said, "Roll over"', and as we went through each verse, giggling, even Dad joined in.

At breakfast, Mam would tell me not to wolf down my Frosties and to take my time. I only chose Frosties because I was saving enough tokens from the back of the packets to send away for a pack of Tony the Tiger playing cards, as I'd already collected enough for some Tony the Tiger pyjamas earlier in the year. With breakfast done, I always ran out of the back door of the house into the farmyard. I was six years old and I ran everywhere. Why walk? That was what old people did. Up the farmyard I went. I ran past the hens, as I was really quite scared of them and was subsequently ridiculed for this fear. My heart was racing and when I reached the end of the farmyard, I stopped dead in my tracks. Standing in front of me was the only thing that scared me more than the hens: the peacock. There I was, in my little blue shorts and racing car T-shirt, shaking and petrified of this bird that everyone else seemed to find so beautiful. If there was enough room, I would take a deep breath and run past it up the track that led to the road. If it was blocking my path and had its tail up in a spectacular fan, I beat a hasty retreat to the house. There were times when the peacock shed a tail feather and I picked it up and ran down to the house clutching it in my hand, waving it in the air above me. Mam wouldn't allow peacock feathers in the house and used to make us take them over to the coal house, where she would store them. At some point, she passed them on to friends, who used them for their flower displays, but she never dreamed of allowing one to pass her door as she firmly believed that they brought bad luck.

My fear of birds, in particular the peacocks, wasn't as irrational as it seemed at the time. As I grew older, I was told by Grandma how one sunny morning when I was about three months old, Mam put me in the pram and left me just outside the back door, pulling over the white cotton canopy to protect me from the sun. After ten minutes, she heard my screams and rushed from the kitchen only to see the peacock up on top of the pram and pulling at my clothes with its sharp beak. In the pecking frenzy it had apparently flipped me over onto my front. Grabbing the broom in her hand, Mam soon sent that peacock packing before lifting me out of the pram. Thankfully, there was no real damage done and I have no recollection of the event but, suffice to say, I'm still petrified of peacocks to this day.

We had quite a lot of hens on the farm and many of them were kept in the hen house, which was the rickety old attic room above the pig sty. Every day, Roger and I had to climb up into the hen house to collect eggs for Mam. Braver than me, my little brother would pull back the piece of sackcloth which hung over the front of each nest to see if there was anything to collect, while I stood nervously by the door staring at the layers of chicken excrement on the floor, a couple of inches thick. During the summer months, Mam often sold the eggs to people who knocked at the door, but most of the time with her endless baking she found uses for them. Sending the two of us out looking for eggs around the farm kept us out of her hair for a while and taught us both that no matter how young you were, everyone in the family had to do their bit and contribute.

Our farm was of a modest size at less than two hundred acres and Dad ran it with the help of Mam, our elder brother Richard and the one farmhand he could afford to pay. Dad had been born at Stanhope Hall and had lived in that one house all his life. Like generations of the Mews family before him, farming was in his blood.

Dad had a beautiful horse called Robin, a mix of Arab stallion and Fell pony, who was kept in the small stable, which was also home to our two sheepdogs, Rob and Roy. He had bought them as a pair of pups and named them after the Rob Roy stagecoach, which the Mews family used to run up and down the Dale decades earlier. The stable was an old two-storey building in the lower farmyard, where the animals lived downstairs and the hayloft with its precarious rotten floorboards sat above. This meant that anyone attempting to access the loft played a game of roulette in an effort not to fall through the floor. One afternoon, Dad managed to do just that and following lots of loud swearing, he was carried out and duly carted off to hospital, his pride probably more damaged than his collarbone.

Above the door to the stable outside was a horse's head carved in stone, which bore witness as the blacksmith came to change the shoes on Robin every three months. We all watched the master craftsman effortlessly wield his hammer, crashing it down on the anvil. I had been taught to show horses respect and here was this magnificent creature placing its trust in a man who was now gripping its ankle in between his knees as he scraped and gouged away at the hoof with his thick knife. All around me were the adults, my father, grandfather and Uncle Harold, all of whom had witnessed this scene on dozens of occasions in their lifetime but here they were, completely in awe of the blacksmith's skill. I wondered why the horses didn't feel pain as the blacksmith hammered the inch-long nails into their feet, sweat flying off his brow as he held the remaining nails in his mouth, the way my grandma did with her pins when hemming the curtains. Once he was done, the horse would be led around the yard, proudly clipping along like a schoolboy showing off a shiny new pair of shoes.

As a young boy, Dad had been ill with tuberculosis and

had spent almost three months in the isolation hospital on the outskirts of Stanhope. Once he had recovered from the TB, the doctors urged Nana to give him goat's milk rather than cow's, and with that, my grandparents bought two goats. Ever since then, a small number of goats had been kept at Stanhope Hall. They were always getting out of the old stable and munching their way through the variety of bulbs and flowers in Mam's garden, causing her to come running out of the house shouting at them. On other occasions, they managed to escape over the wall onto the Dilly Hill and into our neighbour Mary's garden. We listened to Mary over the wall giving the goats a telling-off as if they were small children, while Roger and I giggled naughtily. We weren't alone, as Dad and Richard also found this hilarious, much to Mary's annoyance but she could never remain cross with them for very long, being such a loyal friend and neighbour.

One day, Mary called round and let herself in through the front door, which we all did with each other's houses back then. She wasn't happy about the new cockerel that Dad had bought the previous week.

'Alma, that cockerel woke us all up this morning with its crowing,' she said. Dad, who was sitting in the chair by the kitchen fire, looked up from his newspaper and sarcastically replied, 'Really, Mary? A cockerel crowing? Early in the morning? Never in this world, and on a farm as well!'

Mam threw him an annoyed look – she didn't like Dad teasing her friend. She would placate Mary with some reassuring words as they sat having a cup of tea together and a catch-up. The cockerel problem was soon forgotten about and Mary didn't mention it again, even though it never stopped crowing to announce the arrival of each new day, the way that cockerels do.

We had one bull on the farm. That was all we needed and like most bulls, it had a temperamental nature. Dad described it as a 'bad-tempered bugger'. As with any farm, there would be incidents of walkers straying from the public footpath and cutting across the field only to find themselves being chased by an angry hulking great brute with a brass ring through its nose. One afternoon, the bull got out of the bottom field and into the adjoining caravan site by bashing through the gate. Roger and I watched from a safe distance while Dad and Richard attempted to coax the stubborn beast back into the field. After a lot of waving and swearing from Dad, the bull eventually went for him and knocked him flying to the ground before running off back to the field. Bruised and battered, Dad managed to get back on his feet while swearing profusely, with Roger and I giggling at his use of words like 'bugger' and 'bastard'. Poor Dad was left hobbling and dusting himself down – the 'bad-tempered bugger' had certainly knocked the stuffing out of him.

Although there were different jobs to be done on the farm depending on the time of year, the morning coffee break always occurred at half past ten with military precision. Dad, Richard, Grandad and Uncle Harold made their way to the back door, removing their wellies before heading in for mugs of hot milky coffee and homemade cake. Coffee break would always present Roger and I with an opportunity to get up to mischief. Once the men were ensconced in the kitchen, we took it upon ourselves to relieve our bladders outside the back door, in Dad's and Richard's wellies. We would never dream of doing it to Grandad or Uncle Harold, who were too old, but Dad and Richard were always fair game and gave us the reaction we desired. Back in the kitchen, the men sipped their coffee and chatted with Mam, completely unaware as to what the two of us were up to. As the last drips were deposited into the chosen wellington boots, Roger and I legged it up to the top of the farmyard to hide round the corner and await the reaction. Even on a cold winter's day, Dad and Richard never seemed to notice the last vapours of steam rising from their wellies as they emerged from the farmhouse. It was only when they had put at least the first of their feet into a boot and put their full weight on it did they discover, what with the moisture now penetrating their thick wellie socks, that Roger and myself had left them a little gift.

'Bloody little buggers!' one of them cried.

'What's happened?' shouted Mam, rushing out the back door to see what all the commotion was about.

'Little bugger's pissed in me bloody wellies!' Dad yelled as Roger and I witnessed the scene from our safe vantage point. It took Mam every effort not to laugh in front of Dad and give the appearance of being annoyed by the prank. I'm sure Richard is still a little hesitant even to this day before he puts on a pair of wellies.

Dad was right: we were two little buggers who always got up to mischief. Most days he would take Roger and I to feed the sheep on the fell high above the village, where he would let me steer the Land Rover as he chucked the hay out of the back. On climbing back in, his nose would tell him that all was not well. Less than ten minutes later the Land Rover screeched to a halt in the farmyard as Dad jumped out, coughing and spluttering.

'Alma, Alma!' he shouted as Mam appeared at the back door.

'Little bugger's shat his nappy!' he said as Roger, who was sitting next to me, grinned out the window, totally unfazed by the smell he had created.

Of course, it was Mam who changed his nappy; it always was. There was one occasion several years before when Dad had attempted to change one, mine to be precise. Mam had gone out to a Young Wives meeting at the Church Hall, leaving me in Dad's care. His good friend Robbie had called round that evening and they were sitting in the kitchen having a whisky when they noticed a smell coming from the playpen in which I was sat. As Robbie lifted me out, he didn't need to hold me anywhere near to his nose to tell him that I was the source of the stench.

'By God, I think he's filled it,' Robbie said as he held me, making sure to keep me at arm's length. 'You're going to have to change him. Alma won't be back for another hour,' he informed my dad.

After a bit of scrabbling around in the bathroom, Dad came downstairs with a clean terry towelling nappy before plonking me on the polished kitchen table. He almost choked as he removed the offending dirty nappy and ran to the back door, throwing it onto the ground in the dark. Back in the kitchen, I was still sitting on the table, looking bewildered. Dad cursed as he realised that in the rush to throw the nappy out, he had left the pins attached to it. Not only that, he had also forgotten to wipe me first, so now I had smeared my mess all over Mam's good polished table.

'I don't know what Alma uses to wipe him,' Dad muttered to Robbie. 'Hold him still,' he told Robbie, while he ran into the pantry, returning with a bucket, a floor cloth and a tin of

Vim, which was a scouring cleaner Mam used for the bath. After wiping me down with the floor cloth, Dad went to apply the Vim before Robbie stopped him.

'You can't use that on his arse, he'll be red raw,' he told Dad, who now went upstairs to the bathroom in search of talc. Lots of clashing about and swearing could be heard as he ransacked the bathroom in search of the Johnson's Baby Powder. Eventually he found it and returned to the kitchen, visibly stressed yet triumphant. With my bottom wiped, and powder applied, the table resembled something from Mam's baking day, when it would be covered in flour. Dad now tried to figure out how the nappy was folded so that I could wear it. All this time, Richard was stood at the kitchen door, laughing silently as he watched these two grown men attempt to put a nappy on a toddler. They tried different methods of nappy origami before settling on something they were happy with. Only then did they remember that they no longer had the safety pins to fix it in place. Dad put on his coat and dashed out the back door up to the stable, returning a couple of minutes later with a length of baling twine.

When Mam returned home a short while later, she found Dad and Robbie sat in their chairs with replenished glasses of whisky, surveying their handiwork. She cast her eyes across to the kitchen table, where I was still sat on top. I had the most dishevelled-looking nappy tied loosely around my waist with a length of baling twine, surrounded by a heavy dusting of baby powder that covered the table, its once polished surface still caked in smeared faeces and talc. The floor cloth was hanging over the sink, not yet rinsed, just as they had left it.

That was the one and only time Dad ever changed the nappy of any of his sons, as Mam made sure never to ask him again.

CHAPTER 3

The Caravanners

There were two small patches of wood on either side of the farmyard, which were used as caravan sites. The introduction of caravans was Mam's brainchild, an idea that she had come up with to supplement the farm's income. Tired of having to ask my dad for money, she took it upon herself to earn her own and the caravan sites were her solution. The caravans were predominantly owned by families from Sunderland, who would make weekly pilgrimages to Stanhope for the weekend. Leaving behind the comforts of home such as electricity, baths and flushing toilets, the 'caravanners', as we called them, would make do with washing their kids in the ceramic sink next to the sheep pens. If they wanted hot showers, they would use the public swimming pool along the road in the village. Despite having to keep their milk cool in the stream or lugging gallons of water to the caravans from the communal tap, they never felt that they were roughing it. They were together, as families, on holiday and that was all that mattered. It didn't take long before Mam and Dad became firm friends with many of them and soon a little community formed against the backdrop of this busy working farm.

Each morning during the school holidays, Roger and I would make a beeline for the small yellow-and-white caravan in the corner of the field, which belonged to Jimmy and Theresa Devitt. Jimmy and Theresa were from Sunderland and had arrived at Stanhope Hall two years previously. Their three daughters, Karen, Julie and Louise, were similar ages to us three boys and we all got on brilliantly together. After only two years, they were like my second family. Since the Devitts would be on their holiday at the caravan, they wouldn't get up until after nine, as Jimmy deserved a lie-in from his regular early mornings at the shipyards. As I knocked on the caravan door, Theresa answered and let Roger and myself in to the cosy living area. Karen and Julie were curled up in their sleeping bags on the sofa seats, while little Louise would be sleeping in a travel cot on the floor between them. The caravan was warm and the smell of the bacon frying in the pan on the gas stove was intoxicating.

Of the many things that our two families had in common, one was our sense of humour and as a family, the Devitts constantly teased each other. Nobody was exempt from their jokes and we were all fair game. There were many afternoons that summer when Theresa and Karen would be sunbathing on the sun loungers next to the caravan. As the sun belted down, the temptation would prove too much for Richard and his friend Terry, resulting in the pair being soaked with ice-cold water from the hosepipe. Not the type to let it go, revenge would be swiftly exacted and the lads were duly chased around the field by Theresa and Karen wielding buckets of water, with us kids running alongside, shrieking with laughter and goading both sides on.

One of Jimmy's party tricks was being a 'hen whisperer'. Sitting on the step of the caravan, he used to coax the hens towards him with cornflakes, before picking one of them up and gently rocking it backwards and forwards. Within a minute, the hen would go limp and he would tuck its head under one of its wings before placing it gently on the warm patio slab, where it laid motionless. He then repeated the trick and before too long, he had five or six hens all sleeping in a row.

'Philip, come and see this,' he would whisper to me, holding a sleeping hen.

As I approached, he threw the hen in my direction, whereupon it squarked and flapped its wings in a panic, sending me running across the field, screaming and everyone else into fits of hysterical laughter.

When they were going out for the day in the car, Jimmy and Theresa always offered to take Roger and I along with them, allowing Mam to carry on with her work. They crammed us kids into the back and took us all over for picnics to Barnard Castle, Kirby Stephen and further afield to Lake Windermere. The days were filled with fun and laughter and even on the journey home as the car rumbled over the cattle grid, us kids would squeal, shouting, 'Who's farted?' at each other in fits of giggles. Sometimes we would get to have sleepovers at the caravan and this would be reciprocated the following night by the girls coming down to the farmhouse to stay.

There were other families that we also became great friends with on the caravan site. John and Betty Pratt were a lovely couple who often took Roger and I out for days with their two daughters, Estelle and Lyndsey, both of whom were obsessed with horses. With his slicked-back hair, their dad, John, was a tall, handsome man and like many of the caravanners, he would head home to Sunderland on the Sunday evening and return the following Friday while Mum, Betty and the girls would stay at the caravan all summer long.

As kids, we spent our days hanging out together, living a carefree life and never once getting bored. We occupied ourselves with running around the farm, playing on the Tarzan swing that my brother Richard had rigged up for us with some old rope and a car tyre, catching tiddlers in the stream with our brightly coloured nets, building dens or playing hide and seek around the barns. One of our favourite things to do was to go to the open-air swimming pool in the village. The mothers, including my own, took it in turns to take all the kids down there, allowing the other mums the chance of some peace and quiet. The whole place was a sun trap and during that summer of 1976, it was heaving from the moment it opened until six o'clock in the evening when the last stragglers would be turfed out. Although I still couldn't swim properly back then, I was happy to climb into the little pool with my inflatable arm bands and splash about. At the end of our afternoon-long swimming session, when we were starting to get tired, we would buy hot Bovril from the refreshment counter and sip it from a polystyrene cup while dunking a cream cracker into the hot, steaming liquid. Towels would be wrapped around our small wet bodies as the sun went down and the evening beckoned.

If we weren't at the pool, we went for walks up the Dene, a stretch of woodland that ran along both sides of Stanhope

Burn. A winding path took you along for a mile or more, skirting around large tree stumps and over smaller streams, and for a short time each summer part of the wood was covered in bluebells. Often there were at least six or seven kids in our 'gang' and we were generally accompanied by an adult. We picked small posies of flowers that would be taken back to grateful mums and placed in jam jars on the windowsill in the caravan, or in our case, at Mam's kitchen window.

Walking up the path to the Dene, it eventually turned down to a small concrete footbridge that took you across the shallow burn. Next to the bridge was the entrance to an old lead mine tunnel, with a wire mesh grid over the front. I was fascinated by this place. To see the remnants of the old train tracks emerging from the small tunnel and leading into the river, all rusted and decaying, it evoked a sense of a different life that had once been led here. Mam always told us it was where the fairies lived and it was stories like this that gave the place a magical feel.

Across the bridge and up the steep steps was a single-track tarmac road that was followed for the rest of the walk. Dotted along either side of the road were small entrances to abandoned mines that ran deep into the ground amongst the scarred faces of the quarry walls that provided the backdrop. We scavenged the ground around the mine entrances and heaps, looking for pieces of fluorspar. With their purple and pink crystals embedded into the pieces of rock, we collected small pieces and stuffed them in our pockets to take home. Water had collected at the foot of the small disused quarries and formed marshy ponds, which became the perfect habitat for numerous forms of wildlife, including frogs. I used to love looking for frogs with Roger, Estelle, Lyndsey, Julie and Louise on those sunny afternoons. Running up and down the mounds of earth next to these vast ponds, we scared each other with stories about giants and witches who lived in the abandoned mine tunnels. We freely let ourselves and our imaginations run wild and it was wonderful.

Summer months on the farm were spent 'hay-timing'. For us kids the real fun started when they began to bale the hay. A hay baler was attached to the rear of the tractor and with spokes on the underside, it scooped up the hay from the ground and digested it before pumping out tightly formed rectangular bales from the rear. These were collected in a large metal sledge attached to the back of the baler. Roger and I would stand on the rear gate of the sledge with Terry, who worked for Dad. As the sledge filled with bales of hay, we leapt off the gate and ran to the side as Terry released the handle allowing it to swing open to the side, leaving the bales behind us. The tractor continued without stopping, with Terry running behind and grabbing the gate, swinging it shut as Roger and I followed excitedly behind him, trying as best we could to catch up and jump back on the gate. Panting and giggling, ten minutes later the whole exercise was repeated. It was the stuff of Health and Safety nightmares, but back then we were encouraged to use our common sense. If we didn't get off the back of the gate in time, we soon knew about it as we swung round and fell off onto the prickly stubble of the hay field. Had we cried or complained, we would no longer be allowed to stand on the back of the sledge and the fun would be over.

Grandad's job on the hayfield was to pile up the bales into a large stack or 'stook' as we called them. They had to be stacked in a particular manner in order to fit into the loader which,

when attached to the back of a tractor, was reversed in
and its great metal arms tightly clamped around the ste
Grandad, who was in his late sixties, had no trouble hoisting
the heavy bales onto the top of the stook. With his flat cap
to protect his head from the sun, he brushed the sweat from
his forehead with a hankie and would take a breather after he
had completed each stook. Like Grandma, he was a grafter and
years of working down the coal mines, combined with having
spent most of World War II in Burma and India, had done
nothing to quash his energy and thirst for hard work. This
was his family's livelihood and it put food on the table, so my
grandparents saw it as the responsibility of every member of
the clan to do their bit to help. As the stooks were deposited
in the farmyard with a small gap between each one, a maze
was inadvertently created with a labyrinth of passageways wide
enough for small children to fit through. Once the yard was
full, we were free to run through the passages, chasing each
other and playing hide and seek, again occupying ourselves for
hours on end.

The hay-time tea was an event in itself. At some point after
four o'clock, Mam would be seen driving across the field in
the Land Rover and tractor engines stopped. Dad, Richard,
Grandad and the hay-time helpers made their way towards the
spot selected by Mam, where she had parked up and started
to serve the tea. She had a large basket containing a variety
of sandwiches under a colourful striped tablecloth. Slices of
white bread filled with chopped boiled egg and tomato or
thickly carved ham and mustard were passed around in plastic
Tupperware boxes. Milky tea was poured from the large white
enamel urn with its chipped blue trim, which must have been

used to serve tea in the hay fields for generations before us. Once the sandwiches had been devoured, home-baked scones filled with butter and strawberry jam were handed out, along with coconut rock buns. Mam, like Grandma, was an exceptional baker and she ensured everyone was well-fed.

Although it was already late in the afternoon, the men needed to get back to work while there was still daylight. Weather in the North East, like the rest of the country, could be temperamental and farmers predicted it on a day-by-day basis with an air of caution. Having been out in the hay fields for the entire afternoon, Mam took us kids back to the house with her and so another summer's day on the farm drew to a close. Tired from playing out all day with our wonderful friends from the caravan site, we went to bed safe in the knowledge that we could do it all over again in the morning.

CHAPTER 4

Weekends

Every other weekend, we received a visit from Grandma and Grandad, who would drive up from Brandon in their old Hillman Minx on a Friday teatime to visit their daughter and her family. Grandad helped Dad on the farm doing small jobs and he and Grandma would babysit, allowing our parents to go out for an evening with friends. They brought bags full of goodies such as home-baked apple pies, cakes and my favourite, Grandma's cheese and onion pie. In the pantry, Grandad unpacked gigantic cabbages and cauliflowers wrapped in newspaper from his garden. Fresh home-grown flowers cut and tied together with pieces of old baling twine were handed to Mam, who filled numerous vases around the house. Sometimes Grandma brought new pyjamas or jumpers from Chester-le-Street market for Roger and me. Despite only having a state pension to live on, like most people their age, Grandma and Grandad took great pleasure in bringing these things by way of helping out the family. They were all we had in the way of grandparents, as my dad's mother and father had both died seven years before I was born.

Every Saturday morning, Mam went to the hairdressers in Stanhope (and in later years, Wolsingham). That was her weekly treat and she had more recently adopted the shorter style popular in the seventies, which required a weekly shampoo and set and was topped off with an ozone-busting gallon of hairspray. A self-confessed Mammy's boy back then, I would get upset if I was not allowed to accompany her to the hairdressers every week. Roger, on the other hand, much preferred to stay on the farm and accompany Dad as he tended to the animals. Being allowed to tag along with Mam to the hairdressers of a Saturday was the highlight of my week.

On entering the shop, the eye-watering aroma of perming solution and hairspray hit me and on inhaling for the first time, it caught the back of my throat. Many of the ladies were sitting with a cigarette in one hand and a magazine in the other while cooking their heads under the dryers. With all that lacquer being sprayed around, it's a wonder the shop never went up like the *Hindenburg*. As Mam sat chatting to her friend Valerie, who did her hair, I amused myself by twisting a variety of long, thin rollers into my short hair before sitting under the dryer, with my legs crossed and pretending to smoke a felt-tip pen. I was described as a 'sensitive boy' back then.

At teatime every Saturday, with her hair done, Mam made the tea while the TV was on in the kitchen and we watched the football scores on *World of Sport*. Dickie Davies, silver streak in his hair, read the sports bulletins while half a dozen women sat behind him thrashing away at typewriters and trying not to look at the camera. Listening to the football scores being read out had a hypnotic effect and it was as if the results took on a rhythm of their own. After they had finished there was the wrestling. For those who had never seen it, British wrestling on TV in the seventies was very different from the American-style wrestling that is popular today. Back then, millions of people tuned in every Saturday teatime to watch Big Daddy, Kendo Nagasaki or the enormous Giant Haystacks take on each other in the ring. I was glued to the box each week, watching them throw each other around and jumping from the ropes onto their opponent. Although I was a little scared of Giant Haystacks, it was Kendo Nagasaki who fascinated me. He paraded around the ring dressed as a Japanese Samurai warrior complete with face mask. The illusion was shattered years later when I discovered that beneath the mask he was an Englishman called Peter Thornley. Sometimes it's better never to peek behind the mask, or behind the curtain as Dorothy did, for that matter.

The sport was followed by *The Basil Brush Show* or *Jim'll Fix It* and *Doctor Who*, before the family would gather round to watch Bruce Forsyth's *Generation Game*. Saturday nights back then were the setting for the best light entertainment shows on telly and with only three channels to choose from, families in their millions watched BBC1 or ITV, resulting in audience figures that television executives can only dream of today.

As a child, I hated Sundays. There wasn't an aspect of the Sabbath that I actually liked, except we sometimes had an ice cream that day. Other than that, Sundays were awful and they started with Sunday School. Mam insisted I wore a smart camel coat that she had bought for me to wear to Sunday School every single week. I didn't have to wear it any other day, only on a Sunday, but I thought it made me look like Walter the Softy from *The Beano*. As a result, each Sunday morning I would have a 'to do' with Mam about the coat. The fact that she always got her way didn't deter me from my protests. Roger, on the other hand, never once complained. He quite happily let me create all the drama. Every week, we were picked up by the Rutherford girls, who lived in the house at the bottom of our front garden, and by the time we left for Sunday School, lunch was in the throes of being prepared, Mam already having the veg on a rolling boil.

Sunday School was run by a group of well-meaning ladies who would instruct Bible stories, songs and prayers to a dozen or more small children, numb with boredom and who were all in attendance under duress. We were taught songs by memory so that we could sing them to our parents when we got home. The one that I actually liked singing was 'Lord of the Dance'. I would quite happily belt out the lines of the chorus – 'Dance then, wherever you may be, I am the Lord of the Dance Settee!' – completely unaware that I had misheard the words to the song while envisaging Jesus and myself bouncing up and down on the old battered sofa that sat in our farmhouse kitchen. I remember thinking even if Mam told me off for dancing on the furniture, she may have been more lenient had she known that the Son of God was next to me, also jumping up and down like an idiot. Relief came when it was time to go home. Once we had put on our coats, Roger usually made a beeline for the door and ran off up the street. I was chasing after him and as he wasn't yet four years old, there was a danger that a car wouldn't see him if he went near the road. Eventually I would catch up with him and escort him back to the car, where the Rutherford girls would give us a lift.

Once home, I would run into the kitchen carrying some terrible drawing that I had done of Jesus either nailed to a cross or walking on water, only to find myself engulfed in a room full of steam. Pans were still rattling away on the cooker with steam billowing out as the last traces of colour, flavour or nutrients were boiled out of the assortment of vegetables for dinner. Mam must have topped up the water in those pans several times over. I ought to point out that she was, in fact, an excellent cook and, in her defence, this was the seventies so the fashion of boiling veg for hours on end was normal for millions of housewives across the nation.

There were always a lot of places set at the kitchen table and sometimes we spilled over onto a second table normally used for playing cards. Most weeks, a neighbour – Brian – walked across the field to come and have his Sunday dinner with us and more often than not, there was an assortment of other people joining us. But it wasn't a major event and we didn't feel the need to stand on ceremony as anyone who has experienced the hospitality of Dales farmers will stand testament to their generosity. Mam put out numerous tureens of vegetables ready to eat and soon the table was groaning with food. Once everyone was seated on a selection of chairs of varying heights, she served a large platter piled high with Yorkshire puddings, all cooked to perfection.

Here in 'The North', lunchtime was more commonly referred to as 'dinner' and as my dad worked at home, our main meal of the day was always at lunchtime. I was an incredibly fussy eater at that age and Sunday lunch provided me with a multitude of challenges. The only thing I liked that was on offer was mashed potato and despite Mam trying to tempt me with roast lamb and other vegetables, I would stick with the mash. There was one particular Sunday when, as we were all ready and seated at the table, Mam carried a large joint of beef over and laid it down in front of Dad, ready for him to carve.

'Have you got the knife, Alma?' he enquired.

'I've bought a new one. It's electric,' she replied, passing it over to him before he plugged it in suspiciously. His first thought was probably wondering how much it had cost. Before Mam even had the chance to pass him the two blades out of the box, Dad had switched on the knife, without any blades inserted, and proceeded to try and carve the beef. The rest of us were sitting around the table, initially trying to stifle our giggles. But it wasn't long before we erupted into howls of laughter as he continued to try and cut the meat without the blades. Had he bothered to look up, he would have seen Mam holding out the two attachments vital to the working of the knife and even she couldn't keep a straight face.

'You'd be better off with the old knife, Alma,' he muttered, before looking up and realising his mistake. Ever faithful, Mam handed him the old knife in an attempt to save him any further ridicule. Muttering something about wasting money, he pushed the new contraption to one side and took hold of the trusted old carving knife and began to carve.

Sunday dinner over, Dad always had a lie-down on the old battered sofa next to the kitchen fire and it wouldn't be too long before he would shake the room with the vibration of his snoring. If the weather was fine we went out to play, but in the winter there was little to do as Dad would be sleeping in the afternoon and Mam took a well-earned rest watching some old film on the telly.

In the summer months, when it got to teatime, Dad would jump up and say, 'Come on, you lot, we're going for a ride out.' We would collectively groan in response, because his idea of a 'ride out' was to pile us all in the car, drive up out of the Dale onto the moors to a high point overlooking the valley and sit there and take in the view. Dad occasionally remarked on its beauty but most of the time, he would sit like the most contented man in the world with his wife and kids. Looking back, I now appreciate his passion for nature's landscape and I certainly envy his contentment. He had lived all his life in Weardale and never once tired of its beauty. I may have described an idyllic Sunday to many of you but as a six-year-old boy, all I remember was how dull it was.

Many a Sunday afternoon, it wasn't unusual for us to get visitors. These days, in an age of mobile phones, text messaging and social media, we wouldn't dream of dropping in on friends unannounced, but back in the seventies we often heard a car pulling up into the farmyard, followed by a knock at the door. It could be any one of Mam's dozens of cousins or aunties from Brandon, who would be standing there with eager faces. Dad remained fixed to the spot, listening in to detect whether his blissful Sunday afternoon of rest was to be ruined or not.

'Eeeeh, hello Alma! We were just having a ride out in the car and I said to Bill that we should pop over to Stanhope Hall to see Alma and Harry, didn't I, Bill? I says to him that they're bound to be in. Have you had your dinner? I hope we're not disturbing you,' the woman said without coming up for air.

On this occasion it was Auntie Norma, one of Mam's many

cousins. The one thing that my dad hated was having to sit and make small talk with people. Don't get me wrong, he was a sociable man and enjoyed nothing more than being sat around the dinner table with friends or down The Grey Bull having a drink. When it came to Mam's aunties and cousins, he had more difficulty with some of them as they were pretty much all Methodists and never touched a drink. On this occasion, he needn't have worried as the one thing you could guarantee with a visit from Auntie Norma was that you wouldn't get a word in edgeways.

Mam was the perfect hostess. She disappeared into her pantry and in no time at all the kitchen table was set and laden with food to feed her guests. She never once complained when people came to visit and everyone who called in at Stanhope Hall was shown the best of Dales hospitality. Mam genuinely loved seeing members of the family and was touched that people wanted to call in and see her.

There was a story that has been recounted to me over the years when, one day back in the sixties, Mam received a phone call to say that the women from the Methodist chapel in her home town of Brandon were planning to call in at Stanhope Hall. On the day itself, a coach pulled up in the farmyard and thirty ladies shuffled down the steps while coo-ing and ooh-ing. A generous spread of sandwiches, cold pies and cake was laid on by Mam and Grandma. After their lunch, the house guests crowded into the large sitting room, where they said prayers and rounded the afternoon off with a medley of their favourite hymns, accompanied by Mam on piano. With their visit finally over, they filed out of the house while continuing to coo over the furnishings and carpets.

'Eeeh, that's real Axminster, Betty,' and so on. After another half an hour of thank yous and chatter, they boarded the bus for the twenty-mile journey back to Brandon. No doubt the journey back home involved a toilet stop somewhere, considering the gallons of hot tea they had collectively consumed. They talked about that day for decades to come, so clearly Stanhope Hall had left a lasting impression on them. Having experienced the Dales hospitality for themselves, they had put Mam on a pedestal in the local community back in Brandon and even asked her to open the annual church fete for several years running and present the prizes. I have a copy of an old poster from such an event, which announces rather grandly that the fete will be opened by 'Mrs Mews (of Stanhope Hall)'. The fact was, anyone who had ever met my mother would confirm that she was a very down-to-earth, hard-working woman, who bore no airs and graces.

And so, with the visitors gone, Sunday night arrived. Roger and I always had to be bathed of a Sunday evening, particularly if we were going to school the next morning. Another weekend was over and a new week lay ahead of us on the farm.

CHAPTER 5

Showtime

In the 1970s, the highlight of Weardale's social calendar was the Stanhope Show. Falling annually on the second weekend of September, the agricultural show ran for three days and had an even longer build-up. Grandma and Grandad often came up to stay for the show, arriving the previous weekend so they could lend a hand in getting everything ready. Mam bought in cases of beer along with bottles of whisky, vodka and gin, much against Grandma's disapproving Methodist principles. Large joints of beef would be roasted in advance, as well as ham shanks that were boiled in large pans along with muslin parcels containing split peas used to make the local delicacy, pease pudding. The house was cleaned from top to bottom, with beds made up for guests and brasses polished so that they gleamed against the Jacobean panelling in the kitchen.

The show people arrived on the Tuesday and began erecting

the fairground rides and stalls along the street through the centre of the village. There were roundabouts with brightly painted designs, some with rocket ships and others with simple swings suspended on long chains. These rides were punctuated with an array of stalls, where punters would hook a plastic duck, throw a dart or toss a ping-pong ball into a bowl in an effort to win a teddy or one of the many goldfish hanging in bags of brightly coloured water.

The fair was all we talked about that week at school as the playground buzzed with excitement. Friday afternoon eventually arrived and when we got home we were made to eat our tea before we could head out to the fair. The wait was almost too much for Roger and I, as we were both giddy with anticipation. Stanhope Hall was a hive of activity, as Mam and Dad always adopted an open-house policy at the farm during Stanhope Show, where anyone passing was welcome to call in for their tea, regardless of whether they knew them or not. In the many years since, people have continued to remark to me about the generous hospitality they were showed at the farm, particularly at this time of year. My parents weren't alone, as farmhouses up and down the Dale were prepared for their guests to arrive for their tea.

One year, I think it must have been 1975, Mam's younger sister Brenda and her husband Ron came to visit with their daughter, Gaynor. As usual, in the days leading up to the big weekend, the house was bustling with activity and it was down to us kids not to get under anyone's feet. Luckily, with a house the size of Stanhope Hall, that wasn't too difficult. We had been playing a game of hide and seek and had somehow ended up in the dining room, which lay at the end of a long passageway.

With Gaynor and myself hiding from Roger, a passing adult had locked the door, not realising that two of us were in the room hiding behind the huge curtains.

Unperturbed, Gaynor and I made use of our time incarcerated and thought we would help the adults with their preparations for the show. Underneath the sideboard were four slabs of cans of McEwan's Export beer, bought in readiness for visitors at the weekend. We jointly (neither of us can remember whose idea it was, so we now collectively take credit) decided that it would be a huge help to everyone if we were to remove the ring pulls from the cans of beer and that would save them the effort and work of doing it in two days' time and so the pair of us set to work. Meanwhile the adults had become aware of our absence and began to search the house for us. By the time the latch on the dining room door was unhitched and they found us, we had successfully managed to remove the ring pulls from two full cases of beer and were now making steady progress through the third.

Although Gaynor and I were delighted with our efforts to help, for some reason Mam and Dad were less than impressed. Being from the war generation, they didn't want to waste anything, so a group of Dad's farmer friends was invited over later for a 'dress rehearsal' of the weekend's festivities, with Grandad and Uncle Ron joining in. Grandma and Auntie Brenda, being Methodists, drank tea.

Stanhope Show day arrived and the visitors made their way from all directions, walking down the street towards the river. In the distance through the trees, the peaked tops of the white marquees could be seen and the approaching crowds could already hear the muffled voice of the announcer on the show field talking through the tannoy loudspeaker. Children skipped energetically along the riverside walk towards the footbridge that led to the entrance of the show field, with the announcements getting louder after every step.

Down on the show field, the central arena hosted the main attractions, with a sloping bank rising along the south side to form a natural grandstand. There was always a 'Fur and Feather' tent, where a variety of chickens, rabbits, guinea pigs, ferrets and other animals would be on show, the highest-scoring ones proudly displaying their winning rosettes and certificates on the front of their cages.

Across the opposite side of the field, a bandstand made up of wooden staging had been erected for Stanhope Silver Band to play. The band made their grand entrance, having walked through the village playing traditional brass band tunes before walking across the stepping stones at the ford, carrying their instruments. Next to the bandstand, children were already playing games and rolling down the hill. This was often followed by a telling-off from their mothers for getting their good clothes 'up the eyes' (covered in dirt) before running off to re-join their friends.

The farmers were up early on the Saturday morning, loading the sheep and other livestock into trucks and driving across to the field. The animals were placed in their respective pens ready to be judged later on. What could be guaranteed every year is that Stanhope Show would be pretty much the same as the previous year. Essentially, it has changed little over the decades and that is one of its endearing qualities in a world that is changing at breakneck speed. A weekend at Stanhope Show serves to remind any visitor of times when life was simpler and people made time for each other, to see a community truly come together. There are always exciting new attractions to enjoy in the main arena, from one year to the next, but the essence of the show has remained constant.

As the livestock judging took place, the women could be found in the industrial tent, which was run by the ladies committee. This was where the real competition was at. Forget the livestock and small animals, the baking and homemade produce was where titles were defended and won, as baking and jam-making reputations were at stake. The garden produce was shown in the same tent, as onions, marrows and other vegetables of gigantic proportions were neatly laid alongside one another. Once each person had set out their entries in the numerous categories, they took a sneak peek at the competition alongside them, smiled politely and then vacated the marquee to allow the various judges to get started.

At the Hall, Mam spent the morning of the show helping Grandma put the final touches to the cakes and desserts for the tea later before she went upstairs to get us and herself ready to head across to the show field.

'I hope your dad isn't drunk yet,' she would say to me.

At eleven o'clock, it would be safe to say that he had already sampled his first whisky of the day. Once he and the two Harrys, Robbie and Ivan, who were amongst his closest farming friends, got together in the members' beer tent, a bottle of whisky wouldn't last very long, particularly where my godfather, Harry Pickering, was concerned. Some of the Dales farmers such as Harry could drink whisky for hours in the pub and still manage to get themselves home in one piece. Their drinking was legendary, although not all farmers could keep up with them, including my dad and my other godfather, Ivan Peart. Nevertheless, Stanhope Show Saturday was for them the most important day of the year, even more so than Christmas, and they fully entered into the spirit of the occasion. Although the arena was where the main attractions for the show were held, the place most of the locals concentrated on getting to was the beer tent. Like my dad and his friends, the first people in the beer tent each year were often the usual suspects. By lunchtime, it had filled up and by mid-afternoon, several drinkers were making their annual attempt to climb the thirty-foot support pole to the roof of the marquee, egged on by a cheering crowd.

As the farmers in particular would have spent the best part of the afternoon drinking in the beer tent together, they were usually somewhat the worse for wear by the time they arrived at the Hall for their tea. Grandma, despite not approving of alcohol, patiently waited on them, attempting to offer them cups of hot tea to drink in as much of an effort to sober them up as anything else. Grandad, on the other hand, was only too willing to hand around the beers and spirits to guests while very much entering into the spirit of the occasion himself. Later on, fed and watered, some of the more inebriated guests staggered from the house down into the village, usually not getting much farther than The Grey Bull, the first pub they came to. Stanhope's pubs were packed with revellers from the show field who continued their drinking until the late hours.

In recent years, I have been told the story by a family friend of their first ever Stanhope Show. Bill Holden and his wife Nancy had recently arrived in Stanhope with their baby son and had moved into one of the modest houses along the bottom of Stanhope Hall's drive. Having only moved into their new home that week, they knew very few people and it was on this Saturday afternoon of Stanhope Show, back in the early sixties, that there came a knock at the door.

'Hello, I take it you are Bill and Nancy?'

'Yes,' they replied, not knowing who the gentleman was.

'I'm Robbie. Harry and Alma up at the Hall said you've to go up for your tea.'

No further explanation was given. It was simply an invitation to new neighbours who had just moved into the village.

With that, Bill and Nancy duly made their way up to Stanhope Hall and on entering the kitchen, they were greeted by the sight of a crowd of people sat around a long table, tucking into boiled ham and pease pudding. At the top of the table was my dad, fairly inebriated from an afternoon in the beer tent, in his shirt, tie and tweed sports jacket, holding a carving knife and fork and a huge joint of ham in front of him.

'Ah, Bill and Nancy! Sit yourselves down,' said Dad, with all the familiarity as if he had known them twenty years, before introducing them to his friends. This was the start of the ongoing friendship between our two families.

This highlights what I mean when I write about the 'Dales hospitality'. Even in changing times, there is still such a strong sense of community and in recent years when I have returned to Stanhope Show, I might not know as many people but I never fail to receive an invitation to 'come back for your tea' after the show. It's usually the lure of my friend Susan Gowland's banoffee pie that wins me over every time. The people of Weardale know that what they have there is wonderful. That one weekend every September is something rather special and is treasured in the hope that the traditions will be passed down to future generations for many years to come.

Unfortunately, on a rare occasion, things don't go to plan. Back to the September of 1976, with the longest and hottest summer in living memory having drawn to a close, the long hot summer days made way for torrential rain and storms. As the marquees for Stanhope Show were erected, storm clouds were brewing in the distance. No sooner were they up than the heavens opened and once opened, they didn't stop. Not for days. With the rain came gale-force winds and together, they were determined the show would be a non-starter that year. Within hours, the show field became a quagmire, with even the largest tractors struggling to get through. With the forecast looking increasingly dismal, there was no hope of the show going ahead and for the first time since World War II, the committee took the decision to cancel.

As an active committee member, Dad had gone over on the Thursday afternoon to survey the disaster scene. Wearing his wellies, anorak and carrying a large black umbrella, he and other friends were greeted by a television crew from the local ITV news. As word got back to the house that Dad had been interviewed, we crowded round the television set waiting for the local news to start at six o'clock. At a quarter to six, the power went off and my elder brother Richard seized the chance to be the man of the house, springing up and running to check the fuse box.

'A power line must have gone down,' said Mam.

A quick phone call to her friend Betty at the other end of the village confirmed that their electricity was still on. Throwing on our coats and bundling us in the car, Mam sped off to Betty's farmhouse in the driving rain. We made it just in time as we all crowded round the TV to see the news report. While the soaking-wet television journalist stood giving his report, the camera cut away to a shot of Dad, staring uncomfortably at the camera and before we knew it, they cut back to the studio.

'Is that it?' I said, having expected Dad to speak to the camera.

'Your dad's not one for many words, Philip, especially if some television camera is pointing at his face,' Betty observed drily.

Having witnessed Dad's glittering yet short-lived television career, we drove back home only to find the back road to the farm was now blocked by a large tree that had blown over and crashed through the wall, blocking the entire Hall Road. With the weather being so bad, we had no option but for Mam to reverse out and park the car around the front of the house. The following day, Richard and Dad managed to clear the road with a couple of chainsaws. Once they were done, Mam was relieved that the road was clear again while Dad was more visibly relieved that he wouldn't have to shell out any money for a truckload of logs that winter.

CHAPTER 6

Red, White
& Blue

1977

As 1976 drew to a close, everyone at Stanhope Hall geared up for the busy festive season, including Grandma and Grandad, who were staying with us. Christmas at the farm was so magical and as the seven-foot tree was dragged in from the yard and set up in the corner of the sitting room, Mam engaged my little brother Roger and I to help her to decorate it. She took us both up to one of the spare bedrooms at the top of the house where, underneath the window, sat a large wooden chest. As she lifted the lid, the old hinges creaked a little, revealing the boxes of decorations containing baubles and tinsel. I can still recall the Christmassy smell and I still keep the Christmas baubles in that same wooden chest today. We were so lucky to live in this big old house with its roaring log fires, Christmas tree twinkling with coloured lights and plenty of food and presents. I don't think that I ever stopped to think there might be other children who were less fortunate, but as the years passed I realised just how lucky we were.

On New Year's Eve, Mam and Dad had arranged to go out with their friends while my elder brother Richard went 'first-footing' around the Dale with local farmer's lads Robin and Tom Bell. Having seen the New Year in on babysitting duty, Grandma and Grandad made breakfast for Roger and I on New Year's Day. Not long afterwards, once Mam and Dad had surfaced, Richard, along with a friend, appeared at the kitchen door, looking decidedly the worse for wear and holding out his left arm, which was wrapped in a blood-soaked tea towel.

'What the…?' Mam cried out, incredulous at the gruesome sight before her eyes.

My sixteen-year-old brother had, with the rest of his friends, gone back to Robin's house, where he somehow managed to plunge his arm through a glass door pane. In no time at all, Mam whisked him off to hospital in Bishop Auckland, where he underwent surgery. The surgeon removed the tendons from two of his fingers and transplanted them into his arm to replace those severed in the accident. It was a tricky procedure that subsequently required him to remain in hospital for two weeks. Because Richard had missed so much time at school, and with the ongoing physio needed on his arm, he never went back to Wolsingham Comprehensive and decided his time would be better spent as Dad's apprentice on the farm.

Dad was now teaching his eldest son many of the skills of being a farmer, as his own father had done to him many years before. If I'm honest, I will say that I now envy Richard this time that he got to spend with Dad, learning from him, getting to know him as an adult. Even at the age of six, I never showed any real interest in being a farmer but, on occasion, I wish that I could go back in time and see for myself what made my dad tick. There is a sadness that I feel at times like this that I never had the privilege of knowing my parents as an adult like Richard did. I use the word 'privilege' as I have never taken for granted that our parents and those we love will be around forever. Each day that we have with our loved ones is precious and before too long I would come to learn that for myself.

There was one event in 1977 that the whole country was talking about: the Queen's Silver Jubilee. From the start of the year, Union Jack flags and Jubilee merchandise appeared in the shop windows and at school we started to make Jubilee decorations as early as February. I was now at a new school in the village of Wolsingham after Mam moved me from the local primary school in Stanhope, where I had been in a class of about forty pupils. My new school, St Thomas's, was a very small Catholic primary school with only thirty pupils, where the infants were all taught together in one class and the juniors in another. The school was run by Sister Di Pazzi, a nun with boundless energy and a thick Irish accent despite having lived in Weardale for many years. Although the school was Catholic, myself and many of the other kids were baptised Church of England, but that didn't once come into question. First and foremost it was a community school and parents were very much encouraged by the dynamic Sister to be as hands-on as possible. I preferred it because we got the afternoon off on Saints days, of which there were a lot.

During the Easter holidays, Mam had not been well and following a visit to the doctors, she was referred to hospital for further tests. All they could find was that she had a weak heart, but the doctors were unable to pinpoint anything more specific than that. Due to the physical work that Mam had to do on the farm and in the house, it was decided that they would get someone in to help her with the cleaning once a week. That's how Hilda came to work at Stanhope Hall. Hilda was quite a character, a kind woman who always had a chirpy demeanour and took a keen interest in Roger and I. She was a good help for Mam to keep on top of the housework in the huge house. It was a bonus that they got on famously and were good friends too.

In the May of that year, the school organised a coach trip for the pupils to Barnard Castle, a beautiful market town in the heart of neighbouring Teesdale. Mam came along with me that day, bringing Roger with her. Following a wander around the Bowes Museum, we had a picnic on the green outside the ruins of the castle. Mam had made a lovely lunch for us of ham sandwiches, scones and fruit, which we spread out on a blanket on the grass. She'd even brought some cans of 'One-Cal' lemonade as she was trying to lose a little bit of weight in light of her recent heart trouble.

Lunch was followed by an excursion to High Force waterfall, which we were informed was the highest in England. As soon as we arrived, everyone decided that the view would be better if we climbed the steep set of steps up to the top. Mam had no choice but to stay at the bottom as she didn't dare to take the risk with her heart. Roger and I reluctantly left her behind and climbed the steps. As I turned to look back down at her sitting on the bench, I couldn't help but think something was seriously wrong. I didn't know exactly what, but my intuition told me something wasn't quite right.

Roger and I were disappointed to leave her sitting on her

own when the other mothers were climbing with us to the top of the waterfall. To be truthful, she looked scared. Having made it to the top of the waterfall and had a quick look from a safe distance at the water plummeting over the edge, Roger and I made our way back down, jumping the steps as quickly as we could, eager to get back to Mam. She was still there waiting at the bottom as the both of us rushed towards her and hugged her so tightly.

A couple of weeks later, Mam announced that we were going to go away to Blackpool for a long weekend with herself, Grandma and Grandad. As Dad and Richard were so busy on the farm, they would have to remain at home. This then raised the issue of the driving. Grandad was no longer confident enough to drive such a long way as Blackpool, so Mam asked her friend's daughter Anne to come along and help. Having booked us all into a ground-floor flat, Mam discovered on our arrival in Blackpool that the owner had mixed up the bookings and put us on the second floor. There was no way that Mam was going to manage all those stairs in her condition, so a compromise was met: she and Anne would share a spare bedroom on the ground floor while the rest of us stayed in the upstairs flat. As Mam would still need to come up the stairs to our flat several times a day, I wasn't quite sure how this arrangement helped her in any way, but she was tired after the long drive and accepted the situation so that we could properly begin our holiday.

I had never experienced anywhere like Blackpool before. The colours of the shops and the stalls were so bright and inviting. Shelves were covered in sticks of brightly coloured candy rock, candy canes, even candy dummies on ribbons. Enough candy and sugar to rot the teeth of a generation of children, but it looked wonderful all the same. Everywhere was festooned in Union Jack flags and red, white and blue bunting. Mam bought Roger and I a plastic Jubilee flag each, which we waved in the air as we skipped along the promenade, marvelling at the sight of the trams and the famous Blackpool Tower. It had been my birthday a few days earlier and for my birthday present I had wanted a Batmobile toy car. Unable to find one in the local toy shops, we agreed that we would probably get one in Blackpool. The first large toy shop we came across had only one in stock and it was more expensive as the box contained the Batboat as well as the Batmobile. But Mam had decided that I deserved the upgraded toy, as I had waited patiently since my birthday; and hating to leave Roger out, she bought him a Batcopter as well.

I loved my Batmobile, especially because it could fire matchsticks out of the back, something I never grew tired of for years to come. I see from eBay that these toys are worth hundreds of pounds if you keep them in their boxes in immaculate condition, but to me, the pleasure I got out of playing with them as a little boy was priceless.

While we were in Blackpool, we had been invited to a Jubilee party on the street where our flat was. Street parties to mark royal occasions were a very British tradition and as the Silver Jublilee was the first big royal event in my lifetime, this was to be my first one. As much as it looked like tremendous fun, I was terrified at the thought of having to interact with so many people as I was such a shy child. Sadly, I ended up spending most of the afternoon watching from the downstairs hallway of the flat, despite Mam's best efforts to coax me to come and join in. Roger, on the other hand, had no problem mixing with strangers and although I admired his confidence, I was secretly envious of his ability to overcome shyness and enter into the spirit of the day. As I looked on through the open front door, I felt imprisoned by my own fear. It would take many more years for me to gain the confidence required to mix with large numbers of people and I longed for the day when I wouldn't punish myself by standing on the sidelines.

I don't think we will ever see the likes of those street parties ever again, certainly not on that scale, but that whole period of the Jubilee really gave me my first sense of what we believed it was to be British. I recognised a culture that, at that time, bonded the country together as one. With the Jubilee celebrations over, we left Blackpool behind and returned home to Stanhope.

The summer holidays approached and our grandparents offered to take Roger and myself away for a week. Mam's friend Heather owned a small two-bedroom chalet in Silloth on the Cumbrian coast and she kindly suggested that we have the use of it for a week. Mam drove the four of us across the Pennines and eventually the car pulled up on a small windswept field. The chalet was a basic affair and I don't recall that it had electricity. The rooms were lit by gas lights and I remember being horrified that there would be no television for a week. Today, as an adult, a week in a seaside cabin without electricity, phones, internet and television sounds heavenly but back then, I would take more convincing. Grandma, on the other hand, was more horrified that the cooker was gas.

'I've never used a gas cooker before. I don't trust gas, you never know if it's switched off properly,' she said, looking at it suspiciously while not daring to physically touch it.

Grandad had served in the army out in Burma, so to him our living quarters for the week were nothing short of luxury. Every morning we walked along the worn path that led across the windswept sand dunes to the shop to pick up the essentials. Although we could have bought enough for a couple of days, the daily excursion on foot provided us with something to do. Silloth was the antithesis of Blackpool. Here were the quiet, deserted beaches bordered by sand dunes with no sign of fairgrounds, candy rock or trams. Grandma made up picnics every day, which we took to the beach, sitting huddled against the dunes for shelter from the wind. To anyone passing we would have looked ridiculous, but we were on our holiday at the seaside and no matter what the weather was, we were going to sit on the beach and eat our sandwiches! With the cold wind blowing in from the Irish Sea, we must have consumed our fair share of sand, which had been blown into our meat paste butties.

The beach was almost empty every day and I could only assume most of the locals had gone to Blackpool for their holiday. On the deserted beach, Roger and I scavenged the shore, picking up shells, including razorfish, with their long, sharp edges, and depositing them in our little plastic buckets. One afternoon, Roger went to pick up something that looked like a big lump of clear jelly until Grandad managed to grab him at the last minute. It turned out it was a huge jellyfish and he explained the dangers of touching one. But that didn't stop Roger and I curiously prodding it with a stick and exclaiming 'Urgh!' at regular intervals, running away and then running back to prod it again.

Back at the chalet, with clumps of seaweed hanging up in the porch, still damp and caked in sand, to take back home and hang up outside the back door, we tipped out our haul of shells onto the tiled floor and happily sat sorting them into sizes, colours and shapes. Considering we were two boisterous little boys who were used to having an entire farm to run around, we were content without a television and although the weather wasn't great, I still carry with me the fondest memories of that week in Silloth.

Back at home on the farm, our friends on the caravan site had returned for their summer holidays. Estelle and Lyndsey were there, along with the Devitts, and both caravan sites were a hive of activity. One morning, Mam was sat having a coffee with her friend Theresa Devitt in her caravan and they got on to the subject of Lourdes. Theresa and her family were Catholics with a strong faith and they often went on summer pilgrimages to Lourdes with their local church. Mam had mentioned that her sister Brenda was interested in going, so Theresa suggested that she might like to go along with them on their next trip, as there were still places available. Within the week, Auntie Brenda was on a train with the church group, passing around the sandwiches and sipping on their flasks of tea. Having never been abroad before, this was a big deal for her. She didn't travel well normally and would get travel sickness on the twenty-mile bus journey from Sunderland to Durham, so for her trip to Lourdes she packed enough travel sickness tablets for a trip around the world.

On her return, Auntie Brenda brought us a bundle of souvenirs: sweets in a plastic cup with the Virgin Mary on the front and holy water for Mam and Grandma in bottles shaped like the Virgin Mary, where you screwed off her head to open it. In addition, there were various other treats, all with a Virgin

Mary theme. This was the start of a family association with Lourdes and, every year, friends returned with yet more holy water in plastic bottles of various shapes and sizes. I'm not sure what we used it for, but there seemed to be a bottle in every room of the house, 'just in case' as Grandma used to say. I probably still have one somewhere.

As we hung out with our friends on the caravan site, we spent most of the summer building dens, playing on Tarzan swings and going to the swimming pool. These days, Mam seemed to have much less energy, so our day trips out with her were less frequent than they had been the previous summer. Despite this, life on the farm continued pretty much as usual. Once the hay-timing was over, Mam and Dad decided that Richard was responsible enough to be left alone on the farm for a week while we went to visit Uncle Harry and Auntie Sylvia on their farm in Hampshire. Uncle Harry was Dad's cousin and they had been best man at each other's weddings; he managed a large arable farm just outside Winchester.

After a long drive down the A1, we pulled into the farmyard in the scorching heat. Auntie Sylvia was there to greet us and it wasn't long before Dad was catching up with his cousin and Mam was engaged in conversation with Auntie Sylvia, getting all the latest family news from both sides.

Their farm was so different to what we had at Stanhope and also considerably larger. Although it was on the Downs, much of the land lay in vast flat expanses, making it easier for the enormous combine harvesters to operate. I had seen these machines, on the television and in some of Dad's farming magazines but nothing had prepared me for the sheer scale of the mechanical beasts. When I came face to face with one,

I stared up at the metal giant, slowly reaching out for Dad's hand for reassurance, afraid the combine would suddenly lurch forwards and grab me as if it had a will of its own.

From the experience of having people stay at the farm for holidays, Mam and Dad were all too aware of how annoying it can be when guests fail to appreciate that they are staying on a busy working farm. As hosts, it's not always possible to down tools and entertain people every day when there's work to be done. Day trips to Bournemouth, Winchester and the New Forest gave us plenty to do and Roger and I went on each one wearing matching outfits. At the New Forest, we were both sporting brown shorts with lion T-shirts. Another day, it would be matching blue shorts and Wombles T-shirts. Mam took great pride in having us smartly dressed, which was a radical change from the two feral children who ran around our own farm, climbing into everything and returning home a complete state.

As the end of the week approached, we travelled to the National Motor Museum at Beaulieu. I was so geared up for the visit as I knew this was where the Bluebird car was on display. The car was Donald Campbell's Bluebird-Proteus CN7 and I was fascinated by the pictures that I had seen of it in a book of cars I had at home. Mam and Dad decided that it would be better to head straight to the Bluebird, if only to stop me from pestering them for the rest of the day. The car looked even more amazing than I could have dreamt and I would have been happy standing there all day staring at it. After fifteen minutes and having indulged me for long enough, Dad took hold of my hand.

'Come on, your Mam's feeling tired,' he said. 'Let's go and see if we can get a ride on the monorail, shall we?'

It was while queuing in the baking sunshine for the monorail that Mam said, 'Harry, I don't feel right, can we go to the car?'

Taking one look at her, Dad could see that something was wrong. Within five minutes we were sitting in the car park. Mam had loosened the buttons on the front of her summer dress and Dad rummaged in the boot to find some water to give her. A concerned passer-by came over to see if there was anything that he could do, but Mam by this point wanted to get back to our aunt and uncle's as soon as we could. Determined to try and protect Roger and myself from the truth, she reassured us that she was fine and was simply feeling sick. Dad, on the other hand, knew that the situation was rather more serious.

Back at the house an ambulance was called, as Mam said that she felt worse. As I stood behind the door in the passage, I heard someone utter the words 'heart attack' and even at the age of seven I knew this was serious. I didn't say anything to Roger. My protective instinct towards my little brother told me that I needed to shield him from the reality of the situation, or as much of it as I could understand myself.

Shortly afterwards, the ambulance pulled up outside. By now, Roger and I had been sent to our room out of the way. I was standing at the top of the stairs looking down and witnessed the two ambulance drivers carry Mam out, strapped into a chair. Turning to look up at me, she raised a hand to them to stop.

'I'm going to be all right, bonny lad. You be a good boy for Auntie Sylvia. Look after Roger. I love you,' she said to me. With that they carried her into the waiting ambulance, with Dad following close behind.

Not wanting to cause any further worry, I went back into the bedroom and threw myself face down on the bed. Unable to keep up the façade for Roger any longer, I sobbed my heart out into the pillow while attempting to stifle the noise and not alert any of the adults downstairs. Within a minute, Auntie Sylvia came into the room. Not necessarily because I was crying, but because of instinct: she wanted to check that Roger and I were OK. She sat down on my bed and put a comforting arm around me while beckoning Roger over to join us.

'Your Mam is going to be fine. They just need to take her to the hospital for a day or two so that the doctors can make her well again,' she said reassuringly.

Mam was taken to hospital in Winchester and following a series of tests it was confirmed that she had suffered another heart attack, which was a shock considering she was only forty-two. It was decided that we would spend at least another week in Hampshire as we would need to wait until the doctors consented that Mam would be fit enough for the eight-hour drive back home to Weardale.

Dad drove us into Winchester each day to see Mam. The first time I saw her laid in her hospital bed she had wires and tubes connected to her and her normally immaculate hair was flattened and scraped back. At first I could barely recognise her and could do nothing to stop myself from crying. When the matron's back was turned, Mam invited Roger and I to jump up onto the bed for a cuddle, taking care not to sit on or knock the wires. She told Dad that the food was horrible but she didn't want to say anything as the nurses were working so hard to care for her. When each of these visits drew to a close, I didn't want to leave her. I didn't make a big song and dance about staying as I was determined not to make things more difficult for Dad as he already had enough to cope with. I suppose this was the first time that I learned to just keep my head down and get on with it; I was growing up.

Back at my aunt and uncle's, Roger and I tagged along with Dad as he went round the farm with Uncle Harry. Gone were the fun day trips, so we had to be a little more inventive in occupying ourselves. Across from the farmyard was a row of cottages and we made friends with a couple of the kids who lived there. Uncle Harry's two youngest sons, David and Michael, were a pair of lively characters and always seemed to be up to mischief. They had a motorbike that they would ride around on and one day they had constructed a makeshift sidecar from a welded metal frame, wheels and a sheet of wood as a base. With one of the brothers on the bike and the other crouched on the attached wooden platform, they took the contraption on its first test drive. As they went speeding down the empty private road on the farm, the 'sidecar' worked itself loose from the bike and the two became separated, sending one of the brothers crashing into a ditch on the rickety wooden platform. It was like a scene from a Norman Wisdom film. Roger and I laughed hysterically. Auntie Sylvia, however, didn't find it funny and the boys' attempts at breaking the world land speed record were put on hold for another day.

Towards the end of that week, Mam was finally discharged from hospital and returned to the farm for one night before heading back up north. Naturally, she was pleased to be back under the same roof as her family and I think that she was also relieved to have a decent meal. I was sad to leave Hampshire. It had been an eventful holiday for the four of us, but what none of knew at the time was that it was to be our last family holiday together.

CHAPTER 7

Dark Days

B ack in the seventies, the Miss World beauty contest was hugely popular and drew television audiences of millions in the UK. Along with the Oxford and Cambridge Boat Race and Trooping the Colour, the annual Miss World pageant was seen as a 'television event' punctuating the British calendar.

It was a particularly cold November evening and Dad's friend Harry Pickering and his wife, Norah, called in at the Hall to see him. Such visits were inevitably accompanied by the opening of a bottle of whisky. Everyone knew that when these two old friends got together, it was never going to be an early night and there wouldn't be much whisky left in the bottle the following morning, if any at all. Mam got Roger and myself ready for bed in our room next to a portable Calor gas heater, which struggled to keep the cold bedroom at a decent temperature. Sporting matching blue dressing gowns with ladybird buttons down the front, Roger and I went back downstairs to see Dad before we went to bed. Still on his first glass, I asked him if I could stay up with him and Harry and watch Miss World on telly.

He laughed gently. 'It's on too late for you, bonny lad. You go off to bed now and I'll see you in the morning,' he said. He hugged me and kissed Roger and I goodnight and off we went. 'Watch the bed bugs don't bite,' he shouted after us. He said that every night without fail.

I kept waking up during the night, hearing movement in the bedroom next to us and in the passage outside my bedroom door. This was the room that Grandma and Grandad stayed in when they visited but as they weren't staying that night, I did wonder why people were in there. Being so sleepy, I soon drifted off again. Now I was dreaming and I can still remember that dream all these years later. I dreamt that I woke up in bed and that Dad was sat on the large deep windowsill in my bedroom, looking at Roger and I in bed. I have no recollection of whether he said anything but I do remember him sitting there, wearing his blue pyjamas with the brown stripes. I woke up again, this time still hearing noises farther away in the house. Aware that it was still the middle of the night, I climbed out of the toasty warm bed and after putting my dressing gown on, wandered along the dark cold passageway to my parents' bedroom. The light was on and I opened the door to find Mam sitting on the end of the bed, crying.

'Mammy, what's wrong?' I asked her.

Attempting to stifle her crying, she beckoned me over to her and I duly did so, sitting beside her on the pink floral-patterned eiderdown.

'Oh Philip, my bonny lad,' she said through her tears

and slipping an arm across my back. 'Darling, your daddy died tonight.'

No parent ever dreams that they are going to utter those heartbreaking words to their seven-year-old child, but here was my mother doing just that. I cried. I cried so much. I don't remember saying anything, only crying. Words didn't come to me, and when they did, they weren't what you would imagine a child would say in that situation. All I could utter was, 'I need the toilet.' Nothing more eloquent than that. I'd like to say that I said something far more poignant, but all I wanted to do was go to the loo.

Sitting on the toilet, I tried to take in what Mam had just told me. She came down after a few minutes to check that I was OK and she was sat on the stairs waiting for me when I unlocked the door.

'I think it's best if you go and sleep in Richard's room with him tonight,' she said.

'Where's Daddy now?' I asked, suddenly needing to know some finer detail.

'He's lying on the bed in Grandma's room,' she replied, probably wondering if it was a good idea to impart such information.

My elder brother Richard was also sat on the stairs waiting for me, his eyes still wet and raw from crying. He held my hand and took me upstairs. I was normally scared of going up to the top floor as it was so spooky, but on this occasion he reassured me. His bedroom was noticeably colder than mine. I climbed into his big bed and snuggled up to him underneath the multitude of blankets and the thick, heavy eiderdown. We lay there in our shared grief. Age aside, we were two boys who had just lost their father. Two boys aware that their little brother lay fast asleep downstairs, oblivious to the tragedy that had occurred in the house. I still recall Richard's words of comfort that night before I fell asleep.

'Do you know, Philip? We had the best dad in the world,' he said.

I couldn't agree more.

As I lay in bed, I tried for just one moment to imagine how Dad had died, but thankfully my young brain couldn't comprehend the reality of such a situation. It was many years before I could summon up the courage to ask Richard what had happened.

Once Dad had bade Harry and Norah goodnight and they drove off out of the yard, Dad went up to bed. He'd been pleased to see his old friend after being ill for the past few weeks and as he began to undress in the bedroom, he complained of a pain in his left arm and found himself unable to remove his shirt. Mam instinctively ran up to the top floor of the house to wake Richard. He phoned the doctor who arrived at the back door fifteen minutes later. Dad was sitting on the bed and having great difficulty in getting his breath, so Dr Hill gave him an injection to relax his muscles and aid his breathing. The doctor went out onto the landing to call an ambulance and when he returned to the room, Dad said that he needed the toilet. They helped him downstairs to the small toilet on the landing, leaving him for a moment sitting on the loo to give him some privacy, but on hearing a loud thud, they rushed back in to find him on the floor. Both Richard and the doctor did their utmost to resuscitate him, but he was gone. He had died there and then and nothing could be done to save him.

He had taken his last breaths in a room that was just along the passage from where he had taken his first. He had suffered a massive heart attack.

Harry Mews, our father, born in Stanhope Hall, lived in Stanhope Hall, loved in Stanhope Hall, sung and danced in Stanhope Hall, died in Stanhope Hall.

I must have fallen asleep eventually. My head was spinning with the events of that night, not knowing what lay ahead of us. Life would be different when I woke up in the morning.

It was still dark the following day when Mam came upstairs to the top floor and sat with me as I awoke.

'I want you to go to school today, darling,' she said.

Naturally, I didn't really feel like it and did my best to convince her otherwise, but she assured me that I had to be a good boy and that by going to school, I would be helping her.

'I also don't want you to tell Roger. He doesn't know about his daddy,' she said.

'But why can't Roger know that Daddy has died?' I asked.

'I will tell him at the weekend but I want you to go to school with him today. Grandma and Grandad are coming up from Brandon and I need to organise things for your Daddy. Please do this, bonny lad, for me.'

Looking up into her tired eyes, I agreed and hugged her once more.

I'm sure that I ate breakfast, but I don't remember. I do remember Mam phoning Mrs Beckett and asking her to call to the house as she would be doing the school run that day. When Mrs Beckett arrived, I waited at the back door to the farmhouse while Mam went outside to the car and updated her on the events that had happened during the night. The way that Mrs

Beckett looked at me that morning, it was a look that required no words to go with it. I knew exactly what she meant. It was a look that I was to become all too familiar with in the coming years.

School was quite unremarkable that day. I was dying to speak to somebody to tell them what had happened the previous night, but as Roger was in the class next door, I knew that I couldn't discuss Dad's death with my classmates. After all, I had promised Mam that I wouldn't say anything to anyone. Sitting at my desk during the Friday afternoon art class and unable to contain myself any longer, I approached my teacher, Miss Swinbank.

'Miss, my daddy died last night,' I whispered.

She put a comforting arm across my shoulder and quietly said, 'I know, Philip. I'm so sorry. You need to be a brave boy and keep this to yourself as Roger doesn't know yet.'

She meant well but it was tying me up in knots not being able to talk to anyone that day as I looked around the classroom at everyone carrying on as normal, completely unaware of my news. It was as if I'd had to press the pause button on my emotions until I went home.

CHAPTER 8

Staring Death in the Face

By the time that I had returned home from school that evening, the house was busy. Normally we would have been dropped off at the end of the lane but due to circumstances, Mrs Bumby, another lady who took it in turns with Mam for the school run, had driven round to the farmyard. Her green Land Rover pulled up into the yard and I could see that there were more cars than usual parked outside the stables. Mrs Bumby's youngest son Adam was busy squabbling with my classmate Karl in the back as she came round to open the rear door. She held our hands as Roger and I jumped out of the back into the yard before turning to look back at Adam and Karl.

'Enough of that carrying on, you two. I want quiet.'

Adam looked scolded. 'But Mummy, it was K…'

'*Now,*' she said assertively.

Nobody ever messed with Mrs Bumby. Switching from

her stern face to a smile, she led us down to the back door of the farmhouse. Mam came out, wearing an apron over a black jumper and skirt. She looked tired. I noticed her clothes straight away, as she never normally wore black. Kissing us, she told Roger and I that Grandma and Grandad were here and to go inside. She remained out the back door, chatting to Mrs Bumby for a couple more minutes before appearing at the kitchen door.

In the kitchen, I ran over to Grandma, who was also wearing black. She sat at the table, which she had covered in newspaper, and a selection of candlesticks and horse brasses were set out while the stench of Brasso permeated the room. Standing and holding her blackened hands up in the air out of our reach, she bent down to give Roger and myself a kiss. She must have changed her mind and realised that her grandsons now needed a cuddle and that was far more important than worrying about Brasso stains on our clothes. I got in there first and she held me so tight at that moment. Of course, she knew that I knew about Dad. She knew exactly how I would be feeling, as she had lost her own father when she was seven years old.

Letting go of me, she gently moved me to one side to allow little Roger in for a cuddle. Encasing his tiny, thin frame in her arms, I noticed that the movement in her arm seemed much improved following her stroke. The adults in the room were talking in muted tones, almost in code. I had to constantly remember that I hadn't to let the cat out of the bag and tell Roger that our dad was dead. Out of the corner of my eye, I saw Mam walk down the passageway towards the dining room and I went after her. The next thing I knew was that Grandad had scooped me up in his arms and carried me into the sitting room. He closed the door behind us, put me down and led me over to the settee next to the roaring fire.

'You can't go in there, bonny lad,' he said gently.

'Why not? I was going to help Mammy,' I said.

'Mr Tinkler and his son have moved your daddy into the dining room this afternoon,' he said, perhaps wondering if he ought to have told me this. My immediate thought was why would they move Daddy into the dining room when there was no bed in there for him to lie on?

'Can I go and see him?' I asked, without really thinking of any consequence that seeing my dead father would have. All I wanted to do was make sure that he was OK. Even in death, I needed to know that he was OK.

'That's not a good idea,' he replied. 'It's not the place for a little lad like you.'

He turned on the TV, where Sooty and Sweep sprang to life on the screen. Grandma opened the sitting room door a moment later with Roger and left him with Grandad and I to watch the telly. Soon Roger was laughing as Sooty and Sweep, who were supposed to be baking a cake, had transformed the scene into a full-on flour fight. Looking across at Roger and then at me, Grandad gave me a half-hearted smile. I wanted to talk to someone about Dad and yet I couldn't. I'd not been able to say anything at school and now I was home, I still couldn't talk about it. I had questions that I wanted to ask as well as trying to process the situation in my head. There was a moment when I was jealous of Roger, jealous of his innocence. I wished that I could have been laughing at Sooty and Sweep but instead my mind was in the dining room, thinking of my dad in there.

Later that evening, I was in the bathroom washing my face

and brushing my teeth when Mam came in to check I was OK. Now that there was just the two of us, I decided to ask her.

'Mammy, Grandad said that they moved Daddy into the dining room. Please can I go and see him?' I said.

'That's not a good idea, darling,' she said, trying to hold back yet more tears. 'Perhaps it's better if you remember your daddy the way he was.'

Ever persistent, I wasn't going to accept this offer: I wanted to see him. He would be asleep, so what were they trying to protect me from?

'Please,' I said.

Clearly desperate to appease me and get me up to bed, she said that we could discuss it in the morning. I can't remember what they told Roger to explain Dad's absence that evening as we went to bed, not in our own room but in Mam and Dad's room. We always had a bedtime story and tonight was no exception. Mam was trying her best to retain a sense of normality.

Morning soon came and I got up wondering if this was the day when I would get to go and see him. By the time that I went downstairs into the kitchen, the telephone was ringing and there were people calling at the front and back doors. It was hard to know exactly what was going on. There were lots of serious and sad-looking faces amongst our visitors and conversations would suddenly stop with an uncomfortable silence when I walked into a room. Cautious as not to ask in the vicinity of my brother, I pleaded with Mam several more times to let me see Dad until she eventually relented.

'Once you've had some Frosties and a cup of tea, I will take you to see him,' she said.

Upon discovering that the body had been moved to the

dining room, my mind began to conjure up images of what he would look like. I assume that this was a defence mechanism in my head to prepare me for what I was about to witness. As a seven-year-old, I knew nothing of death, nothing of the paraphernalia that accompanies a death, so I really had no idea what to expect. After breakfast, as my mother led me along what seemed to be the endless passageway from the kitchen to the dining room, I expected to see the dining room set up as normal and his body simply placed in a slumped position in his chair. I expected him to be dead, but sat at his rightful place at the head of the table.

I gripped Mam's hand tightly as she led me up to the dining room door. There was a catch at the top of the door to keep the room locked and as she lifted it from its resting place, the door slowly opened. My heart was pounding and going ten to the dozen. Nothing could have prepared me for what I was about to witness. The biggest initial shock was that the dining table had been dismantled and placed at the far end of the long, cold room. In its place stood a long wooden box with brass handles along either side. The next thing to startle my senses was the smell – it wasn't a bad smell, but a smell that ultimately was alien to my young self. I don't know if it was the wooden box or something that the undertaker had used. Was it the smell of death?

'What's the box for?' I asked, trying to take it all in.

'It's a coffin, darling,' Mam replied, further tightening her grip on my hand, possibly to reassure herself as well as me. This did nothing to slow my heartbeat as she slowly led me closer to the side of the coffin. Out of the corner of my eye, I saw a wooden lid propped up against the wall next to the fireplace.

'Is Daddy in there?' I asked her.

'Yes, he is. He will just look as if he is sleeping, sweetheart,' she said, holding my hand tighter than ever. Once I was next to the coffin, I could clearly see that there were a number of gold silk squares placed along the top of it, each one edged with its fine decorative tassels covering part of Dad's body.

Unsure of the decision that she had made, Mam asked me, 'Are you sure you want to see him? It's alright if you've changed your mind.'

But I had come this far and agreed that it was what I wanted. She leant over to pull back the golden square of silk that covered his face. If I could rewind back to any point in my life and change the course of events, this is, without doubt, one of those points. Little did I, let alone my mother, know that this image that I was about to see would come to haunt me in my dreams for decades to come.

He looked asleep. Asleep and unshaven. He was wearing his blue pyjamas with the brown stripes, the same ones that he had worn in my dream the night he died. I tried to take it in. I would never speak to him again. I would never again go off in the Land Rover with him up the fell to feed the sheep. I would never hear him screaming 'the little buggers!' after we had peed in his wellies. I would never hear him sing 'Two Little Boys' to Roger and I as we sat on his knees. I'm a little ashamed to admit that I didn't take much notice as to how Mam was feeling at this point. Seven years old is too young to lose a parent, but forty-two is also too young to lose the love of your life.

I didn't dare to step any closer. I'm not sure what I was frightened of, looking at Dad lying there so peacefully, but despite this, my feet were frozen to the spot. They wouldn't move, yet my heart was beating faster than ever. The smell, I was still conscious of the smell. The smell was too much to take – I had to leave.

Mam, so tuned in to me and my feelings, had already sensed that I had been there long enough. She put her arm around me and said that it was time to go. I'm not sure that I ever said goodbye as sadly, I was far more conscious of getting out of there. She took the piece of gold cloth and carefully laid it back across his face. That was it, I would never see him again. I was all too painfully aware of the finality of the moment as she slowly led me out of the room. I knew that I wouldn't be coming back into this room, at least not while he was lying there anyway.

As she shut the dining room door behind me, I was aware again of other people in the house. I could hear Grandma clattering dishes in the pantry and Roger playing a game of Snap with Grandad at the kitchen table. My little brother was still blissfully blind to the heartache that the rest of us were feeling at this moment. Roger was only two years younger than me, having only just celebrated his fifth birthday, and although two years is a fairly small age gap between siblings, at this moment it seemed as if there was a gulf of years between us.

CHAPTER 9

Tea & Sympathy

Several minutes after my life-changing ordeal of seeing Dad lying dead in his coffin, the mundanities of everyday life would kick straight back in.

'Has the bairn had his breakfast?' Grandma asked my mam. Grandma referred to all us kids as 'the bairns'.

'Yes, Mam,' my own mother replied.

'Has Brenda called? Is she coming up from Sunderland?'

'I spoke to her last night. They're coming this afternoon. Her neighbours are bringing them up in the car.'

My Auntie Brenda was Mam's younger sister. She lived in a small red-brick house close to the beach in Seaburn, along with my Uncle Ron and cousin Gaynor. I was particularly close to Gaynor, as we were almost the same age, although whenever this was mentioned she would be quick to assert that she was actually six months older than me. Auntie Brenda and Uncle Ron didn't have a car, as they went everywhere by bus. A visit from my aunt was just the boost I needed right now, as she had a tremendous amount of energy and lit up any room that she entered.

Looking back towards the dining room door, I couldn't get the image of Dad lying in that box out of my head. I felt sick and had a sudden urge to get out of the house, so I grabbed my coat and hurried out into the farmyard as quickly as I could, not only because I needed some air but also to avoid having to take Roger with me. I really needed to be on my own just now. My head was spinning as I tried to make sense of what had happened. Having to lie to Roger, who kept asking where his daddy was, had proved so difficult. I wasn't sure why Mam had decided not to tell him yet, although I readily accepted that she had enough to deal with in that first couple of days. I don't remember when she did tell him, but I imagine that it was over that weekend before the funeral.

I walked up the farmyard and wandered into the byre full of Dad's beef cattle. Looking at the cows, I thought to myself, *Do animals know death? Are they aware of what death brings when it visits?* As I tried to get my head around the fact that my dad wouldn't be coming up here to feed and muck out any more, my thoughts turned to more insecure fears. What was going to happen to the farm? What would happen to our family? For the first time in my so-far short life, I felt my future was uncertain. Previously, I had never given much thought to the future as I was always far too absorbed in the here and now. There was always so much going on in my life to keep me occupied, and yet here I was, stood in a byre crying, alone with my thoughts.

Scared by the feeling of absolute desolation, I ran out of the byre and out along the track that trailed along the back of the caravan site in the Top Wood. With it being November, the caravans were empty for the winter. Standing in the middle of the small field, I looked over at each caravan in turn, wondering if any of the occupants knew about Dad yet. Jimmy and Theresa, had they been told? What about Lyndsey and Estelle's family? They probably wouldn't know. I know that the phone had been busy since yesterday morning. It had never stopped ringing as Richard stood in the passage talking very seriously for hours on end. In a close-knit community like Stanhope, it never took very long for news, particularly bad news, to spread around the village and beyond into the Dale. I walked slowly across the empty field, which looked bleaker than ever on this cold overcast day and into the old ramshackle shelter next to the sheep pens, where Dad stored his old red David Brown tractor.

A couple of years had passed since the tractor had last seen active service on the farm and recently it had been consigned to sit here to gather dust and to decay beneath the leaky old tin roof. I climbed up and sat myself in the seat as I held onto the steering wheel. All I could think about was Dad, lying in that box. There wasn't much room for anything else in my head at that moment. As much as I tried to picture him living, my mind kept throwing up the image of him in the dining room, lying still in his pyjamas, devoid of life. Less than an hour had passed since I had been in to see him and already I was having regrets. The rain started to come down and soon it was making a racket on the corrugated tin roof. Only last summer we had been playing here with our friends, Julie, Louise, Estelle and Lyndsey, and in the paddling pool, having water fights and enjoying the long, hot, carefree days. I realised at this point that my life had changed forever.

Auntie Brenda and her family arrived sooner than expected and by the time that I had walked back down to the house, she and Mam were already embracing each other in the tightest of hugs. So much crying, the like of which I had never witnessed before.

'Is this how it was going to be?' I asked myself. This house, which had known so much love and laughter, was now immersed in grief and tears. I found it all too intoxicating and the added tradition of everyone wearing black only added to the gloomy atmosphere.

Following more tea and tears, I took my cousin upstairs to play in my room while Mam escorted her sister down the passage to the dining room to see my dad. *Why do people do it? Why do they want to see someone they love very much lying in a long wooden box so cold and empty?* All these thoughts were churning around in my mind as I continued to try and eradicate the image from my head.

At the end of another very long day, I went to bed considerably less innocent than I had been when I woke that morning. I'm not sure if the nightmares started that night or over the next couple of nights before they buried Dad, but it wasn't long before the haunting scenes began invading my sleep. I'd always been prone to bad dreams, all of a very similar nature. Usually I was being chased up the stairs at Stanhope Hall by a strange man, who looked like Inigo Pipkin (from kids' TV series), making a loud, sinister laughing sound, much like the 'ghosts' on the *Scooby-Doo* cartoons. I was never sure what he would do if he ever caught me, but he used to frighten the life out of me nonetheless.

Following the scene that I had witnessed that morning in

the dining room, the scary man disappeared from my dreams only to be replaced by my dad. I couldn't comprehend this for a second. Why would Dad, my dear beloved father, be the scary man in the dreams coming to get me? The scenario bore no relation to his personality or the relationship that I had with him.

As the nightmares continued night after night, I became increasingly traumatised by the visions. I don't know why I was running away from him, because if I had possessed some magic power that could bring people back from the dead, I would certainly have found myself rushing into his arms rather than running away from him. So was this what it was going to be like? Surrounded by death twenty-four hours a day? The days would be filled with my longing for him, the grief and anxiety of those around me, the confusion of my little brother struggling to understand that his daddy wasn't going to walk through the door and scoop him up in his arms. Meanwhile, the nights would be spent lying in bed haunted by the dreams that would plague me for years to come.

On the night before the funeral, more visitors arrived at the farm to see Mam and to pay their respects to Dad. Their close friends Harry, Marjorie, Ivan and Sheila called at the farm, so Mam escorted Ivan and Harry into the dining room to see Dad while I remained in the kitchen with Sheila and Marjorie. I wanted to make Mam stop crying by doing something nice for her, so as I sat with a hairbrush and a bag of hair rollers, I told Sheila and Marjorie of my plans to do Mam's hair as a treat for her so that she would look nice for the funeral the next day.

Later that evening, Uncle Alec called at the farm. He was

married to my Auntie Olive, who was Dad's younger and only surviving sister. Many people focus on the feelings of the widow and children when someone dies, but rarely do the surviving siblings receive such sympathy. Thinking back to this time, I try to imagine the effect that this devastating news must have had on my aunt who, now in her forties, had buried her sister and parents in the last twenty years and now she was having to say goodbye to her only brother. A person can have many people around them, but grief can take you to a lonely place, especially if you are the only remaining child, having lost your parents. I didn't really know anyone on my dad's side of the family up until this point, so Uncle Alec's visit that night paved the way for us to become reacquainted. It's funny how despite such dark times in people's lives, there can be positive outcomes for which we can be thankful.

Over the weekend, Mam took Roger to one side and gently broke the news to him. Naturally he was devastated, once he had grasped the reality that his daddy was gone and wouldn't be coming back. Dad's funeral came and went without my being present. Mam decided that the grim Victorian formality of a funeral and burial would be too much for Roger and I, so in an effort to spare us further trauma, it was decided that it would be best for the both of us to go to school on that day. Richard and Mam led the mourners into the crowded church, followed by Auntie Olive and Uncle Alec, with my grandparents close behind.

The church of St Thomas in Stanhope market place was full to standing on the day they buried Dad. As the cortège moved slowly through the village, people stopped outside their businesses, bowing their heads in respect, while the local constabulary lined up outside the police station as the hearse crawled past.

I've never asked anyone about the funeral service itself, as such questions only serve to open up old wounds and remind people of the heartache they felt at that difficult time.

Dad was buried in the new cemetery located on a hill above the village, surrounded by his beloved Weardale countryside and the sheep grazing on the heaps casting a watchful eye over the dead lying beneath the ground.

Following Dad's funeral, his obituary appeared in the *Stanhope Parish Magazine* of January 1978:

> *21st November 1977: Henry Harrison Mews, Stanhope Hall, Stanhope*
>
> *It was indicative of the esteem in which Harry Mews was held that the Parish Church was full to standing on 21st November. A great wave of sympathy went out to Mrs A. Mews, Richard and other members of the family in their great loss. The most telling tribute came from a fellow member of the farming community, expressed in the simple words: "He was a good man". We trust that Alma and her family will draw strength from precious memories and the assurance of the goodwill of the community.*

CHAPTER 10

Smiling in the Face of Adversity

I would like to say that life on the farm was beginning to get back to normal, but that wouldn't be the truth. As a family, we had started to settle ourselves into a new way of life, one with a different rhythm. Roger and I went to school each day, while Richard began to find his feet as the farm manager. With her three sons getting on with their lives, Mam did her best to put on a brave face, but she wasn't kidding any of us. From time to time, the mask would slip to reveal a young woman wracked with grief and desperately trying to keep herself and her family emotionally afloat. I would walk into a room as she swiftly wiped away any sign of her being upset. Sometimes I loitered outside a door on hearing her sobbing, which was muffled by her hands and several tear-drenched handkerchiefs. A black cloud was sitting above our lives and none of us had any idea when or if it would lift. Roger coped as well as you would expect a five-year-old to in such a situation and there were many days and nights that he cried for his dad, as did myself and Richard. Thankfully, the three of us had each other for comfort. There may have been a gulf of years between us, but we were united in our common grief, each of us hurting in the same way.

During the initial months after Dad's death, money was tight due to the farm's accounts being frozen. As he had died without leaving a will, it took a number of weeks for the solicitors to sort out the probate status of his estate. Grandma and Grandad came up almost every weekend, laden with essentials and goodies as they always did, but now on each visit they brought cash that they had withdrawn from their savings to try and help Mam through this cash flow crisis. The whole financial aspect of losing Dad must have made this period even more excruciating for my mother.

Christmas was fast approaching and Mam had confided in her parents that she was worried where she was going to get the money to pay for it. Of course, Grandma and Grandad were not going to see us deprived of a visit from Santa Claus and if anything, we needed Christmas more than anything right now. A new Cash & Carry warehouse had opened in West Auckland and they sold items in bulk with a fairly hefty discount. Armed with a small loan from her parents, Mam took the opportunity one day in the December to go there with her good friend Joan Woodhall and buy what she could for Christmas. Joan and Mam had always been close friends and had often gone on shopping trips together over the years. She had proved to be a tremendous support to Mam in the weeks since Dad's death and on that particular day, she helped her get everything she needed for a family Christmas.

Stanhope Hall had plenty of visitors throughout December, as many of Mam and Dad's friends would call in to offer support and comfort to the family. The women would sit with Mam while the men chatted with Richard in the farmyard to see how he was managing and offer some well-meaning advice. It's easy to overlook my brother's contribution at this stage, because most of what he did was outside the house on the farm. He managed to put to use the knowledge that he had gained from Dad to running the farm alone. Of course, he had help from Grandad, who could do some small jobs, but the bulk of it had to be done alone. Plenty of good advice was dispensed by these older farmers and Richard accepted it graciously. It can't have been easy for him knowing that the spotlight was on him and that almost every decision he made would be scrutinised.

Christmas came and went and the house was full of family, with Auntie Brenda and her family from Seaburn staying, along with Grandma and Grandad, of course. On Christmas morning, Roger and I ran downstairs with our usual excitement at the thought of Santa's visit. I remember turning into the dark passage and momentarily thinking that as it was Christmas morning, Dad wouldn't be chasing me from the dining room, where I'd last seen him. We burst into the sitting room and switched on the big light to reveal two plastic Santa sacks, each with our name written on it, sitting in front of the piano. I was so excited to delve into mine and retrieve the Operation and KerPlunk games I had asked Father Christmas for. Mam followed us downstairs to see our faces as Roger and I squealed with excitement opening our presents. I would like to think that she was able to take pleasure from her two youngest boys revelling in their Christmas thrills, but somehow I doubt that. I imagine that as she stood there in her dressing gown, she was all too aware of the vacant space at her side and wished that Dad was there with us as he had been on Christmas morning the previous year.

Later that morning, once everyone had eaten breakfast, we gathered around the tree to unwrap the gifts from friends and relatives. As Mam passed out gifts to the family, she picked out a particular parcel from under the tree and started to cry. Handing the gift to Grandma and Grandad, she apologised that it was such a meagre present, but due to the farm's accounts being frozen, it was all she could afford. More tears came in response as her parents hugged her in reassurance, knowing the true value of a gift was the love in which it was given. Grandma unwrapped the green-and-white plastic tea tray with a seventies floral design. She loved it and treasured that tray for many years to come. Every time we used it, she repeated the story of how Mam came to buy it for her, getting herself upset in the process.

Christmas passed and 1978 arrived with muted celebration at the farm. For Mam, relief came when the probate process had been completed on Dad's estate and she could start to move on with getting the farm's finances in order. Grandma's birthday approached at the start of February and Mam was pleased to be able to buy her a more substantial gift, not only to make up for the tray at Christmas, which of course required no apology or explanation, but as a thank you for being a solid rock in these difficult times. We decided to have a tea party in celebration of Grandma's birthday and I was put in charge of doing the sausages, pineapple, cheese and pickled onions on cocktail sticks and inserting them into a halved orange. These were the staple of any birthday party in the seventies, the decade of kitsch cuisine. With Roger helping me, on this occasion we decided to mix the concept up a little by adding Polo mints onto the cocktail sticks, creating a somewhat bizarre mix of Polos and pineapple. Grandma, Grandad and Mam thought it was hilarious and for the first time in ages, Stanhope Hall was ringing with the sound of laughter. At tea, we presented Grandma with her present – a gold dress watch – and as she opened her gift, she was truly overwhelmed.

CHAPTER 11

Storm Clouds Looming

1978

It was an average Sunday evening as we were sitting in front of the television. Roger and I were bathed and in our pyjamas, Roger having taken medicine for a hacking cough, watching a new show, *All Creatures Great and Small*, in the sitting room with Mam while Richard was sitting alone in the kitchen, having a cigarette. He had only recently started smoking and although she was a smoker herself, Mam wouldn't allow him to smoke in front of Roger and I. On the TV, Christopher Timothy was elbow-deep inside a calving cow when Mam started to panic.

'I can't see! Philip, get Richard, I can't see anything!' she cried.

I ran through to the kitchen to get Richard.

'Richard! You've got to come. Mammy can't see,' I said, sounding scared.

Jumping up and throwing the half-smoked cigarette into the fire, Richard rushed through to the sitting room.

'Mam, what's wrong?'

'It's my eyes, I couldn't see. My vision went blurry for a moment. I can see a bit now. It's fine, I'll be fine,' she said, catching her breath as her panic slowly subsided.

'I'll phone the doctor,' Richard said.

'No. Don't, Richard. I said I'm fine,' she told him and that was the end of it. She held her thumb and forefinger against her eyes for a few minutes before taking another sip of her drink and we continued watching the telly. I looked over at her to check that she was OK and apart from occasionally rubbing her eyes, she seemed to be back to normal.

The next morning, Roger's cough had got worse, so Mam called the doctor's surgery to see if she could get an appointment for him. As we were running a bit late that morning, she told Mrs Beckett not to wait for me at the end of the road but that she would take me to school herself. Pulling up outside the school gates, she gave me a kiss goodbye and off I went. There was nothing particularly memorable about this moment at the time.

Later that day, on our way home from school, we were jumping around in the back of Mrs Bumby's Land Rover, as we regularly did on the six-mile journey home. Always boisterous, we battered each other with our satchels, testing the patience of the poor adult who was lumbered with the school run. After being dropped off at the road end, I raced along the lane and up the front path to our house. As soon as I got in through the front door, I heard the television playing cartoons. I went into the sitting room to see Roger sitting transfixed by *Scooby-Doo*.

'Mammy's in the hospital,' he said. 'She went in the hambilance.'

What started as a mispronunciation a few years ago, Roger still continued to pronounce the word 'ambulance' this way and was all the more endearing for it. I walked into the kitchen, where Hilda was doing some ironing.

'Is my Mammy in hospital?' I asked.

'Yes, honey. She's going to be all right. Richard has gone to Bishop to see her and your grandma and grandad will be here soon.'

'OK,' I said. I had a bad feeling. 'Can I go out to play?' I asked, looking to get away into the fresh air.

'Do you not want your tea? I was going to do you fish fingers,' Hilda said.

'I'll only be a short while.'

'Put your coat on then and I'll ring the bell when your tea's ready.'

I walked out of the back door into the farmyard. It was already getting dark, but I was scared of something much worse. As I shut the door behind me and stepped out into the cold, I could hear Roger's pleas wanting to follow me outside. *He doesn't know*, I thought to myself. *He really doesn't know.*

Out in the farmyard, the snow was beginning to fall, although the ground wasn't quite cold enough for it to settle. Up in the distance at the top of the yard, I could make out the silhouette of Uncle Harold and the two sheepdogs walking down the track. Above them I could see the regular small puffs of smoke coming from the old man's pipe. I walked up the back yard to meet him on the track.

'Now then, young Philip, is that you just in from school?' he said.

'Yes,' I replied. He must have sensed my glum mood. 'Where's the car? Is your mother out?'

'She's been taken to hospital in Bishop. Richard's gone to visit her.'

With the dogs jumping around at our feet, eager to be fed after their walk, I accompanied him back down to the stable. Scooping the bright yellow flakes into the two battered enamel bowls and puffing away on his pipe, he took the opportunity to give me some words of advice.

'Your mother needs you to be really strong now. Richard may be the eldest but she will need you to be man of the house and support her. Your father was a good man and you'll be like him one day,' he said.

Not really sure what to make of this, I simply nodded. The slurping feeding frenzy of the two hungry dogs was broken by the arrival of a car coming into the yard. It was Grandad's old Hillman Minx. Grandma got out of the passenger side in a swift movement. I threw my arms around her, as I always did. At the same time, Hilda shouted from the back door, with Roger standing at her side, 'Philip, your tea's on the table.'

Once we were in the house, Grandad ushered Roger and I into the kitchen to have our tea. Grandma seemed a little put out to see someone else cooking in her daughter's kitchen, but graciously acknowledged Hilda's kind and well-meaning efforts to feed us. She shunned her coat and went straight to get her pink tabard from the drawer in the large sideboard. Running the hot water tap, she set about doing the dishes while we ate our fish fingers. Clearly, her way of coping was to go into domestic overdrive. They had only been in the house ten minutes when a car screeched into the farmyard and Richard came running down into the house. With his red eyes and unshaven face he looked as if he had the weight of the world on his shoulders when he entered the kitchen. He beckoned Grandma and Grandad out of the kitchen and into the passageway. I left the table and moved closer to the door so that I could listen in on the hushed voices out in the passageway. As my brother came back in, I jumped back to my seat at the table. He whispered to Hilda briefly, as she nodded with a grave look on her face. Grandma hurried back into the kitchen, taking off her tabard as she went and taking her coat off the hall stand.

'Grandad and I are going to see Mammy in hospital,' she said to Roger and I.

'Can I come?' I asked.

'No, bonny lad, you stay here with Hilda. We won't be long. Give me a kiss and be a good boy,' she said as she briefly hugged me. She did the same with Roger before hurrying out of the door. As they left the house, I could hear her already issuing her instructions to Richard.

'You go canny on them roads. The last thing we need is more of us in hospital,' she said and a moment later, they sped off up the track. The phone didn't stop ringing throughout the evening. Hilda was relieved by Auntie Mary from next door, who busied herself in the kitchen doing the ironing until my grandparents returned. Both of them looked tired and weary as they came into the kitchen, removing their coats for the second time. Roger and I were playing a board game at the kitchen table. Grandma came over and kissed us both on the head.

'Your Mammy is being looked after in the hospital. She said

to tell you that she loves you and that you have to be good boys and get ready for bed.'

'Is Mammy coming home tonight?' Roger asked.

'Not tonight, she has to get better before she can come home. It won't be long. She will be home soon, in a day or so,' she said.

I wasn't convinced. Her words may have told me one story but her face gave a completely different version away. Looking at her and seeing Grandad standing behind her, wiping away his tears, I knew this was serious. Everyone jumped as the phone rang and Richard darted out into the passageway to answer it. After a moment he put the phone down and came back in the kitchen to grab the car keys that he had left on the table.

'Richard!' Grandma shouted. 'Who was it? Was that the hospital?'

With tears streaming down his face, he could barely muster a reply.

'The hospital called. It's Mam. I need to go…' he tailed off as he headed out the door without stopping. Once again, I heard the car tyres screech as he sped off out of the yard. Shortly after, both Grandma and Grandad tucked us into bed. We had moved out of our own bedroom after Dad's death a couple of months earlier to sleep with Mam in her bed. Prayers were said with conviction that night but considering the circumstances, the nightly bedtime story was dispensed with and without any complaint from Roger or myself. It was a strange night's sleep and again, I was aware that there was a lot of movement going on in the house as I kept waking up during the night. Thankfully, Roger was fast asleep. It seemed strange having that space in the bed next to us, but she would be back home soon.

CHAPTER 12

Darker Days

I suppose that it made sense to wait until we had finished our breakfast before they told us. Hilda had arrived to help with the cleaning, which was strange as she normally only came on a Friday and today was Tuesday. I looked towards the door to see Roger being led into the kitchen by Grandad, carrying his bright orange teddy bear in his hand. I know that I hadn't overheard anyone saying anything, but I knew what was to come. Richard sat us both down on the battered old settee and looked at us both. He was trying his best to fight back the tears.

'What's wrong, Richard?' Roger asked.

'Come here, bonny lad,' he said as he pulled us both closer to him. He took a deep breath. I noticed that his other hand was shaking. Drawing us even closer towards him, he went for it.

'Mammy died last night. We've lost her,' he said.

I closed my eyes and threw myself against the back of the settee. I can still remember that exact moment. Roger was already in tears. I held out without crying, almost as if I was not going to be the first, but inevitably, the emotion was too much for me. There were several people in the kitchen that morning who witnessed these two little boys being told that their mother had died. You wouldn't envy any of them. Nobody had seen this coming. She was forty-three and this was only ten weeks after we had lost Dad.

I was numb. But I soon stopped crying and as I wiped away my tears with the sleeve of my jumper, I looked around me: everyone was looking at us. Desperate to get away from the audience that we had, I took Roger's hand and we went through into the sitting room. I shut the door, sending out a clear message that we needed to be alone. The fact that nobody tried the door handle told me that the message was received and understood, at least for a short while. My main concern was Roger. I wasn't convinced that he really understood what was going on – he was only five, after all. As long as I could be there for him, that was as much as I could do. The reality was that I needed him just as much as he needed me.

The phone rang all day, with people sending condolences and offering support to the family. The whole community was in shock. Aunty Mary from next door called round and was visibly distraught. She and my mother had been great friends and had called in to see one another on a daily basis.

Later that morning, Grandma announced that Auntie Brenda had arrived. Richard had driven to Sunderland to pick her up in Mam's car and I was standing at the back door, watching her slowly walk down the yard towards the house. On her face she had a look of utter devastation that I will never forget. Previously, I had never seen her with any other expression than a smile and the Auntie Brenda that I knew and loved bore little resemblance to the grief-stricken woman in front of me. I barely recognised her. Her hair and clothes were as they had always been but her face was different. Gone was the happy smile that beamed with energy and in its place were tired features. Her eyes were red and puffy from crying, but she did her best to muster a smile on seeing Roger and I. Looking past us, something had caught her eye. Grandma and Grandad appeared behind me and the sight of them meant that Auntie Brenda could hold out no longer. It was as if the full reality of the death of her big sister hit her right there and then. Brenda had always been the little sister, and some would say that she had spent much of her life in my mother's shadow. This would have caused other siblings to fall out, but such was the strength of the relationship between these two sisters, such was their love for each other, pedestals and shadows could never come between them and the inseparable bond they had with each other.

Now everybody was crying and I could do nothing to help. What I do recall is the practical help that everyone offered. Consumed by her grief, Grandma initially refused any form of support or assistance offered to her, but she soon realised that people were only being kind and that it would be churlish to turn such offers of generosity and sympathy away. In the days that followed, the postman delivered large bundles of sympathy cards. Here was yet another symbol of death that I had to get my head around. Every spare bit of surface on furniture in every room was covered in these cards, each and every one containing a genuine heartfelt message of condolence.

The next couple of days blurred into one. Adults busied themselves with making funeral arrangements. A lot of crying was done, a lot of hugs given and received and copious amounts of tea made and drank. Even in times of death and the grief that follows our house was as hospitable as ever and no visitor left without being offered their dinner or tea.

Stanhope Hall felt different. Not just the absence of those we loved, but there was something else. Strangers were coming and going. Post would arrive in official brown envelopes addressed to 'The late H.H. Mews'. That word, 'late'. I had never seen it used in this context before and asked Grandma to explain it to me. After she did, I wished that she hadn't. *Another 'death thing',* I thought. Not only did everyone's behaviour change, as you would expect, but the clothes they wore changed too. The morning after Mam died, Grandma changed into black and she remained dressed in mourning for years to come. Mr Tinkler, the undertaker, called in to speak with Grandma and Grandad to make the arrangements for the funeral. Thankfully, it was deemed unsuitable for myself or Roger to be involved in this process. We were taken to the shops in the village by my uncle, while the remainder of the adults stayed sat in the kitchen choosing hymns, flowers and a coffin.

Having returned a while later carrying a small haul of sweets and crisps, I dug out my game of KerPlunk in the hope that someone would play with me. Maybe it was a case of the child trying to distract the adult rather than the opposite.

That night, when we were washed and dressed in our pyjamas, both Grandma and Grandad took us up to bed. Even as we climbed the two flights of stairs to Mam and Dad's room, Grandma was fighting back more tears. This was the future now. They had to look after us and there was no doubt that they wouldn't have anyone else come in and take on that task.

At the age of almost seventy, fate had set them a new path and an important job to undertake. They tucked us into the large double bed as Mam had done only two nights earlier. Neither of them could envisage how they were going to get through the next week, never mind the months and years that were to follow. One thing was certain: not getting through this wasn't an option.

CHAPTER 13

Jam Tarts & Buckaroo!

L ess than five days after Mam passed away, her family and friends gathered together in Stanhope to say farewell to her. Her body was to be interred in the grave that had barely had a chance to settle since it had been dug for Dad only ten weeks earlier. It was decided that it would be better if Roger and I did not attend Mam's funeral that day. Aside from sparing us the trauma of having to walk into a crowded church behind her coffin, it was felt that Grandma and Grandad had enough to do to cope with their own grief during that long, cold, torturous day. I did not complain at the decision and it didn't even occur to me to question it. Roger, too young to understand, willingly obliged.

It was a busy house at breakfast that morning, with a constant stream of people coming and going. The stainless-steel electric kettle that sat next to the cooker was rarely off the boil at any point. Grandma asked me if I would like to go and see my mam to say goodbye, as she was aware that I had been to see Dad.

Because I had never told her about the subsequent nightmares I had endured in the past ten weeks, she had no idea that I might not be willing. I was non-committal in my answer but she pressed me for a response. I didn't know what to do. I was torn in that I did want to see Mam one last time but the memory of seeing Dad in his coffin was still very raw.

Before I knew what was happening, I was being led along the passage to the dining room. I felt sick and my heart was pounding faster than it had ever done before. Grandma held my hand tightly, probably to reassure me, but I found that I couldn't pull away from her. We were now on the steps outside the dining room. Her hand reached up to lift the catch on the top of the door. I was going to be sick; I couldn't do it and I panicked. I started to scream and pull away from her as she turned the door handle. I managed to break free from her hand and ran back to the kitchen, screaming and crying. Everyone was staring at me, not knowing what the hell had happened, while I buried my face in a sofa cushion and sobbed. I knew that seeing Dad in his coffin had brought on the nightmares and there was no way I could cope if Mam started doing that in my dreams. Not my beloved Mammy, to whom I was so close.

Once I had eventually calmed myself down, I expected Grandma to have a sympathetic ear. But she didn't. She was upset that I didn't want to see Mam, especially since I had been to see my dad in his coffin ten weeks ago. In the years that followed, she never really understood why I chose not to see Mam that final time. In later years, I tried to explain the reasons to her and all she could say was, 'Your Mammy wouldn't ever hurt you.' I told her about the nightmares but she couldn't comprehend them so I felt that it was better if I just kept them to myself. The nightmares never, ever went away and I still live with them all these years later, although a lot less frequently.

Cars pulled up in the farmyard and just as I was being hurried upstairs to wash my face, several ladies made their way through the back passage, led by Richard, each carrying a floral display. The scent of the flowers hit me as I paused on the staircase to take in the sight of the procession. Grandma followed up the stairs to make sure that Roger and I got washed and dressed properly. We normally washed in the bathroom, but as we had a house full of guests staying with us, the bathroom was busy so instead we washed in the bedroom, Victorian-style. Once we had dressed ourselves and Gran had done the final checks with our hair, we went downstairs as Auntie Brenda invited Mrs Beckett through the back door and into the busy kitchen. Looking around her, Mrs Beckett made her best effort to produce a smile for Roger and I.

'Are you boys ready to come up to our house?' she said.

'I need to find Bongo Bear first,' Roger said, looking around him for his teddy.

'What's the bairn looking for, Harry?' Grandma asked her husband. She was now looking anxious, as she was aware that along the passageway, people were coming and going to the dining room, where her daughter's body lay.

'His teddy, the one that Alma got him for Christmas,' Grandad said.

'Mammy didn't buy it for me, Santa brought it,' Roger said innocently.

Realising that they had narrowly escaped the Father Christmas faux-pas, they joined in the search for the orange bear. On any other day, Roger would have been told to leave it at home but today nobody was going to deprive a five-year-old of the comfort of his teddy, especially when his mother was lying in her coffin just along the passage.

A day of alternative activities was offered by Mrs Beckett, who had arranged to keep her own kids off school so that my brother and I could go up to her house to play with them. As the mourners would be coming back to the farm following the funeral and burial, Mrs Beckett thought that it would be nice for us to make some jam tarts to take home and hand out to the visitors.

Those attending the funeral had to withstand the bitter icy temperatures as a thick covering of snow lay on the ground. The empty hearse pulled up along the narrow lane in front of Stanhope Hall. Dryden, our neighbour, had generously sprinkled ashes from the coal fire along the path to grit the surface and prevent anyone from slipping. The undertakers filed up the pathway to the front door, where they were met by my uncle. Around the corner in the dining room, my grandparents, Richard and Auntie Brenda were stood around Mam's coffin, whispering their last goodbyes. Richard had already had some time alone in there as he wrote the card to go on the spray of flowers from us three boys. Grandma had put a pair of red slippers on Mam's feet, the rationale being that they would keep her warm. It was a final act of love. Knowing that the time had come, they could not put off the inevitable any longer. Glancing back at her for the final time, they left the room to allow the undertaker and his son to gently put the coffin lid in place.

The family filed out of the house behind the coffin and down the path to the waiting funeral cars. Stanhope Hall had witnessed some dark, sad days in its long history and this was the latest. Two ladies from the church remained in the house to keep an eye on the place and set up the food for the mourners returning a little later. It was common for funerals in Weardale to be well attended and today was no exception. The family expected the church to be full, but the number of mourners exceeded all expectations. As the funeral cortège slowly moved its way through the village, the streets were quiet. Mr and Mrs Bell, who owned the petrol station, stood solemnly outside the pumps as the hearse passed by. Many of the smaller shops had closed, as the people who owned them had been friends of my mother and so they had chosen to make their way down to the church rather than stay open for business.

Grandma and Grandad were taken aback by the crowds of people stood outside the church as the coffin was lifted out of the hearse and guided towards the four men, decked out in their best suits, each of them family friends, who kindly acted as pallbearers. Conscious of the freezing cold weather, Grandma urged the crowd to go on into the warmth of the church, only to be told that the church was full to standing. Despite being asked to go along to the farm for a cup of tea and some food, the mourners stood in the churchyard throughout the service and were there to greet the family as they emerged over forty minutes later.

In the Dale, only family and close friends traditionally attend the burial, thus avoiding the pantomime of fifty cars attempting to get up the hill to the cemetery. Dad's grave had been opened up to a respectable depth to accommodate his wife's coffin above him and she was laid to rest with the man who had captured her heart only twenty years earlier. They shouldn't have been in there, buried in the ground. They should have been continuing their happy marriage into old age, watching Richard, Roger and myself growing up into men. Life can be cruel and unfair.

Many people had travelled a good distance that day and in addition to the hordes of relatives from Mam's home town of Brandon, people came from as far as Scotland and Hampshire. Grandma stuck to her strong Methodist sensibilities and had arranged to invite all the mourners back to Stanhope Hall for refreshments rather than host the wake in a pub. Many of Mam's friends raised concerns that catering for such a large crowd would be too much for Grandma, but she had a plan. In recent weeks, Mam had filled the chest freezer in the pantry with an array of sponge cakes and pies, the very staple of a Dales funeral tea, so that she was always prepared for the many surprise visitors that called in at Stanhope Hall. Grandma gave cakes from the freezer to Mam's friends, who took them away and duly returned them on the morning of the funeral, defrosted, filled and iced. Joints of beef and ham were also roasted and transformed into platters of sandwiches to feed the scores of hungry mourners.

It was starting to get dark when we drove along the track above the farmyard in Mrs Beckett's car. Due to the large number of cars already parked there, she had to park on the grass verge at the top of the track. Roger and I proudly carried the biscuit tins containing two dozen jam and lemon curd tarts that we had made that afternoon. Roger gave his tin to Mrs Beckett and ran ahead into the house, almost tripping over as he went. Following him in, I could see people everywhere, some standing in the passage, old ladies sitting in the kitchen polishing off scones. Dear old Auntie Bessie sat in her thick heavy coat and hat, licking her fingers and then using them to get the last of the cake crumbs that lay on her plate. She smiled at me warmly. She was a lovely woman who was a regular visitor at Stanhope Hall and I was very fond of her.

Roger and I took the tin of jam tarts around the adults in their dark suits and black dresses. People tried their best to smile at us. I urged Roger to take some tarts into the dining room at the end of the passageway, as there was no way I wanted to go into that room. Ten minutes later, in the kitchen, Roger had dug out his game of Buckaroo! that he received for Christmas. We approached the group of elderly ladies that were seated and asked them to join in the game. They willingly obliged. Auntie Ivy was now eyeing up the large coffee cake that Auntie Brenda had just carried in from the pantry and licking her lips at the prospect of a slice. We set up the Buckaroo! and attempted to explain the purpose of the game to our captive audience. Grandma voiced her concerns that the shock of the plastic horse bucking its entire contents across the sofa could send our elderly guests into cardiac arrest. Nevertheless, the guests humoured us and played along.

In the years that have since passed, people have asked me on several occasions if I attended my mam's funeral and they are somewhat surprised when I tell them that my overriding memory of the day that they buried my mother was that I made jam tarts and played Buckaroo! I will always thank the people who made the decision to spare Roger and I the harsh reality of that dreadful day.

CHAPTER 14

Knights in Shining Armour

It must be noted that the events that took place in this chapter are based on an account told to me repeatedly over the years by my grandmother and not based on my own memories.

It was two days after the funeral when the knock came at the door. Still wearing her woollen headscarf and pink tabard, Grandma answered it while drying her wet hands on a tea towel. A man and woman, neither of whom she recognised, were standing there.

'Mrs Mews?' the woman enquired.

'No,' Grandma said in a quiet voice. 'My daughter died recently. I'm Mrs Close.'

Looking at her leather folder, the woman scrutinised her notes and without looking up she said, 'But you are the grandmother to Philip and Roger Mews?'

'Yes,' Grandma said, still drying her hands, holding on to the tea towel as if it were some sort of comfort blanket. 'You'd better come in.'

She led them through to the kitchen and offered them a cup of tea, which neither of them accepted. The woman pulled more paperwork out of her briefcase. The man still hadn't spoken a word and at this point they still hadn't introduced themselves.

'We are from Social Services and we would like to have a chat with you and your husband about your grandsons,' the woman said.

As they waited for Grandad to remove his wellies at the back door, the room was silent. Grandma knew that they had not come with good news. Wearing his boiler suit and thick woollen welly socks, Grandad walked in and looked at Grandma as if trying to glean some information as to the nature of the visit. He introduced himself to the man and the woman, not shaking hands but holding them up to show that they were dirty from the farmyard and excusing himself for doing so.

'We have received information that due to the recent deaths of your son Henry and daughter-in-law Alma,' looking at the paperwork, 'that the boys are now orphans,' the woman said.

Grandma immediately interjected.

'My *daughter*... Alma was my daughter... *our* daughter,' as Grandad reached across and took hold of her hand.

Making no apology for the error and disregarding the fact that she had upset my grandmother, the woman continued. She talked about the fact that now that Mam and Dad were dead, there was an issue of legal guardianship for Roger and myself. She addressed my grandparents in a cold, unsympathetic manner. As Richard was now eighteen, he was our legal guardian. They thought that being so young and having a farm to run single-handed, the job of raising two young boys would be too much to ask. They also raised the matter of Grandma and Grandad's age, questioning their suitability for the role of bringing us up. Neither of my grandparents was under any illusion now: they were here to take Roger and I away.

Grandma gripped Grandad's hand tightly. She knew that she had to do something and act quickly. Without conferring with her husband, she jumped up from the chair and shouted at the man and woman.

'Get out! Get out of this house now!'

I'm not sure who was more taken aback, Grandad or the couple from Social Services.

'Go on! I want you both to leave!' Gran shouted.

'But Mrs Mews…' said the woman, attempting to respond.

'I've told you, my name is Mrs *Close*!' Gran said. 'My daughter was Mrs Mews and you seem to forget that we only buried her two days ago. My grandsons have just lost their Mammy and Daddy and you are here to try and take them away from us, from their family. You've got a nerve!'

'Mrs… Close, I don't think that you understand…'

'Don't you dare tell me that I don't understand! Do you, either of you, understand what we have been through? What those boys have been through?'

Grandad, who until this point had not said a great deal, looked over at the gentleman, who had also barely spoken.

'Did you say that our older grandson Richard is actually the legal guardian of the boys at the moment?' Grandad said.

'Yes,' replied the man, without needing to refer to notes.

'In that case, none of us can be having this discussion until Richard gets in. He's away getting a part for one of the tractors.'

'When will he be back?' the woman asked impatiently, while looking at her watch.

'He's gone to Darlington, so he could be a few hours yet. Why don't you phone the house tomorrow and arrange a time to come back?'

'Harry! I don't want them coming back here! Isn't Richard...?' Grandma said. But Grandad cut her off and grabbed her hand.

'He'll be away for a couple of hours at least,' he repeated to the woman while staring at Grandma as if to say 'just go along with me on this'.

Grandad escorted the woman and her colleague out the back door and into the farmyard and remained there until they had driven up the track and out of sight. He waited until they had disappeared from view before shutting the door and heading back through to the kitchen.

'Richard's not gone to Darlington, he was in the top barn putting the lambing pens together,' Grandma protested.

'I know that, honey, but they didn't,' he said, doing his best to raise a smile as he winked at her.

Trying to catch their breath after this bombshell visit, they sat for a moment and discussed how they were going to get around this. They had lost their daughter and son-in-law in the space of ten weeks and now they were faced with the prospect of losing their two youngest grandchildren too.

Not sure where to turn next, they decided to call their solicitor, Mr Wills in Durham. Mr Wills had been a friend of the family for many years and although it was not his practice that dealt with the probate following the death of my parents, he was the trusted advisor to Grandma and Grandad. Having spoken to him personally on the phone, Grandad said that he would come up to the farm that afternoon and that if anyone from Social Services called, nobody was to engage in any conversation with them.

Ken Wills, Grandma and Grandad's solicitor, arrived about an hour later. It was a long anxious hour, with Grandma pacing around the house, unable to sit down and relax. Grandad showed Mr Wills into the kitchen just as another car pulled up in the farmyard. Grandma didn't recognise the man who emerged from the second car as he walked down to the farmhouse.

Mr Wills looked through the kitchen door and down the rear passage of the house.

'I took the liberty of calling a colleague of Harry's before I left my office in Durham to drive up here. Mr Humble, who knew your son-in-law well, has come to assist me with these matters.' His voice trailed off as the second gentleman walked into the kitchen, followed by Grandad. Extending his hand, he introduced himself to Grandma as Oliver Humble.

'I was a good friend of Harry... and Alma for that matter. I had intended to visit you tomorrow as soon as I had confirmation but due to events currently unfolding this morning, I thought I had better come straight away.'

Not knowing exactly why he was here and what part he played in the situation with the Department of Social Services, Grandma was more confused than ever. In an attempt to clarify the situation as swiftly as possible, Mr Wills spoke up.

'Mr and Mrs Close, I am here to propose that we swear you both in as legal guardians of Philip and Roger following the loss of the boys' mother and father. As you will have been informed, their elder brother Richard, now being of age, is currently their guardian in the eyes of the law. It seems to be the opinion of our friends at Social Services that being so young and now having to run the farm, that the responsibility of looking after the two boys will be too much to ask of an eighteen-year-old lad.'

'They're my lads, I'm their grandma. We're their grand-parents. My Alma's two lads,' she said, breaking into sobs.

Mr Wills continued, 'Nobody is going to take your lads... the boys... away, Mrs Close. That is what Mr Humble and I are here to prevent happening. The best plan that we can come up with is to change the right of legal guardianship from your grandson Richard to that of yourselves as the grandparents of the boys. Social Services will try to use your age as an argument to remove the boys from the family and we need to counter that somehow. This is where Mr Humble can help us.'

Mr Humble leaned forward in the armchair, holding several pieces of paper folded in his hands.

'Mr and Mrs Close,' he said with a kind smile, 'you may or may not be aware that your son-in-law Harry was a member of the Masonic Lodge here in Stanhope.'

Grandad nodded.

'We used to look after the children when Alma and Harry went to functions at the Masonic Lodge. I used to iron his shirt for his meetings,' Grandma said.

Mr Humble continued. 'Several days ago, I had a meeting with members of the Lodge regarding the boys' welfare and to see if there was anything that we could do to help the family. As part of the Masonic tradition for charitable fundraising, we have a trust, the purpose of which is to support families of members within and outside our community when they most need it. We have approached the Trust to see if there is anything that they can do to help you with the boys and their upbringing.'

Unfolding the letter in his hands, he reached into the outside breast pocket of his sports jacket and pulled out his glasses case. Putting his reading specs on, he scanned the contents of the letter before handing it over to my grandparents.

'The Trust have expressed their wish to help your family by proposing to pay for the boys' education until they come of age. If you are happy to accept this offer, we can get the relevant paperwork drawn up and assist you with making a start, looking at schools,' he said.

Finding it difficult to take in this overwhelming offer of generosity, Grandma was dumbstruck. It was as if she needed reassurance that the plan would work. Years later, she told me that she didn't dare to believe it until she had everything in writing, most importantly, from the people at Social Services. It had never occurred to either of my grandparents that in the midst of their anguish over losing their daughter, they might have to consider the possibility that they could lose their grandchildren as well.

Mr Humble reached across and handed the letter to Grandma. Her eyes still streaming with tears, she was unable to read anything. Grandad took the letter from her and began to read it. He must have read it at least three times, his hand trembling as he held the sheets of paper.

'He's right. It certainly looks to be in order,' he said to her.

'Right then, Mr and Mrs Close. If you could pass me the number for the people at Social Services that came this morning, I will contact them and start putting arrangements in place. We will need to consult your grandson Richard before we can take matters forward, as he is currently the legal guardian for the boys. Is he around at all?' said Mr Wills.

'He's just feeding up in the top byre, Mr Wills. I can go and get him,' Grandad said.

'No, you stay there, Mr Close. I'm sure I'll manage to find him,' Mr Wills said, putting on his overcoat and making to leave the room. 'I'll call you this afternoon with an update.'

That afternoon, Roger and I went next door to Auntie Mary's, carrying our colouring books and crayons, while Gran, Grandad and Richard set off in the car to Mr Wills's office. There, the paperwork was completed and my grandparents duly sworn in, with hands on a Bible, as legal guardians of Roger and myself. Mr Wills the solicitor, the kind people at the Stanhope Masonic Lodge, my grandparents and elder brother all worked behind the scenes to set up a secure future for Roger and I. Richard's contribution was to keep the family farm afloat and running to ensure that we had a home and the family had an income. My grandparents were still wracked with grief, but were reassured that the future of the family was secure and relieved that the social workers had withdrawn from their brief intrusion into our lives.

I am aware that the Masonic community is traditionally discreet and I wanted to ensure that by telling this part of the story that I would not upset any members of the wider community of Freemasons. During the writing of this book, and particularly this chapter, I have been in touch with members of my father's Masonic Lodge, who have reassured me that, in times of more relaxed attitudes, they are happy for me to tell my readers of their involvement in helping Roger and myself at that time and in the subsequent years.

CHAPTER 15

Scrapbooks & Stories

Following that first week after Mam's funeral, we tried to get into the swing of some sort of normality. But first we had to find our 'new normal'. Basic functions such as meals and housework were carried out as though they were second nature. The work on the farm wasn't so straightforward, however. Although Richard had been managing the farm since Dad died ten weeks ago, he was now truly going it alone, which wasn't such an easy task for any eighteen-year-old. Despite the pressure that he was under in addition to his own grief, he managed to get out of bed each day and head out to see to the livestock, with a little help from Grandad, and keep the farm running.

It was at some point during that week that the matter of myself and Roger returning to school was addressed. Who was really to know when would be a good time? After all, there was certainly no textbook or manual on to how to do this. Going back to school for the first time in over two weeks felt a little like going back after being off with the measles. My friends had covered a topic or two in History that I had missed and the class was now reading a different storybook for the group reading at the end of the day. Lots of kids gave me sympathetic smiles as I walked back into the classroom on that first morning.

As it was mid-morning when I went back, I imagine that Roger and I had been taken in a little later to allow the teachers the opportunity to sit the class down and explain that nobody was to ask us about our mother's death. As not one person said anything, this must have been what happened. It was only when my pal David came bounding into the classroom before lunch, after another session with the doctor about the large ringworm scab on his head, that the elephant in the room was addressed. Pushing his black-rimmed glasses back up his nose and wiping a large snot with his sleeve, he spied me sitting across the classroom at my desk.

'Philip! You're back,' he shouted and before Miss Swinbank the teacher could move to silence him, he blurted out, 'Your mam's dead, isn't she?'

'David! You mustn't talk about that. Philip is quite aware of what has happened,' Miss Swinbank said.

Unable to stop himself, David continued: 'She's been buried in a box in the ground, hasn't she? My dad says...'

'David! What did I just say?' Miss Swinbank said in vain, desperately trying to steer him off this course of conversation. 'David, why don't you tell Philip something nice?' she pleaded as he persisted in his attempt to get the details of my mother's death from me.

I remember that I was neither annoyed nor upset at David that day. At least he had mentioned what everyone else was frightened to talk about. Where everyone in that classroom had gone tiptoeing around the eggshells, David had stormed straight in, crunching every one under his two left feet, and to be honest, I was thankful to him for doing so. I decided to change the conversation topic to one that he had plenty of knowledge about.

'Still got your ringworm then, David?' I said.

Our teacher didn't care that he didn't stop talking about his ringworm for the next twenty minutes, because if he was discussing that, he wouldn't be asking for the morbid details of Mam's death.

I don't remember much about the days at school in the months following my mother's death. The evenings were something else, though. Fearing we might start to forget about our parents, Grandma and Grandad decided that we needed to talk about them. Grandad came into the kitchen after tea one evening with a bag containing two large scrapbooks, while Grandma had brought down a large box of photographs from the bedroom. The four of us were sitting around the kitchen table as she lifted a small pile of photos from the box and placed them in the centre of the kitchen table.

'I want each of you boys to pick a photo each, any one you like, but pick out one photo,' Grandma said, drawing in breath in an attempt to steel herself for what would be an emotional hour. Looking across the table at the pile of photos scattered in an untidy heap, numerous faces smiled back at me, many in black and white and occasional ones in colour that looked more familiar. I picked one up of Mam and Dad, taken on their wedding day. Roger chose another one for himself. Richard chose not to sit in on these sessions as he found it too painful to sit looking at photos and in an effort to minimise his tears in front of his little brothers, he found quiet solace watching TV in the sitting room.

Having each made our choice, Grandma or Grandad then took it in turns to tell us a story either about that particular photo or another story about Mam and Dad. Grandma found the task more difficult and had to take breaks, as she would inevitably start sobbing, leaving Grandad to pick up the reins and finish on her behalf. Once the story had concluded, we each stuck the photo into the scrapbook, which was then put away until the following evening when the practice would be repeated. For what became a nightly ritual, this seemed like the most normal thing in the world and when I look back as an adult, it was an inspired move. Those were the days before the widespread existence of bereavement counselling and support services run by professionals. It was a case of families, friends and communities providing support for each other in times of need. By going through the photographs, we weren't just listening to stories about our parents, but Grandma and Grandad made sure we never forgot them. If we were to grow up without them, then surely we should know as much as we could about who they were, what made them laugh, what made them cry and how they came together to create our family.

Dad had had two sisters. Aunt Ida was his elder sister and I knew of her from the times my dad had told me stories about her. She was a tall, beautiful, dark-haired woman, who was an excellent pianist and singer. Such was her talent that she often performed at the Empire Theatre in Sunderland as part of the Sunderland Operatic Society. Her premature death from meningitis at the age of twenty-eight left not only her three-year-old-son and husband, but her parents and siblings devastated. Dad had described her death as 'the darkest day at Stanhope Hall'.

Auntie Olive was four years younger than my father and up until this point, I didn't know her that well. Following Dad's death, Mam had accepted the hand of friendship from Auntie Olive and her family as they joined her and Richard at Dad's funeral. Weeks later, Mam had attended my cousin Chris's wedding only two days before she died.

A week after we returned to school, an invitation came from Auntie Olive. The invitation by telephone was the offer of her taking Roger and I to her house for the day that coming Saturday. The visit would be a dual-purpose one: to get to know her two little nephews better and to give my grandparents a break. There was only one problem: I didn't want to go and I made it quite clear to everyone in the house that I didn't want to go. It wasn't that I didn't want to meet my extended family, but even at the age of seven I was still painfully shy. My greatest fear was to walk into a room full of strangers and have them talk to me. As far as I was concerned, my aunt and cousins were strangers and the closer we got to their farm that Saturday, the more anxious I became, to the point where I was hysterical. On realising that my protestations were having no effect on Richard, who was driving, I started to lash out in the back of the car.

'I don't want to go!' I screamed.

'You're going and that's the end of it,' was Richard's response, his patience wearing thin.

But I was getting desperate and ultimately stooped to a low, even for a seven-year-old. 'It's your fault that Mam is dead. It's all your fault! You... you killed her!' I howled.

Richard slammed the brakes on the car as we jolted forward in the back seat. This time, I had gone too far. Turning around to face me I could see that he had tears in his eyes. He didn't want to be in this situation; he knew that I didn't mean it, but also knew that saying such things was not acceptable and I needed to be reprimanded. He could see that I was a frightened little boy who had gone through so much in recent weeks and here I was, going to stay with people who, to me, were almost strangers. He pulled the car into a passing place on the narrow road to allow a tractor to pass. Switching off the engine, he lit up a cigarette and inhaled deeply. Clearly, he needed to settle his nerves as well as giving me the opportunity to calm myself down. During the whole of my hysterical performance, Roger sat quietly next to me, not uttering a word, but was seemingly engrossed in his picture book that he had brought with him. Five minutes passed. Tears were dried and my nose was blown before we continued the final half a mile along the road to my aunt's house.

Nearly all Dad's side of my family were farmers and Auntie Olive herself had married a farmer. Their farm was much more modern than Stanhope Hall. The straight, tree-lined drive from the road up to the farmyard was neatly trimmed with grass on either side and there were small clumps of daffodils. As the car pulled up outside the farmhouse, Auntie Olive appeared in the glass porch, an apron tied around her waist. She had a warm smile on her face and as we climbed out of the car, she greeted us with open arms, offering hugs and kisses, which we duly accepted.

'How are you, boys?' she greeted in her Weardale accent.

She took us into the house and introduced us to our cousin

Helen, the youngest of her three children. Helen was about five years older than me and wore her mousey hair tied back in a ponytail; she was very friendly and I was soon put at ease. She started by showing us around the house and then took us out into the farmyard to see Uncle Alec. I had met Uncle Alec before when he came up to Stanhope Hall to see Mam on the night after Dad died. A tall, slim man with fair hair, he had a calm manner, immediately welcoming us both and was soon showing us his prized Bluefaced Leicester sheep, which were his pride and joy. I really liked him and soon felt at ease. I was enjoying myself and I don't know why I had made such a fuss in the car earlier. Roger and I had been through a very traumatic time considering we were so young and that trauma manifests itself in different ways, I suppose.

Back at the house, we washed our hands, as lunch was almost ready to be served. As we sat around the kitchen table, Auntie Olive served us cauliflower cheese with bacon. Having always been a fussy eater, I'd always refused to eat cauliflower at home and here I was with a great big portion on the plate in front of me. Not wanting to seem ungrateful, I started to eat it and to my surprise, I really liked it. The rest of the day was spent happily playing on the farm and after our tea, Auntie Olive packed us into her car and took us back up to the Hall.

Full of excitement, Roger and I ran into the house eager to tell Grandma and Grandad about our day out. I think this was the first day that we laughed and smiled after Mam's death and the relief on Grandma's face was obvious. My aunt followed us into the house and gave Grandma a report on how the day had gone, that both of us had eaten our lunch, before handing over a large bag of ginger snaps to Gran that were still warm from the oven. Relieved we had come home in one piece, Grandma thanked Auntie Olive and she drove off out of the farmyard. Back in the kitchen, Grandma sat at the polished table, staring at the gift of homemade biscuits, knowing full well that at times like this, you need all the friends you can get. As for Roger and I, we were already looking forward to our next visit to the farm and seeing our new family.

CHAPTER 16

Short Trousers

Since the previous November, Mam had been giving me fifty pence a week towards the class trip to Edinburgh. On my return to school, I asked Grandma if I could have the money to take in, but she declined my request. Instead, she passed me a note to take to Sister Di Pazzi, our headmistress, telling her that I wouldn't be going to Edinburgh: she was frightened to let me go on the trip for fear of something happening to me. That evening, after we had had tea, Sister Di Pazzi's car pulled up in the farmyard. Under the guise of a pastoral visit to see how Grandma was coping, Sister, as we called her, used the opportunity to talk my grandmother into allowing me to go to Edinburgh as planned. Grandma did take some convincing, but she trusted Sister Di Pazzi's sincerity and reassurance that I would be looked after and finally relented.

The weeks running up to the trip soon passed by and early one morning, we assembled outside the school gates, waiting to board the coach. Being such a small school, we had to share the coach with the Church of England primary school in the village. As we were there first, we raced to secure our seats as close to the back as possible and soon the coach was full of excited kids, screaming and shouting. Miss Swinbank had taught the whole class to sing 'Mull of Kintyre' on the coach in the weeks running up to the trip, as some sort of ill-advised cultural activity, and understandably we received muted applause from the other school.

With a pit stop at Hadrian's Wall and the Roman fort at Housesteads, we arrived in Edinburgh at teatime. We stayed at the Arden Hotel, which sat on an elevated position on Royal Terrace, below Calton Hill. It was a vast, tired-looking hotel that accommodated school parties, with its many rooms spread across several floors. It was only a matter of time before we were running riot up and down the stairs, chasing each other along the long, dusty passageways.

I'd never seen anything like Edinburgh before in my life. I had been there when I was five, but my memory of the visit was hazy. Over the next two days we went to Edinburgh Castle and the Palace of Holyroodhouse amongst many others. I'd never been to a big city like Edinburgh before and at the main tourist attractions, I found myself staring at the tourists from other countries talking in foreign languages. I'd never seen Japanese people before and I'd certainly never heard French or Italian being spoken other than on the TV. Suddenly aware that the world was a much bigger place, I became obsessed with listening to foreigners speaking their own language. At Edinburgh Castle, Sister Di Pazzi had to keep coming to find me, as I lagged behind from the main group, listening in on people's conversations in Japanese or some other language.

I loved Edinburgh and found the city to have such an intoxicating appeal. Above all, the best thing about the trip was that I had three days away from home. I loved my family dearly and very much appreciated them, but it was so liberating to be away from grieving people. At home on the farm, there were constant daily reminders about death. Grandma crying, letters addressed to 'The late H.H. Mews' or even walking past the dining room door every day, knowing that on the other side of the door was the room where my parents' coffins had been laid out. To have this break away was the release that I needed. Once I returned home fully intact and carrying a small amount of Scottish tourist tat, I had hoped that Grandma might begin to relax a little and worry less. Perhaps she would even allow us a bit more of a free rein to go out onto the farm and beyond and play at our daring adventures, as we had done before we became orphans. This was not to be.

That Easter, I went to stay with my Auntie Brenda and Uncle Ron at their house in Seaburn. I spent the entire week playing with my cousin Gaynor, although I don't recall much other than riding bikes and going to the beach, even if the weather was cool and windy. In a letter written at that time, Auntie Brenda did her best to reassure her worrying parents:

Dear Mam & Dad,
Just writing this while we wait for Richard coming. Well,
our Philip has had a good week, he is very precious to me
so I watch him very carefully. I have kept him wrapped
up with his duffle coat and hat. He has got a nose cold
but he has eaten all his meals all week, with a bowl of
warm milk and cornflakes every morning. I think that it

is only cooked joints and veg that he does not like but he likes mince and frozen peas and sliced green beans and an orange yoghurt for a sweet. I have had the bottles in his bed and warm pyjamas. I have given him a good wash every night but I have not washed his hair, with him having cold. So everything has gone off well and Gaynor and him have been fine, not one squabble all week, I can honestly say. She has read him stories every night.

Well Mam, I keep most things to myself. I am not one for many words but like you, my heart aches for our Alma. I do my work every day through a veil of tears. She was my dear sister and I am missing her very much. There is an emptiness inside me that will never be filled. I can well understand how you both will be feeling and it must be a hard job for you to get through each day. There will never be anyone as good and as kind as our Alma and she will always be in my thoughts day and night.

You are going to be busy in the summer holidays getting Philip's things ready for school. It is just as well now that he comes to me as you will have to take him to Barnard Castle for his uniform. I hope that all the papers come through for him to go alright. Philip will be able to come and stay for a fortnight here on his next holiday. He will be alright.

I think that is all for the moment. Should you ever need me, ring June and don't forget the code first, you have it in the book. If you and Dad are ever bad, let me know straight away. I have six weeks holiday from the school and would come straight away. I am always thinking of you both, I feel that I am not much help to you at the moment.

If the boys get to school, they will always be able to come to me for the holidays anytime. I will always see to their welfare and won't let anything happen to them. God be with you both,

Your ever loving daughter Brenda xxxx

Reading back that letter now, thirty-nine years later, I finally understand exactly how my Auntie Brenda must have felt in losing her sister.

The good people at the Royal Masonic Trust for Girls and Boys, along with the Masonic Lodge in Stanhope, had been working in the background since Mam's funeral and one morning, a letter arrived addressed to my grandparents. It was from Barnard Castle Prep School, inviting them and me to come and take a look around. Dressed up in our best clothes, Richard and Grandma took me to visit my potential new school. I'm not really sure at this point that I was fully aware that I was going to board there but, nevertheless, I went along with it.

Barnard Castle is a pretty market town situated in Teesdale on the banks of the River Tees and only an eighteen-mile drive from Stanhope. The school was a large, imposing building and driving past it, with its white wooden 'pepper pot' nestled on top, we slowly made our way up the secluded winding drive and pulled up outside a large Victorian house. Grandma fussed over me, running her gloved hand across my hair in an attempt to straighten out the tuft that always stuck up at the back. Happy that I was in a presentable state, she rang the doorbell, which echoed inside the house. After a moment, a short lady wearing brown trousers, a flowery blouse and large round glasses answered the door. In her well-spoken voice, she queried, 'Mrs Mews?'

Smiling at her, Grandma responded, 'I'm Mrs Close, Philip's grandma. Er… this is Philip Mews.'

Richard followed by introducing himself.

'I'm Mrs Sherbrooke, house mother here at the Prep School. Please do come in.'

As we walked into the large hallway, I looked around, taking in all the detail: the colourful tiles on the floor, the high ceilings and in particular I remember the way that every noise echoed around the room.

She introduced her husband, Mr Sherbrooke, the principal of the Prep School. He was a tall man with a balding head, goatee beard and a warm smile. Pretty much straight away, I was whisked into a small dining room and was seated at the table to perform a number of written tests. It felt like I was in there for an entire afternoon, but actually it only took about an hour. When we were done, I was taken back out into the hall to wait for Grandma and Richard to return. Mrs Sherbrooke, having given them a tour of the facilities, then led me through to take a tour for myself, leaving Grandma and Richard with her husband to chat. I was shown the classrooms and recreational room, where the boys spent most of their time. We entered the cloakroom, where a row of navy mackintosh coats with belts hung on coat pegs. *Was I going to have to wear one of them?* I thought to myself. As if that wasn't bad enough, I then spied the row of caps with the school badge emblazoned on the front. Did people really still wear these? They were like something from the *Just William* show that I had seen on TV.

Now climbing the back staircase, Mrs Sherbrooke led me into a large room, where six identical black metal beds were lined along two walls on top of freshly mopped floor tiles. Confused, I asked, 'Why are there beds in here?'

'Well, this is where you will be sleeping, of course,' was the response.

Reeling, I stared incredulously at the beds in this stark room. I could block out the truth no longer, I was going to go away from home and sleep at school. I was going to have to leave my family.

In the car on the way back home, I could think of nothing else but the strange uniforms and the dormitory with the beds in it. This was all alien to me. Then it dawned on me: this was to help my grandparents. I was going away to school to help them manage back at home and this was part of the deal that ensured our family stayed together. I couldn't complain or protest. That wouldn't be fair, no matter how much I was hurting inside at the prospect of going away. Back home, we all discussed the school around the table at teatime. Roger was disappointed that he couldn't come with me to boarding school and was told that he would have to wait until he turned eight.

In the weeks that followed, preparations were made so that I would be ready to start my new school in September. A list of clothing and other items that I would need arrived from the school. Grandad came home one afternoon with a large old tin trunk on which he delicately painted 'Philip Mews, 625' – the school number allocated to me for my time in the Prep School. This was placed in my old bedroom (now that I was sleeping in my parents' old room full-time) and I went in each day to see what had been bought. As each item was added to the pile I got so excited at small things, such as a plastic blue soap dish, a proper gentleman's wash bag, a clothes brush, etc.

After school every day, Grandad and I headed up to the room and he gave me lessons in the skills that I would need to live independently once I went away. One day he taught me how to polish my shoes, the next we covered tying a tie. For most other kids, this is something they learned on an ad hoc basis when living with their parents, but I needed to start the school with the ability to confidently perform these tasks for myself. With repeat sessions on tying a tie, folding clothes and polishing my shoes, it wasn't long before I was soon ready for my new adventure.

Being so busy with all these preparations actually helped a little to take my mind off losing Mam and Dad. Otherwise, life carried on as normal. As May approached, so did my eighth birthday. Sister Di Pazzi, on one of her regular weekend visits to the farm, had asked Grandma if she would like to have a birthday party for me at the school rather than back at home so as to make life easier. It was practical offers of help such as this that were so welcomed by our family and I'm sure the last thing that Grandma wanted was to have twenty-five children, all high on sugar, running around the house.

On the day of my birthday, Grandma and Grandad pulled up in their little car at the school gates and began to unload the mountain of huge Tupperware containers and cake tins. A couple of hours earlier, Miss Swinbank had the class making decorations to hang up in the small dining hall for my party. Grandad had brought with him a packet of balloons and started to blow them up, much to Grandma's annoyance – she hated balloons, as she was always scared that one of us could swallow one, when trying to blow it up. I remember several years later she had cut out a story from a newspaper where a child had choked on a balloon, trying to blow the thing up. That was something she always did, cutting out newspaper articles that highlighted the dangers of anything from swimming in the river to climbing trees. Of course, it was annoying at the time, but we were lucky to have someone who loved and cared for us so much.

It was decided that lessons would finish early and as the sun was shining on this beautiful summer afternoon, we should play the party games out on the school field. Auntie Olive arrived at the school gates with my birthday cake. A large square orange cake, it was immaculately piped and sported eight brightly coloured candles on the top. Once the games had finished, we all ran down into the dining hall for our tea. Grandma was there with Sister Di Pazzi, mixing large metal jugs of orange squash and standing back from the two long tables groaning with plates of sandwiches, cakes, scones and the obligatory sausages and pineapple on sticks.

After tea, I was handed a multitude of presents and cards by my friends, well aware that I had probably received such extraordinary kindness due to my recent loss as much as anything else. I was overwhelmed by the generosity of people in our community and it really did make a difference. That day my life was full of vibrant colour after the bleak landscape I had been living in for the past seven months.

As the summer term drew to a close, I was a little sad that I wouldn't be coming back in September and really quite daunted at the prospect of going away to boarding school. Final preparations for the school play, *Alice in Wonderland*, were underway and I was cast as the Dormouse. It was during the dress rehearsal while sitting on stage at the Mad Hatter's tea party that I fainted. There was a scramble to get me off stage and before I knew it, Grandma and Grandad were at the school to collect me. I really wasn't feeling very well at all and poor Grandma was petrified that my illness was more serious than it actually was. I was taken home and put to bed. Grandma told everyone that I had pneumonia, which obviously wasn't the case. Nevertheless, I was forced to spend a week in bed with only my books and some jigsaws while my classmates got to perform *Alice in Wonderland*, complete with a Dormouse understudy. I was disappointed to have missed the play and that I never got the chance to say goodbye to most of my friends.

After a week in bed, I was itching to be back outside on the farm and having fun over the summer holidays. The Devitts came up from Sunderland and their new static caravan had been put in place in the Top Wood. We had seen them over the winter, as they had come to the farm when each of my parents had died, but now was the time that we were to carry on where we left off the previous summer. Jimmy and Theresa Devitt wanted to make sure that we all had fun and did their best to entertain us all. Things seemed different without Mam and Dad being around, but everyone made a concerted effort to carry on as normal.

For Grandma, the responsibility of bringing up Roger and myself was one that weighed heavily on her shoulders. She had always been a worrier and was never afraid of vocalising her fears. 'The bairns!' she would shout on a regular basis if Richard or his friends were playing with us in the garden or the house. It was the usual rough and tumble of rolling around and play fighting, etc. that all boys do when growing up, but such antics could always be guaranteed to send her into a fit of panic. At the time, we used to laugh it off, but looking back, it is easy to comprehend her fears: there she was, seventy years old, and having taken on the responsibility for two little lads, she was petrified that something else might could go wrong and that she would lose us. The result was that Grandma was reluctant for us to do anything that might remotely affect our health or put us in any danger. Whereas in previous summers we had gone down to the river with fishing nets, visited the swimming pool with friends and their parents, now such activities were forbidden. Still enveloped in grief, her fear of losing her lads was more than she could bear. We were no longer allowed to go out for day trips with anyone other than the Devitts, and even that was only allowed after Theresa had gone down to the farmhouse and offered reassurance to her.

During the summer holidays, we still had to continue preparations for me going away to school. Auntie Olive took Grandma and myself over to Swinbanks, which was the approved school outfitters in Barnard Castle. It was a typical gentleman's outfitters, where the salesmen were as stiff and formal as the shirt collars they were selling. Upstairs in the school uniform department, several ladies manned the counter as each customer would receive a full personal service. It was like a scene from the set of *Are You Being Served?*, a hugely popular television sitcom at the time, only without the innuendos and cheeky gags.

Holding the list, Grandma explained the situation that I was an orphan and that this would be the first term that I would be going away from home. Having filled in the staff on the state of our family situation and the obligatory sympathetic head tilting had been offered, they set about the business of getting me kitted out for my new school.

If school fees weren't enough of a barrier to stop ordinary people sending their kids to public school, then the extortionate cost of the uniform certainly must have been. With state schools, parents normally had the liberty to get the bulk of the school uniform from the shop that they could best afford and then buy the school badge for the blazer from the official school outfitter. Not here. The grey V-neck jumper, the knee-length grey woollen socks all had the blue and brown piping of the school colours and could only be bought from Swinbanks. A school cap was brought out of a cabinet and tried on my head for size.

I studied myself in the mirror: I didn't like it all and thought it made me look far too posh, but as I looked back at my refection, I caught sight of Grandma sitting on the chair behind me. Beaming with pride, she removed her glasses momentarily to wipe away a tear.

I was handed a dark navy woollen blazer to try on and complete the look. It felt like an extravagance, as it would only be worn for chapel on Sundays. I stood patiently as the lady wrapped a tape measure around various limbs and more and more items were piled up on the counter, such as rugby kit, a Cub Scout uniform with another silly cap. Then came the school trousers – grey, short trousers.

'We get long trousers for the winter, don't we? These are just for summer, aren't they?' I said. The lady simply shook her head. 'But what do we wear in the snow?' I pleaded.

'Wellington boots, with short trousers,' came the reply.

I gave Grandma a pleading look, but I could see that she was already tired and in no mood to have a discussion about this. Those were the rules and all the other boys wore them, I was told by the lady.

Auntie Olive saw her role as being the one to perk me up during the process.

'Come on, Philip,' she said in an encouraging tone, 'you'll look so smart. What a lucky boy you are to have such a lovely uniform.'

Despite her optimistic approach, I couldn't agree but gave her my best attempt at a smile.

The uniform shopping complete, it was all carefully packed into a large cardboard box and two gentlemen from the shop floor downstairs carried it down and loaded it into the boot of Auntie Olive's car outside the shop. I was lucky, as the outlay for all my uniform was covered by the generosity of the Masonic Trust and their grant. I did appreciate, even at the time, that all this had cost a small fortune and that I was incredibly fortunate to be in this position.

Once we were home, Auntie Brenda arrived a couple of days later, carrying piles of shopping bags containing underwear, pyjamas and toiletries to add to the pile of uniform. For days, she and Grandma painstakingly sewed name tags onto every single item of clothing, including towels, while Grandad, with a permanent marker pen, labelled all my shoes, hair brush, clothes brush, wooden coat-hangers, stationery, etc. Each item was then diligently packed into the trunk and ticked off the list.

I needed formal shoes to go with my uniform. There was nothing I hated more than shopping for shoes and Grandma had insisted on new Clarks shoes for school. We knew nothing of designer labels, but if we had, Clarks was about as designer as it got. On this hot August afternoon, Roger and I were sitting in the back of the car while Richard was our reluctant designated driver. Grandma hated going faster than forty miles an hour, so the journey to Bishop Auckland was a long and tedious one in the hot, stuffy car. Because she'd had had an operation on her head years ago to correct a trigeminal neuralgia, which sent severe shooting pain down the side of her face, Grandma always kept it covered with a hat or a headscarf and hated a draught.

On our arrival at Bishop (locals never refer to the 'Auckland'), the car pulled up in the piece of rough ground that posed as a car park. I opened the door and gasped for fresh air, as the car interior breathed a sigh of relief. Richard wisely chose to stay put while we were hauled off to buy the shoes.

Robertson's was Grandma's shop of choice for school shoes. It was an imposing building with a polished brass handle, and as we opened the door, a bell tinkled. We were greeted by a woman in her fifties wearing a neck-tie blouse and so much hairspray that her bouffant didn't move a millimetre. She spun around on her heels to summon her young colleague, who was looking bored and picking at her nail polish.

'Sharon,' she said to the girl, who was clearly deep in thought on other matters. The woman turned back to us and smiled apologetically. 'Sharon!' she barked in a loud voice that made me jump. 'Sharon, would you kindly serve this lady and these two young gentlemen?'

The girl stepped forward, annoyed that she actually had to do some work, and led me over to 'the machine'. She asked me to remove my shoes and place one foot in the mechanical measuring contraption that would engulf it, while she, easily distracted, would leave her foot on the pedal as my toes began to curl under. It was only when I let out a yelp did her attention return to the machine and she released the pedal. Having cocked up this simple process, she had no choice but to start again.

Not trusting her colleague, the older woman now took over and gave orders to the girl, sending her off into the stockroom to fetch numerous pairs of shoes for my approval. It was at this point that the small talk would start. Grandma, still wearing black after six months, would readily offer up the information, 'They're orphans, you know…' That word again – 'Orphans'. It was a conversation that I would become all too familiar with over the coming years.

A letter came from the Prep School for Grandma and Grandad, giving them more information regarding life at the boarding school:

<u>Notes for Parents</u>
These notes have been prepared to give you an outline of Preparatory School life and to provide you with information you may find helpful.
<u>DAILY ROUTINE</u>
The rising bell rings at 7.30 a.m., the boys wash and dress and breakfast at 7.50 a.m. After this, mail is distributed and the boys make their beds and tidy their dormitories. Morning school consists of four periods lasting from 9.00 a.m. until 12.30 p.m. Lunch at 12.30 p.m. is followed by afternoon lessons from 1.30 p.m. until 3.30 p.m., after which the boys are free to play games, make their models or pursue their hobbies. After tea, an activity such as Cub Scouts, rounders or a walk in the surrounding countryside is organised. Supervised Preparation consisting of half an hour written work and half an hour of reading ends at 7.00 p.m., when the boys have supper and prepare for bed. The silence bell rings

at 8.00 p.m. and lights go out at 8.30 p.m. The boys remain in bed during this period and may read their comics.

On Thursdays organised games take place for both boarding and day pupils and after tea, the boys go to Main School for swimming and hot baths. There are no afternoon lessons on Saturday and games are played. On Sunday morning, 45 minutes is set aside for letter writing and at 10.30 a.m., the pupils go to Chapel. The afternoon is occupied by supervised games, expeditions into the surrounding countryside, swimming, etc.

During periods of free time the boys may choose a variety of activities, such as model making, table tennis and indoor games.

THINGS TO BRING

At the beginning of each term the boys must bring with them a weekend bag containing their brush, comb, toothbrush, a pair of shoes, slippers, pyjamas and linen sufficient for three days.

Two items your son will need are an inexpensive fountain pen and a craft board. Boys may bring toys and games but please do not overdo this! We have limited storage space and in addition to the games we provide, your son will share those brought by other boarders.

Pocket money is limited to £4 per term and is handed in to Mrs Sherbrooke upon arrival. £2 of this may only be spent on fruit and the other £2 is "tuck money", which may be spent on anything – sweets, marbles, toys and models.

A weekly fruit order is taken from the boys and is

delivered to the school. Tuck money may be spent at the school tuck shop after lunch on a Saturday. The boys are given complete freedom to spend their money as they wish but most soon learn to spread this spending over the term in a sensible manner.

We do not allow tuck parcels of any sort. All boys have an equal opportunity to provide their own sweets and invidious comparisons are avoided. No money should be sent to boys. Each boy is allowed one comic per week.

LETTERS

We insist that all boys write home at least once a week and a time is set aside for this purpose on Sunday morning. It may be advisable to provide your boy with a number of stamped addressed envelopes for his first letters.

DOMESTIC DUTIES

The only "chores" the boys do are cleaning their own shoes and making their beds. It would be helpful if you gave your boy some instruction in these things if he does not already do them for himself. In addition, please check that he can fasten his own tie.

CHAPTER 17

Twenty-One Brothers

I was about to leave my family and embark on a new chapter of my life. I knew very little about boarding school and so I wasn't really sure what to expect, but I was ready for the adventure.

On the afternoon of my departure, I was sent upstairs by Grandma to change. She had laid out my uniform on my bed and Grandad came up to check that I had done my tie correctly. My grandparents looked at me proudly, as I stood in my full uniform, complete with school cap and the new Clarks shoes. Saying my goodbyes to Roger and Grandad wasn't too emotional, for no other reason than I was too excited to be going to my new school. I had never been away from home or my family before, so I really had no idea how much it was going to hurt to be parted from them. Roger, on the other hand, was devastated that I was leaving. We hadn't really been apart before and my going away to school left him feeling lonely and bereft.

Richard drove me to the school with Grandma sitting next to him in the front passenger seat. I was wedged in the back with one of the car seats pushed down in order to fit in the tin trunk containing my uniform and belongings. I was allowed one weekend bag, which I had stuffed with my essentials, such as some books, a *Beano* annual, my teddy and a photo of Mam and Dad.

Forty minutes later, as the car made its way up the drive of the Prep School, I looked out of the window and already the place had a vague familiarity about it. We pulled up and another boy climbed out of the car next to us. Looking at him, I noticed that he was taller than me and also skinny, which wasn't helped by his knobbly knees sticking out of his grey short trousers. His eyes were red and bloodshot from crying and he was blowing his nose into a large hanky. I could see that his cheeks and his ears matched the redness of his eyes.

'Philip, don't stare! Where's your cap?' Grandma said in a hushed voice.

With my cap retrieved from the back seat, she held my hand and led me towards the front door, glancing behind her to check on Richard's progress with carrying the tin trunk all by himself. I looked back to see the skinny boy crying and trying to catch his breath. His mother attempted to console him while his father looked on awkwardly as he lifted the boy's trunk out of the car boot. Grandma reached forward and with her hand covered in a navy glove, she pressed the doorbell. I knew this was it, there was no going back. Mrs Sherbrooke opened the door once again and greeted us.

'Mews, welcome to Westwick Lodge,' she said. The hallway behind her was a hive of activity with other boys coming and going. Whereas last time she had welcomed Grandma and Richard in and made a fuss of them, on this occasion she kept them on the doorstep. 'Leave the trunk there on the step, Mr Mews,' she instructed Richard.

'Well, Mews,' she said.

I looked at her thinking, *is she talking to me? Why doesn't she call me Philip? Everybody calls me Philip.*

'I think you had better say goodbye to your grandmother and brother now, Mews,' she told me.

I was taken aback. I had envisaged Grandma and Richard being able to come in with me and help me settle in and show them my bed. Judging by the look on Grandma's face, she had been thinking the same. As I turned to say my goodbyes much sooner than I had expected, I tried to keep myself from crying. In one sense it was to protect Grandma and hopefully make her less upset, but also because out of the corner of my eye, I could see the skinny boy still sobbing uncontrollably. Mrs Sherbrooke was getting impatient as I hugged and kissed Grandma and Richard to say goodbye.

'Come on then, Mews, let's get you inside,' she said as Grandma was wiping a tear from behind her glasses. I was used to seeing her cry but it was when I looked at my older brother Richard, his eyes full of tears, desperately trying to hold it together, that I felt my resolve beginning to melt and my own tears welled up too. It was at that moment that I was hurriedly escorted inside and the door shut behind me. Once I was inside the house, Mrs Sherbrooke introduced me to a smiling tubby boy with black hair and green eyes.

'Mews, this is Watson. Watson here will be your minder for your first two weeks. He will help you find your way about and show you how we do things here at the Prep School.'

Watson was about to say hello, but before he had the chance to do so she cut in again. 'Watson's parents are farmers, so I'm sure you will have plenty to talk about,' she said. Turning to Watson, she whispered, 'Mews doesn't have any parents.' That final sentence left me frozen to the spot. I don't think she meant it to come out as insensitively as it did, but it hurt me all the same. Reaching out, I shook Watson's extended hand.

'My mam and dad just died,' I said, keen to correct her. I did have parents, they weren't alive, that was all. I couldn't utter anything else. Watson didn't say a word, and I sensed that he didn't dare to do so in front of Mrs Sherbrooke, as he probably found her as frightening as I did. Instead, he took my brand-new blue Adidas bag from me and led me up the grand front staircase to our dormitory.

'These are the front stairs. This is the only time that you are allowed to use them,' he said.

'Why? How are we supposed to get upstairs?' I questioned naively.

'These are Mr and Mrs Sherbrooke's stairs. Boys have to use the back staircase to the dorms.'

Leading me into the dormitory off the landing, Watson placed my bag on the middle of three beds that ran along the far side of the room. 'This is B Dorm and over here, this is your bed.' A small white sticker reading 'MEWS' had been stuck firmly on the metal frame at the foot of the bed. Staring at it, I thought to myself once more, *My name is Philip*, but I didn't say anything. As I started to unpack my bag, I changed my mind.

'At home, everybody calls me Philip,' I said to him.

'You cannat use your first names in here. She'll gan mad,' a new voice bellowed behind me. A large thick-set lad, about a year or two older than me, walked into the dorm and dumped his large bag on the bed next to mine.

'Theakston, Eddie Theakston,' he said confidently, putting out his hand to shake.

'Philip Mews… I mean Mews,' I stumbled.

Eddie was a farmer's son too, but unlike me, he seemed to know lots about farming, judging by the fact that he never stopped talking about it. He had a cheeky face and no matter what mood he was in, he was always smiling. After about five minutes, Watson said that we ought to go over to the classrooms and on the way he would show me the playroom. Walking back across the landing, I went to walk back down the stairs when Watson grabbed my arm and said, 'Back stairs, remember?' I paused for a moment at the top of the stairs and peered down at the skinny boy, who was now in the hall with Mrs Sherbrooke. He was still crying, sobbing into his tear-soaked hanky. Tugging on my arm again, Watson pulled me away from the staircase for fear of us being seen by Mrs Sherbrooke. I wasn't jumping to conclusions, but I could already see that everyone was quite scared of her.

I was taken on a tour of the rest of the school and with each area I was told which part we were allowed in and which areas, which seemed to be the majority, were out of bounds. The Prep School was housed in Westwick Lodge, a beautiful Victorian house with the original decorative tiled floors still intact. Past the cloakroom at the back of the house lay the playroom, a large room with double doors at the far end and containing a row of toy lockers and a piano. As we walked in, I saw two boys looking through a bag of marbles, lifting each one out and commenting on it. Both of them briefly looked up and acknowledged my presence before returning to the matter in hand. Beyond the playroom lay the small 1960s classroom block, which housed two classrooms and a craft room. Behind this was a large walled garden that ran right up to a tree-covered area known as 'the mound'. At the front of the school lay a tennis lawn and next to that a croquet lawn, which stretched along the front of the large orangery. With the wooded gardens cascading down towards the main road, this place was truly picturesque and would have been more so had we had regular access to it, but as we were constantly reminded, those areas were out of bounds.

As I was shown around the school, I did my best to remember the rules that were being pointed out to me and I was already scared of putting a foot wrong and upsetting Mrs Sherbrooke. When teatime came, I met the rest of the boarders. There were twenty-two of us in total and our ages ranged from eight to ten years old as boys only attended the Prep School for three years before moving up to the Main School at the age of eleven. We lined up along the back porch for tea and Mr Sherbrooke appeared.

'Hello boys, ready for a new term?'

'Yes, Sir,' the group responded in well-rehearsed unison.

'Can I expect you to stay out of trouble this year, Theakston?' he said, singling out my cheeky dorm mate Eddie.

'Yes, Sir,' he replied, grinning.

Mr Sherbrooke smiled as if to say he had been here before with Theakston. He leaned forward and pressed the electronic bell and with that, the queue of boys shuffled forwards to the entrance hall of the house and lined up along the wall outside the dining room. Mrs Sherbrooke opened the door and stood back in front of a large marble fireplace as the boys in front of me stepped forward and stretched their hands out in front of her, palms upward before turning them over for her to check the backs. As Watson had steered me to the toilet to wash mine before we went down, I hoped mine would pass the test. Holding my hands out, I couldn't stop shaking and casting an eye through her thick glasses, she smiled and said, 'Follow Watson, Mews.'

My minder indicated for me to follow him and sit down on the bench at one of three tables that were set up in the room. Our table was known as South Table and of course the one at the opposite end of the room was called the North Table. We all sat down once Grace had been said and then Mrs Sherbrooke addressed us all and asked each of the new boys to answer their name and put their hand up when they were called.

'Hodgson, Mews, Mitchell…' she read out our names one by one.

'Winford.'

Nobody put their hand up as we all looked about the room.

'Winford,' she repeated as she turned her head towards the skinny boy, who was sat at the North Table, his eyes red from crying and holding his hanky.

'Winford, you must answer your name when I call it out,' she said.

The boy was clearly traumatised at the experience of leaving his family, but this was the 1970s and it was drilled into us all that we had to be tough. Boarding schools weren't as sympathetic or as tuned in to displays of emotion back then so it was normal for crying boys to be encouraged to 'pull themselves together'.

That evening, as we went to bed, a bell rang at eight o'clock to signal half an hour of silent reading before lights out. Sitting in bed and holding the photo of Mam and Dad, the true impact of that day hit me like a wrecking ball. Tears streamed down my face and I could do nothing to stop their flow. Watson and Theakston both jumped across to my bed in an effort to comfort me but there was nothing that could be done to console me. Mrs Sherbrooke appeared after a short time to turn the lights out and on seeing me, she told Watson and Wright to get back to their beds immediately, and to me, her only words of comfort before flicking the switch and plunging the dorm into darkness were, 'Come on, Mews, crying isn't going to help you, you're a big boy now.'

As I lay in my bed crying myself to sleep, I could hear the skinny boy sobbing in the next dorm. I wasn't crying because I was homesick but because I was grieving and now I was alone. Nobody there could begin to comprehend what I had been through and how I felt that night as I lay on my pillow, now drenched with tears.

CHAPTER 18

School Life

Despite my initial misgivings, I soon managed to settle into a way of life at Barney (as we now referred to the school). I made some good friends and in particular, I struck up a friendship with Winford, the skinny boy. We had quite a bit in common, in that our birthdays were on the same day, we both lived on farms and both our first names were Philip. He was a nice quiet lad and he, like most of us, was often on the receiving end of Mrs Sherbrooke's bad mood. The Sherbrookes seemed to be such a mismatched couple. He was an optimistic and friendly man with a very down-to-earth nature, whereas she appeared to take great pleasure in making unkind comments and treating people poorly. Who knows what makes a marriage tick? Whatever it was, it worked, and they were married for many years. What's more, both of their children were kind and amiable, thankfully taking after their father.

On my first full day, I was introduced to my class teacher, Miss Willatt, who was in charge of the Lower Division. She was about thirty-five years old, single and kept coloured tissues in the cuff of her cardigan. I really liked her. She had a great deal of warmth and she was patient with all of us in the class, empathising with us younger boys who were away from home for the first time. Miss Willatt taught us everything from how to do joined-up writing with our fountain pens to playing musical instruments. I really enjoyed being in her class and that made being away from home so much more bearable.

Every evening after tea, we were encouraged to go outside and play. If the weather was poor or the dark nights were drawing in, we were allowed to sit in the classroom and watch TV. Mrs Sherbrooke informed us on our first day that we were not allowed to watch ITV as it was considered far too common. So despite there only being three television channels back in 1978, we were restricted to watching the BBC. *Happy Days* and *Magpie* had to make way for *John Craven's Newsround* and *Blue Peter*, both of which I actually enjoyed. The only flaw in her plan came a few months later when the BBC screened a new kids' show called *Grange Hill*. It was a drama series set in a north London comprehensive school and soon we were hooked on the exploits of a group of rowdy state school kids on our TV screens.

'I'm sure your parents will be delighted to be paying out good money for your education to have you sit and watch children misbehaving in a comprehensive school,' she would say, placing particular emphasis on the word 'comprehensive'. In that first week, we were given something referred to as 'prep', which was the posh school name for homework. Each weeknight, we were supervised in a classroom from six o'clock, with the first half hour devoted to doing our prep and in the second half hour we were allowed to write a letter home or read a book (but not a comic).

The first book that I chose to read was one from the Enid Blyton *Famous Five* series. I had inherited most of them from Richard, so had taken two to school with me. Once the bell rang at seven o'clock, we disbanded from the classroom and ran along to the kitchen. Mrs Sherbrooke poured each of us a small glass of milk and we were given a digestive biscuit with it, before going upstairs to get washed and changed into our pyjamas. In that first week while having our milk one evening, Mrs Sherbrooke noticed my book.

'What are you reading, Mews?' she asked.

'*The Famous Five*, Mrs Sherbrooke,' I replied.

'Oh, what are you reading that rubbish for?' she snapped back.

'My mam used to read them to me,' I said quietly, aware that all the other boys were now staring at me.

'Well, Mews, they're very poorly written stories. You ought to set your sights a bit higher and read a proper book. You'll find plenty of them in your classroom,' she said.

I felt terrible. There I was, desperately trying to hang on to any connection that I had with my parents, and she dismissed my mother's reading choices without any thought to my feelings.

Having washed and changed upstairs, we were allowed to play board games and chat before the silence period. Each dorm had a senior Prep School boy who was appointed as monitor to keep order amongst the ranks. Monitors were not permitted to dish out punishments but if anyone were to seriously misbehave, then they would 'report' the offending boy to Mr or Mrs Sherbrooke. In those first days of term there were still a few of us who cried ourselves to sleep in the dorms but as the week progressed, this diminished. One night in the first week, the lights had been switched off for about ten minutes when a loud electronic buzzing noise reverberated through the house. The boys around me jumped up out of their beds, shouting, 'Fire practice!'

The dorm lights were switched on and Mrs Sherbrooke ordered us to put our dressing gowns and slippers on and pick up the travelling rug that each of us had sitting folded on the end of our bed. We were led out onto the landing and into the room next door, which was actually the bedroom of Mrs Sherbrooke's teenage daughter. With the sash window open, we were instructed by Mr Sherbrooke to climb through the window and on to the metal fire escape ladder that dropped vertically on to the path below.

I was nervous as anything and petrified of falling off but with a few words of encouragement, I diligently climbed down, somehow balancing the oversized Otterburn blanket that I was carrying. Once I'd set foot on the ground, relief swept over me. I was directed on to the croquet lawn, where the other boys were assembled ready for the roll call. It was pretty nippy that night and I soon saw the point of the travel rugs as the older boys wrapped them around themselves, with us new lads following suit.

Standing on the lawn in the dark, we were aware of a commotion at the top of the ladder at the bedroom window. Poor Jamieson, another new boy, was crying at the window, absolutely petrified at the prospect of climbing out into the autumn night and down a ladder. After some coaxing, negotiation and a few encouraging words from Mr Sherbrooke, he climbed out and gingerly made his way down the ladder, with the rest of us erupting into applause when his foot landed on the gravel path.

'Well done, boys!' said Mrs Sherbrooke, now herself on the lawn. 'Although Jamieson would have burned to death, had there been a real fire.'

'That fat heffer never climbed down the ladder, did she? She went down the bloody stairs!' Eddie Theakston whispered just a little too loudly. Mrs Sherbrooke looked across at us and in particular at my smirking dorm mate.

'Something you wish to share with us, Theakston?'

'No, Mrs Sherbrooke,' was his response, finding it difficult to stifle the laughter.

In single file we were allowed to head back upstairs via the forbidden front staircase before Mr Sherbrooke came round and did his checks, switching out the dorm lights for the second time that night.

On my third morning at the Prep School, I met Mr Hay for the first time. A red-faced man in his late fifties with a large belly, he was the form teacher for the Upper Division class and his reputation for being a frightening character preceded him. I think both the red face and the belly were attributed to his love of beer. Every day he travelled to school on his motorbike, lighting up one of his Marlboros before he had even switched off the engine. Every Monday and Thursday he took assembly, when all the boys would sit cross-legged on the floor while he read a story from the Old Testament. During my first assembly with him, he stared at me during the hymn and as soon as it was finished, he bellowed:

'You, boy!'

Not sure who he was talking to, I looked around, only to realise that he was talking directly to me.

'What is your name, boy?'

'Mews…' I stammered nervously.

'Hughes?'

'No, Sir… Mews.'

I was now shaking.

'Come here, Mews,' he said.

As the rest of the boys were now sitting on the floor, I was aware of the whole school staring at me. I barely moved.

'Come here, Mews. I don't bite!'

Standing in front of him, the smell of alcohol on him was intoxicating and I could feel my eyes starting to sting from his breath. As he looked down over his gold half-moon reading glasses, I felt my knees wobble.

'Mews, what were you just singing there?' His voice wasn't getting any quieter.

'A hymn, Sir!'

'Yes, Sir! A hymn, Sir.' He mimicked me in a pathetic wet voice. 'Except you weren't singing the hymn, were you, Sir?'

'I don't know the hymn, Sir. I'm sorry, Sir,' I murmured apologetically, ever more desperate to escape his boozy breath, now wafting in my face and threatening to make me retch.

'Don't talk nonsense, boy! How could you not know this hymn? Learn it, boy! Write it out and have it on my desk by tomorrow morning.'

Sitting back down, I started to feel sick, as my nose and stomach were still reeling from the stench of his breath. That was worse than the small taste of public humiliation he had just put me through. One of the older boys told me after assembly that copying hymns out was a punishment at the school and I had succeeded in obtaining my first punishment on my third day.

My first weekend at the Prep School provided a whole host of new experiences for me. On Friday night after tea, there was no prep but we did have Cubs instead. Where most Cub packs around the country spent their time learning skills and earning badges, Cubs at the Prep School consisted of two sixth formers coming over from the Main School and getting us to play British Bulldogs for an hour.

British Bulldogs consisted of the two senior boys who were the Bulldogs standing on the rugby pitch with us Cubs all lined up on one side. The purpose of the game was to run across the field past the Bulldogs without being caught. If you got caught then you also became a Bulldog and joined them to catch the others. The winner of the game is the last player to be 'free'. If it was dark outside, then we did the same thing, only in the playroom instead. I'll admit that at first, I was a little nervous of playing the game, but as I was used to the rough and tumble of playing with both of my brothers back home (yes, even Richard!) I soon took it in my stride. Some of the more timid-natured lads found the prospect more daunting.

As there were no kitchen staff in the school on Saturday and Sunday mornings, it was down to Mrs Sherbrooke to make breakfast. On Friday night, she asked for two volunteers to offer to get up early the next morning and help lay the tables for breakfast. The following morning, she wheeled in a large pan of hard-boiled eggs. We queued up and were given an egg each on a plate – that was our breakfast. There was also often some white bread caked in the nastiest margarine and probably so full of chemicals that it could never go off. While we ate our breakfast, Mrs Sherbrooke would sit on the side table by the window and smoke, clearly in need of a rest after the exertion of boiling a pan of twenty-two eggs.

We had school lessons on Saturday mornings every week so while the rest of Britain's youth were on the sofa at home watching *Swap Shop* or even *Tiswas* (the forbidden ITV again), we were sitting in a classroom learning the joys of long division. Apparently, the payback was that we had longer school holidays in between terms. Lunch on Saturdays was always the same, week after week: half a pork pie, half a jacket potato and a spoonful of Branston pickle. After lunch, Mrs Sherbrooke opened her 'tuck shop'. She covered the table in her private dining room with boxes of penny chews, sherbert fountains, liquorice, foam shrimps, marshmallow flumps, white chocolate mice and lollies. Each boy was allowed to spend ten pence and she jotted it down in her book as we carried our stash of sweeties off to our tuck locker in the dining room. The trick was to try and make this handful of goodies last the entire weekend, although I recall that that never happened.

Once the sweets were bought, we gathered our swimming things and wash bags and went over to the Main School to use the swimming pool and the baths. As there weren't enough baths or showers at the Prep School, we had to use the ones in the Main School twice a week. In the large bathroom there were ten baths, so two of us had to get in each bath and wash ourselves. Mrs Sherbrooke came round and made all of us stand up stark naked and we had to make sure that we were covered in soap suds. Once she was satisfied, we were allowed to rinse off, put on our trunks and head to the pool.

In my first term, my older brother Richard had bought some Linco 'beer shampoo' for himself so I pinched it from the bathroom at home and took it back to school. While I was using it one Saturday, Mrs Sherbrooke picked up the bottle and studied it as I was standing in the bath, covered top-to-toe in shampoo suds.

'Mews, lean forward, please. Let me smell your hair.'

I duly complied and as she leaned in to take a sniff, her face grimaced.

'Mews, your hair smells like a brewery! Borrow some shampoo from Watson and wash it again, please,' she said, unimpressed. She took the offending bottle away and put it in the bin. At the next bathing session, I reverted back to the Vosene medicated shampoo that Grandma had bought me.

I couldn't really swim when I arrived at Barney but within a few weeks, with a lot of spluttering and thrashing from me and a great deal of encouragement from Mr White, our formidable swimming teacher, I was soon a competent swimmer. It did take me some time and as Mr White held the long bamboo pole in the water to guide me along the length of the pool, I must have tested his patience week after week but he never complained. He was one of the most popular teachers at the school, not just because of his patience, but also due to his wickedly dry sense of humour. Years later, I was saddened to hear of his sudden passing while on holiday, having only just retired. It was teachers like Mr White that left a lasting impression on the pupils at Barney.

As my confidence in the swimming pool grew, the more daring I became, and before long I was jumping off the top diving board and doing handstands underwater. Saturday afternoons at the swimming baths were my favourite time of the week. Since Mam and Dad died, Grandma had not allowed me to go swimming with my friends but only with my school, so I treated this time as a bit of freedom.

Tea on Saturdays usually consisted of half a toasted teacake or crumpet each, covered with margarine. We never had cake unless it was someone's birthday, but we did get half an orange with our tea once a week and half a banana on another evening. After that we were expected to fill ourselves up on bread and jam. Only at weekends did Mr and Mrs Sherbrooke and their family dine with us in the main dining room. They were seated at the middle table although they would have proper butter, decent jam and cakes on their table that would leave the rest of us salivating. Once they had finished, we were allowed any leftover bread and butter from their table and this was considered a treat.

On Saturday evenings, we were allowed to watch the only television in the school, which was in a classroom. If we weren't watching Tom Baker flying the TARDIS in *Doctor Who*, we could be found in the craft room, gluing together Airfix models of planes, battleships, or in my case, dinosaurs. I was obsessed with dinosaurs, having started a project on them in my first week at the school. We were allowed to use glue, turps and even Stanley knives in the model room. Looking back, it does amuse me that sharp Stanley knives were totally acceptable, yet Mrs Sherbrooke felt that our welfare was in greater danger from watching ITV. Again, this was the 1970s and where the school was strict on things like uniform, use of surnames, etc., they were more lax regarding the use of knives and flammable liquids. How times have changed. I bet they don't get to use Stanley knives and turpentine unsupervised at the Prep School today.

Sunday morning breakfast was followed by model making or some other activity. In fact, any activity that didn't involve us getting dirty as we had to be ready in our uniforms complete with blazers and caps for ten o'clock. Following a line-up inspection from Mrs Sherbrooke, we filed across to the chapel for Holy Communion. Mam had made me go to Sunday School and I never really saw the point of it and on the occasions when I went to church, I was bored rigid. School chapel would prove no different, I feared.

Holy Communion lasted an hour but it always felt like longer. The Prep School boys always had to sit up in the gallery next to the organ and as the tune belted out from the organ pipes, our ears would take the full brunt of the force. Once we had escaped from chapel and changed out of our Sunday best, we would have Sunday lunch. I was at the posh school now so I wasn't allowed to call it 'Sunday dinner'. As much as I hated Sunday dinners at home, I soon grew to love them at school. Mrs Heavisides, a farmer's wife in her seventies, used to come down every Sunday and cook lunch for 'her boys'. She was a lovely lady who made a point of learning all our names and making time for us. All the boys loved her and her wonderful cooking. Her roast potatoes were astounding and she used to make the most amazing puddings, such as baked apples stuffed with sultanas or Queen of Puddings.

In the afternoons, we often went out for a walk with Mr

and Mrs Sherbrooke and it was on Sundays such as this that we would stay relatively local to Barnard Castle. On other weekends when there was no chapel, Mr Sherbrooke took us all over to the Yorkshire Dales in the school minibus. One of the most popular new television programmes on at that time was *All Creatures Great and Small*, a drama series based on the books by James Herriot about three vets practising in Yorkshire in the 1930s, and all the external scenes were shot around Askrigg, Swaledale and Wensleydale. On many occasions, Mr Sherbrooke drove the school minibus through the water-splash seen in the famous opening titles of the show and I felt such a thrill of excitement. I dearly loved that programme, not only because it was beautifully made but also it was the last TV show that I ever watched with Mam, the night before she died. I was also thankful it was on the BBC and not ITV, otherwise we wouldn't have been allowed to watch it at school.

We always had an hour set aside every Sunday evening for writing letters home while Mrs Sherbrooke sat in the classroom and oversaw the process. All letters had to be placed on the desk in an open stamped addressed envelope. She then proceeded to read each one, in her words, 'to check for grammatical or factual errors'. If a boy wrote in his letter that he had been punished or that he hadn't liked a particular meal, Mrs Sherbrooke tore up the letter in front of him and made him write a new one. I never felt the need to 'reveal all' in my letters home to Grandma, as I didn't want to cause her any undue worry. As such, I followed my usual script of reassuring her that all was well, and to tell the truth, it was. I was enjoying myself and there was always loads to do, so we were never bored.

All the boys would have killed for the chance to use a

telephone to speak to our families, but it was forbidden. The logic being that if we were to speak to our loved ones on the phone, then we would get homesick and it would hamper our ability to settle in. Of course, this would be unthinkable today, but back in the 1970s attitudes were different and nobody ever thought to question the rules. Mrs Sherbrooke continued to censor our outgoing mail and although I didn't really like her, I managed to keep a low profile and not draw her attention towards me.

Each term we could order a weekly comic, which would be delivered to the school by the local newsagent. I had only ever seen *Look-in* or *Tiger* comics at that point, so I ordered my *Look-in*. Billed as a junior version of the *TV Times*, it had comic strips of popular television shows and there was always a poster in the middle featuring the biggest pop stars of the day. More often than not it was ABBA and they were my favourite band at the time.

Having twenty-one other boys living in the same house meant that we all shared our comics with each other. That way, we could ensure that we had a whole range of them and we got to read them all: *The Topper, Beezer, Whizzer and Chips, Buster* and of course, *The Beano* and *The Dandy*. Other boys ordered the likes of *Victor, Warlord* and *Commando* comics, but I was never as interested in those, preferring my comics to have humour rather than stories of shooting Germans and Japanese.

Getting your comic delivery once a week was great, but nothing compared to receiving a letter from home. Grandma wrote to me twice a week and never once missed. Sometimes her letters contained bits of news and on other days they would be more mundane descriptions of everyday life but every single one of them was packed full of love. She would always tell me that Roger would be missing me and I missed my little brother in turn. Every single word that she wrote down was filled with longing to see me again soon. My letters back to her were no more exciting, really, but I would treasure each one that I received, reading them again and again.

Although I had taken a handful of games away to school with me, along with one or two toy cars and a couple of books, the craze sweeping the playground that term was marbles. The boys played against each other and in each game the winner would get to keep their opponent's marble. Such was the nature of the game, it wasn't easy to join in if you didn't possess your own marbles. Not feeling comfortable to ask for anything as I knew Grandma and Grandad didn't have much money, I eventually plucked up the courage to write home, asking if Grandad could buy me a small bag of marbles and promising to pay him out of my pocket money by not getting sweeties on a Saturday for the next five weeks. Four days later a parcel arrived and as I excitedly tore off the brown wrapping paper to reveal a shoe box, I could barely contain myself. One half of the box contained several bags of clear glass marbles, each with their different coloured centres. There were also some white and coloured ones known as 'chinas', along with larger glass ones which we referred to as 'Tenners'. The other half of the box contained a handful of my toy Matchbox cars and a note that read:

Dear Philip,
Thank you for your letter. I'm glad that you are settling in and that you are finding plenty to do. Grandad has

been to the shops and bought you some marbles and Roger
helped to pick them out for you. I hope you like them. I
will write properly tomorrow as Grandad has to take this
parcel round to Mr Robson's and they will drop them at
the Prep School for you tomorrow.

Be a good boy for Mr and Mrs Sherbrooke and I hope
that all the boys are kind to each other. God Bless my
bonny lad.

Your loving Grandma, Grandad, Richard and Roger

xxxxxx

Delighted as I was to receive the marbles and eager to go out and play with them, reading Grandma's note made me feel homesick as I was really missing them. I had to put on a smile but it wouldn't be long before I was back home for the weekend and could see my grandparents and my brothers. We were allowed home about every three weeks, which seemed like a lifetime to an eight-year-old boy to have to wait. At the Prep School we had lessons on Saturday mornings, so the weekend would only start properly at 12.30 p.m.

My little brother Roger remained at Stanhope Hall when I went away to school. He lived there with Grandma, Grandad and Richard. Despite my absence, life carried on pretty much as normal for him. He continued to go to school in Wolsingham, where he was taught under the guidance of Sister Di Pazzi. On the weekends when I wasn't home from school, he would go with Grandma and Grandad to Brandon. They had decided to keep their own home in Brandon village following Mam's death. It was a lovely three-bedroom house that faced on to a neighbouring farm, with its fields directly opposite. On a clear day, from an upstairs window, you could see the top of Durham Cathedral and in the far distance, Penshaw Monument. Grandad went there every fortnight to check that everything was in order. He had to light the coal fires to ensure that the house was aired and tended to his prolific vegetable garden at the back of the house. Grandad cooked most of the food on the coal fire rather than use the electric cooker as it saved money. Kettles of water, pans of milk and even the chip pan was used on the fire, the latter thankfully without incident.

Mrs Bumby and Mrs Beckett were now doing the school run between them and every morning, Grandad walked Roger down the front path and along to the main road to meet the lift. Roger loved school, making many friends there, and when he returned home every afternoon, Grandad was waiting for him at the end of the track at the front of Stanhope Hall. Later, he would tell me he would always check to see if a letter had arrived from me and he longed to hear how his big brother was getting on at boarding school.

In September 1978, my grandparents received an update letter from Mr Humble at the Masonic Lodge:

Dear Mr & Mrs Close,
Enclosed is the birth certificate, which was sent to me in error.

I can confirm that all the particulars and the Lodge recommendation have been forwarded on to the Grand Lodge and as I have already informed you, although nothing definite as to the amount of grant to be made,

I am given on good authority it will be only what is thought to be that which the estate can afford. They are very generous and liberal.

The first month at school will soon be over and after your first visit, I shall be glad to know how Philip is settling in.

Yours Sincerely
Oliver Humble

Judging by the letter, they must have still been sorting out the paperwork for my schooling. I expect these things took a long time to arrange.

CHAPTER 19

Grease is the Word

I'd already received letters from Grandma and Auntie Brenda to say that I was to spend most of my half-term holiday at Seaburn. As the mid-term break approached, I grew more excited at the thought of coming home and seeing my family, especially Roger. My cousin Gaynor would be getting the same week off as me so we could spend a few days of the week-long holiday together.

Throughout the summer of 1978, there had been a huge buzz about the film *Grease*, starring John Travolta and Olivia Newton-John, which produced the songs 'You're The One That I Want' and 'Summer Nights', both of which became massive number one hits. Newspaper headlines such as 'Olivia Neutron Bomb' whipped the British public up into a frenzy and the whole country was going daft over this film, including me. The TV and newspapers reported that queues to see it were stretching over several streets in towns and cities across the UK. Back in 1978, we didn't have video recorders and once a film had been on at the cinema, it took an average of three to four years before it would be screened on the television so it was either catch it at the pictures or have a long wait.

As kids we didn't care. We had spent the summer singing along to the songs on the radio and on *Top of the Pops* and we were desperate to finally see the film. Auntie Brenda thought it would be a good idea to get there early and as the cinema only had the one screen, the queue was already around the block. Giddy with excitement, Gaynor and I stood in a queue that didn't seem to move. Eventually, cheers could be heard from around the block and the people in front of us started to shuffle forwards. For the next twenty minutes our chances of getting in were looking good. Not for long. Our hearts sank as a man came out and informed us that the cinema was full and that it would be another two hours and fifteen minutes before they could let us in for the next showing. There was only about fifteen people in front of us as we collectively sighed.

'I think we should go home and come back another time,' Auntie Brenda suggested.

'I suppose so,' I reluctantly agreed, all too aware that I was returning home the following day and then back to school. I would have to wait four years to see this film.

'I'm not moving,' Gaynor said, assertively. 'We've queued for ages. You two can go home and I will wait and go in on my own,' knowing fine well that her mother wouldn't agree to that in a million years. In a bid not to disappoint us, Auntie Brenda agreed that we could stay.

Eventually, after almost five hours of queuing, Auntie Brenda breaking a tooth on an éclair and Gaynor getting peeled paint stuck under her fingernail, we were admitted inside. This was the first time I'd ever been to the cinema, although like most others back then we called it 'the pictures'. All I can recall is that we sat at the front and that it was difficult to hear much of the film due to the audience wolf-whistling throughout. We loved every minute of it and as Danny and Sandy's 'Grease Lightning' car took off into the sky, we grabbed our coats and sang the songs all the way home on the bus.

CHAPTER 20

Winter Marches On

I soon slipped back into the daily routine at school following the half-term break. As the chilly autumn days unfolded, the playground became awash with a golden sea of dead leaves, blowing about as we played games of marbles or yard cricket. Staying inside during playtime wasn't an option and we were regularly reminded that being out in the cold while wearing short trousers would serve to toughen us up. I'm not sure that any of us really gave the impression of being softies, as surely the emotional wrench of living away from our families at such a young age proved that we were tough little boys indeed.

Bonfire Night was always a major event at the Prep School, the older boys assured me. Parents were encouraged to donate a handful of fireworks each towards the display that was to be held down the orchard. Grandma hadn't been able to find any fireworks for sale in the village, so she donated some money so that Mr Sherbrooke could buy some in the town. The shop-bought fireworks had nothing on Mr Sherbrooke's homemade creations, though. Packed full of all sorts of powdery chemicals, his fireworks were by far the loudest, brightest and most impressive ones that were set off that night. They were probably also the most dangerous and I imagine the shops would never have been allowed to sell them, had they been commercially available. As I've said before, this was the 1970s and we weren't so concerned with Health and Safety back then.

As the weeks progressed towards the end of term, we made preparations for the Christmas festivities at school. Miss Willatt transformed herself into a *Blue Peter* presenter as she issued each of us with scissors, masses of coloured paper, old milk bottle tops and empty foil pie dishes. Our task was to transform the classroom into a festive wonderland, decorating the windows, walls, and making a variety of paper lanterns smothered in paint and glitter. We also made hats to wear at the class Christmas party and I was in my element happily sloshing copious amounts of paper glue onto coloured paper and everywhere else. I loved that white glue, purely because once it dried on your hands, you could peel it off like a second skin. It was a pleasure that many of that generation still talk about fondly, peeling the glue off your fingers. It's funny the things we get sentimental and nostalgic over.

Learning new Christmas carols to sing at the end-of-term Nativity play became a daily activity. Back home we had only really sung 'Away in a Manger' and 'Once in Royal David's City' and yet here I was learning new carols, the sound of which would permeate my Christmases for years to come: 'O Little Town of Bethlehem', 'Hark the Herald Angels Sing' and the one that would become my favourite, 'God Rest Ye Merry Gentlemen'. Time and time again, Miss Willatt thumped out the tunes on the piano in the playroom until we knew them off by heart.

At Barney, it was also traditional to decorate the dormitories in the run-up to Christmas, with the proviso being that the decorations had to be homemade. Fast forward to us sitting on our beds, two of us cutting strips from old comics and magazines, while the other four boys in our dorm stapled them into loops to create paper chains. It didn't matter to any of us that we didn't have brightly coloured paper like they did on *Blue Peter*. The excitement of creating our own decorations from what was effectively rubbish was more than good enough for us. Standing on the shiny metal bed frames, we stretched as far as we could to pin the paper chains up and in no time at all the dorm was transformed with our homemade creations.

Mrs Sherbrooke had selected a handful of boys to assist her with decorating the large Christmas tree that had been delivered that morning and was now in place in the entrance hall downstairs. With the string of multi-coloured lights shining amongst the tinsel and glass baubles, the scene was set for the Christmas celebrations that would take place in the final ten days of term. That evening after supper when we were in our pyjamas playing board games in the dorm, Mr Sherbrooke came in and told us to put on our dressing gowns and slippers and make our way down the forbidden front staircase. As we all sat on the stairs as instructed, the lights were turned off. Mr and Mrs Sherbrooke were only visible to us from the twinkling coloured lights on the Christmas tree as they stood in the hall. Outside beyond the front door we could hear voices singing, the tune growing louder by the second. Mr Sherbrooke opened the door and the sound of Christmas carols filled the hallway as the carol singers, made up of sixth formers from the Main School, entered.

Wrapped up in their thick coats with scarves and gloves, each of them carried a traditional lantern which lit up their faces and enabled them to read from their carol sheets. I can still picture the scene so vividly after all these years. I remember looking at the sixth formers with their lanterns and thinking, *that will be me one day*. It was a wonderfully festive moment and at some point each Christmas, I find myself casting my mind back to that very evening.

Once we had joined in with singing several carols, all of us were invited into the dining room to have a mince pie and a glass of milk while Mr Sherbrooke poured a beer for each of the sixth formers as their reward. The Prep School was always the first stop for the carol singers as they made their way to the varying houses around the school and the town where the headmaster, chaplain and various others connected with the school lived. At each house, they would receive a glass of mulled wine or something stronger and by the time they finished up at the pub, their voices were sounding far more like a rugby team after a winning match. A few years later, one or two of the boys got themselves into a drunken state while at the headmaster's house, so by the time I reached the sixth form myself, years later, the tradition was sadly no more.

Performing the Nativity play was another tradition that I loved, having done them at my previous schools. Yet again I was a shepherd. I always seemed to be a shepherd, wearing my dressing gown with a towel on my head, while other boys aspired to the more glamorous roles of the Three Kings. Because the Nativity play was not held on the last day of term, it was only really the parents of the day boys who were able to attend and even then it was just the mothers. This being the 1970s, it was long before the time that fathers even considered taking time off work to attend their children's afternoon school play.

Having looked forward to the Nativity so much in the previous weeks, seeing all the mothers of the day boys there in the audience made me feel so bereft. As I stood in front of them in my shepherd's costume, I scanned the expectant faces in front of me, hoping that for just one fleeting moment, I would see my mam's face amongst the others: she wasn't there, of course. In the midst of this wonderful Christmas celebration I was immersed in a deep sadness. These sudden pangs of grief would hit me from time to time, but I never got used to my loss.

The final few days of term approached and our tin trunks were brought up from the cellars beneath the kitchen and placed at the end of our beds. As we packed our clothes and belongings away, we really felt as if the holidays were almost upon us. The dorms were bare as we took down all our Christmas decorations. Being young boys, we didn't do this carefully and diligently but rather by jumping from bed to bed with arms outstretched and ripping the paper chains from their moorings on the wall.

With one last Christmas celebration awaiting us, we walked in file across to the school chapel that evening for the Christmas carol service, more formally known as the Festival of Nine Lessons and Carols. As we sat up on the balcony, looking down onto the chapel, the lights were extinguished. Somewhere beneath us, the treble section of the choir sang the first verse of 'Once in Royal David's City'. Lit only by the candles they were carrying, they processed up the centre aisle of the chapel and into the choir stalls. Suddenly, as the last verse began, the lights were switched on and the organ bellowed into action, making a deafening noise that made us all jump out of our skins. It was this, the theatre of the school chapel celebrating Christmas, that I instantly fell in love with. At the end of the service, I felt elated yet sad when the final chorus of 'O Come All Ye Faithful' was belted out by over four hundred boys in the chapel that night.

As all the boarders and masters filed out into the chilly December night, us Prep School boys ran back to Westwick Lodge, singing carols and high at the thought of going home the next day. In our dorm that night, with our trunks packed, none of us could get to sleep and before too long, Eddie Theakston had started a pillow fight, with us running around the dorm, jumping from one bed to the next until Mr Sherbrooke came up and switched on the lights.

'Now then, boys,' he said, unable to suppress a tiny smile. 'Settle down and get some sleep.'

'Goodnight, Sir!' we chorused in reply, Theakston much louder than the rest of us.

There were no proper classes the next day, with the normal morning Assembly abandoned in favour of the end-of-term Prize Giving. The only way in which it differed from our regular Assembly was that we wore our Sunday blazers and all the teachers were present, including Mrs Sherbrooke. The trophies were handed out one at a time and each presentation accompanied by hearty applause. I didn't win anything, but after all, this was only my first term. With the ceremony done and lunch eaten with a greater than usual enthusiasm, the boarders assembled near to the entrance hall and waited for our families to come and collect us.

Lots of the boys had guardians who were often their aunts and uncles but in some cases, the guardians were people who were paid to look after them in the holidays because their parents lived abroad. I wasn't happy when Mr and Mrs Sherbrooke referred to Grandma as my 'guardian' even though they were technically correct. To me the term 'guardian' seemed so impersonal and I would have much preferred that they said 'grandmother'. But I was an eight-year-old boy and not in a position to correct Mrs Sherbrooke and I was also smart enough to know that it wasn't worth getting on the wrong side of her.

Each time the sound of the front doorbell echoed through the entrance hall, my heart jumped, thinking it was my turn. As the minutes dragged on and countless boys were reunited with their parents, my mood began to sink. I was almost the last boy to be collected when Mrs Sherbrooke opened the door to reveal my brother Richard standing there, dressed in his farming clothes and wellies. She looked him up and down as she bade us a 'Merry Christmas', closing the door behind us. Once she was out of sight I felt my shoulders relax, as this was the moment I had been waiting for: I was finally going home to my family for the Christmas holidays.

In her most recent letter, Grandma told me that Roger was so excited about my coming home for the holidays. He had been keen to put up a Christmas tree and decorate it, but had been told that he must wait until I returned home.

The journey home across the moors seemed to take no time at all and although the road was clear, there was already a good covering of snow on the fells, which only served to add to the wintry beauty of the stunning landscape around us. The snow started to thin out as we started our descent down Softly Bank and into Weardale. Now bare, the trees did nothing to block the sight of Stanhope Hall in the distance. As we pulled into the farmyard, I could see Roger jumping up and down with excitement at the back door. Uncle Harold emerged from the stable, presumably having fed the dogs and without removing his pipe, welcomed me home for the holidays.

'Now then, Master Mews, how's school?' he enquired.

'Good, thank you,' was my brief response, all too aware that I was stood in the freezing farmyard still wearing my short trousers.

As I grabbed my weekend bag out of the Land Rover, I left Richard to tackle the trunk and I ran down to the farmhouse. The smell of Grandma's home baking almost hit me as quickly as Roger did when as he ran to greet me, launching himself at me with an excited fervour. 'Philip!' he yelled as he then proceeded to run off a list of things that he had been doing, such as being a sheep in his own school Nativity play.

'Roger, give the lad a minute to get in the door,' said the warm familiar voice of Grandad as he stepped out of the pantry, carrying two cake tins. He put them down at the bottom of the stairs to enable him to give me a huge hug and a kiss on the cheek.

I hadn't made it past the back passage of the farmhouse and already I was intoxicated with the sights, sounds and smells that reassured me that I was home. When I walked into the kitchen, there was Grandma wiping her hands free of flour on a tea towel at the kitchen table. Her eyes were already brimming with tears while her face could not hide the utter joy that she felt at that moment to welcome me home. I ran into her open arms, which she quickly wrapped tight around me as I pressed my face into her pink nylon tabard that was dusty with flour.

I inhaled the smell, which was unmistakable: a combination of Yardley Freesia talc and home baking shot straight up my nose as she continued to hold me tight.

Amongst the cacophony of voices to be heard in the kitchen, Grandad, Roger, Richard and now Uncle Harold, who had just walked in, the one sound that I focused on was the gentle quiet sobbing of my grandma. She eventually released me from her tight hug and took a step back as she held both sides of my face in her careworn hands, the tears running down her cheeks. As she inspected me, checking for scuffs and scratches, she must have felt a bittersweet mix of emotions – the joy at my having returned home and the sorrow that it should have been Mam and Dad stood there, welcoming me back for the holidays. But it did not do to dwell on this at that moment but rather embrace the positive and celebrate that I was finally home for Christmas. There had been so little to smile about in Stanhope Hall for the past twelve months, so this rare moment of happiness was cherished by every person in that room.

During the first couple of days of the holidays, I gently eased myself into a revised routine peppered with home comforts as I managed to get up, eat and eventually go to bed without being summoned by a bell. Grandma made a start on emptying my school trunk and putting every single item through the wash. Wheeling out the twin-tub washing machine over to the kitchen sink, the marathon washing session would begin, which was no mean feat without a tumble dryer or central heating. Despite other family members telling her to pace herself, she ploughed on and wouldn't rest until she was done. One of her biggest fears was that she would 'take bad' and that I would return to school with a trunk full of clothes in a less than pristine condition. She wasn't going to give anyone an excuse to criticise her ability as a parent, despite her age and sure enough, forty-eight hours later, my trunk was filled with freshly pressed laundry, ready for my return to Barney in January.

I was under strict instructions from Uncle Harold to call in and see him and Auntie Ethel when I arrived home for the holidays. They lived in a detached house at the bottom of the drive of Stanhope Hall and were both now in their seventies. Never having had children of their own, they doted on Roger and I and treated us as if we were their own grandchildren. We were accustomed to giving the back door a small knock before letting ourselves in and as usual, Auntie Ethel was busying herself preparing lunch.

Stepping over the threshold, I looked around the country cottage kitchen with its low ceiling, scrubbed pine kitchen table and Aga belting out the heat. The smell of pipe tobacco smoke lingered in the air, giving me the strangest sensation on my lower gums and teeth, causing them to tingle.

Now that I had been afforded this privilege of being privately educated, both Uncle Harold and Auntie Ethel were keen to hear of my progress and how I had found my first term away from home. Uncle Harold especially would drum into me the importance of education and to make the most of the opportunities laid before me. They regularly gave Roger and I a pound note each and would call it our 'pocket money'.

As soon as we had been to see them, we called in to see Auntie Mary and Uncle Dryden, who lived next door to us at Stanhope Hall. I loved going to see them and again, they were like additional grandparents to Roger and I. With his cheeky smile, Uncle Dryden would be so pleased to see me home from school and was keen to hear about what mischief I had been up to, while Auntie Mary smiled and told him not to encourage me. She had been good friends with Mam and she still missed her very much. Dryden and Mary both took it badly when my parents died but they made a huge effort to be upbeat with us when we called round to visit. They had an old mill at the bottom of their garden path and Roger and I used to clamber up behind the bushes to the side so that we could look through the large hole in the wall. Inside was a huge old wooden water wheel, sitting quite still, many years having passed since it had last seen active service, while the stream of water continued to run beneath it, echoing around the damp old stone walls.

It was now a week away from Christmas Eve and my grandparents were keen to maintain as many of the family traditions as possible. My elder brother Richard heaved a large seven-foot tree out of the back of the Land Rover and placed it in a tub full of logs in the corner of the sitting room. Many of the baubles in the box had been in the family for years, right back to the 1930s, and as each one was unwrapped from its dusty yellow newspaper wrapping, it felt like greeting an old friend, one you only see at this time of year. In amongst the decorations was a box of bell-shaped baubles that Mam had bought the previous Christmas, our first without Dad. In many ways, I would come to treasure these baubles more than any other as they were one of the last things I remember buying in a shop with her.

Despite these emotions floating to the surface, Roger and I took it in turns to hang the decorations on the tree while Grandma busied herself baking the first of many batches of mince pies through in the kitchen. I never really liked mince pies before but since my first term away at school, where I was forced to give every type of food a try, I had developed a liking for them. Being a strict Methodist, Grandma refused to add any alcohol to her mince pies, Christmas cake or Christmas pudding, but at the time we didn't really care. They were homemade and the best kind you could ask for.

We traditionally decorated the pictures around the house with sprigs of holly so when Grandad had finished his jobs for the morning, he took us up the field to the site of the old limestone kilns, behind which grew several holly bushes. With Grandad in charge of the secateurs, we collected a large amount of holly, which we carefully placed in an old plastic fertiliser sack and set off back down the pasture to the house. There had been another light snowfall overnight and the ground was frozen solid. As we slowly made our way back home, Roger and I took it in turns to jump onto the frozen puddles, breaking through the ice and squealing with delight as the mucky brown water underneath splashed up against our brightly coloured wellies.

In the previous week while I had been away at school, Grandma had received a phone call from Nancy Holden, one of Mam's closest friends. The Young Wives, a local church group, of which Mam had been secretary, were hosting a children's Christmas party in the church hall in the village and Roger and myself were invited to attend. That afternoon, with the house now festooned with freshly picked holly and the tree all decorated, Grandma got us both ready in clean outfits and Richard dropped us off at the church hall. At first I was quite nervous and afraid there wouldn't be anyone that I knew there, but as we walked tentatively through the door into the hall, I instantly saw at least six other kids that I recognised from my old school. There to greet us with the warmest of smiles was Nancy, accompanied by her eldest daughter, Sarah, who was there to lend a helping hand.

After handing in our coats, we were directed over to the centre of the floor in front of the stage, where there was already a group of children assembled. David, my old pal from Sunday School, was there and quick on the mark to enquire how I was finding boarding school. A lady sat at the piano at the side of the stage was leafing through some books of Christmas sheet music and began clinking away at the keys, belting out jolly tunes like 'Deck the Halls' and carols like 'The Holly and the Ivy'. We were given homemade party hats and before too long, were in the throes of the Christmas party games. Oranges and Lemons was the one that I remember, as two of the children joined hands and held their arms aloft while the rest of us paraded in single file, ducking underneath them and all the while hoping that the music wouldn't stop when it came to us. With more party games and food to follow, I was sad when it was time for us to go home. Grandad appeared at the entrance to the hall and waited alongside the other parents. As he watched us enjoying ourselves, I do think that it must have been comforting for him to see us smiling and laughing again. We were each given a present as we were leaving, with strict instructions to place it under our Christmas tree until the big day, and so we climbed into the car, each clutching our parcel, giddy with excitement as we looked forward to the rest of the festivities that lay ahead.

On the evening of 23 December, a car pulled into the farmyard and a minute later, it was followed by a knock at the door: Ivan and Sheila Peart, two of Mam and Dad's closest friends, had called to bring Christmas gifts for Roger and myself. As well as being my godfather, Ivan and his wife had known Dad for over thirty years and when Dad met my mother, she and Sheila struck up a strong friendship. For one reason or another, many of the friends of my parents eventually drifted away after their death but Ivan and Sheila called in to see us at least every Christmas for many years to come and they certainly never failed to remember our landmark birthdays. Grandma was sometimes dismissive of her daughter's friends, particularly those who enjoyed a drink, but she never disapproved of Ivan and Sheila. Comforted by their kindness and friendship, she always ensured that they continued to receive a warm welcome at Stanhope Hall.

Always keen to see both Roger and I, on this occasion they were eager to hear of my exploits during my first term away at boarding school. Adding their gifts to the pile of presents that was rapidly growing beneath the Christmas tree, I was all too aware of the kindness that we had received from such a large number of friends and family for that particularly difficult first Christmas without both of our parents.

On the morning of Christmas Eve, Grandma had been up early to make sure that she had the spare bedroom ready for Auntie Brenda, Uncle Ron and their daughter Gaynor arriving. By now, Auntie Brenda was a regular visitor to Stanhope Hall, having travelled up on the bus almost every other weekend since Mam's death, back in February. She was a bolster of support for her own parents, now in their seventies, who were tasked with the responsibility of looking after three boys (albeit one of us was now an adult) and a farm. As they were bringing a large number of parcels with them for Christmas, Richard had driven to Seaburn to pick them up rather than have them spend four hours on the buses. Gaynor skipped down from the car to the farmhouse followed by her mother, leaving Uncle Ron to supervise the unloading of stuff from the car boot. Although I hadn't realised it at the time, we were all very quickly ushered into the sitting room on the premise of showing Gaynor the Christmas tree. This gave Richard and Uncle Ron the opportunity to secrete the presents from 'Santa Claus' up in a bedroom on the top floor, which was then locked to prevent entry by little ones with prying eyes.

Come teatime, it was our turn to repeat another annual tradition of going up to the barn with Grandad and selecting a bale of hay to put outside the stable for Santa's reindeer. I know that many other families left out carrots for the reindeer, but Santa's reindeer always got nice dry hay to eat at Stanhope Hall and this year would be no different. Grandma had made yet another batch of mince pies that afternoon to offer the constant stream of visitors we had at the farm. I selected one from the cooling rack to place on a tea plate with a sherry glass filled with Grandad's homemade ginger wine. Auntie Brenda herded the three of us upstairs to get changed into our pyjamas before coming back down to the kitchen to eat our supper of cornflakes with hot milk. The stockings were hung and Grandad read us a bedtime story before urging us to go straight to sleep.

An hour later, we were still wide awake and my elder brother Richard came up to our bedroom to encourage us to get some sleep: 'I've seen Santa by the Pack Horse [the village pub] and he said he's not coming if you don't go to sleep now.' Astounded by this revelation that he delivered with such conviction, it didn't take us long to nod off. Waking up at two in the morning was never part of the plan.

Grandma was asleep in bed next to Roger as I went over to wake him up and get him to come downstairs with me to see if Santa had been yet. I wasn't aware of what exactly the time was, but we crept downstairs and into the sitting room. It was quiet, with no sign of Santa having been yet. Back in the dark, cold passageway, I slowly pushed open the kitchen door, with Roger behind me clinging to my dressing gown. On the sofa and armchair in the kitchen was a pile of presents. Over in the other armchair in front of a roaring log fire, Grandad was sitting fast asleep in his pyjamas and dressing gown. He woke with a start at our yelps of joy. Having warmed some milk in a pan, he encouraged us to take one toy back up to bed to try and get more sleep. Gaynor's presents had been laid out on the sofa and like mine, they weren't wrapped up in Christmas wrapping paper, so I could see clearly what she had got from Santa. I bounded back up the stairs and headed straight for her room.

'Gaynor! Gaynor! He's *been*, Santa's been! You've got a Sindy buggy, *Charlie's Angels* dolls…' and I continued to ream off a list of at least six of her Christmas presents. Needless to say, she was less than impressed and almost forty years later, she still hasn't forgiven me.

The toys that still stick in my mind more than any others were the space hoppers, the giant rubber balls you could bounce along on. Auntie Brenda must have known that Roger and I were getting them for Christmas, as she had packed Gaynor's existing one and brought it up with her. The arrival of the space hoppers at Stanhope Hall that Christmas brought chaos. Always in search of daring adventure, we came up with the insane idea of conducting space hopper races from the very top floor of the farmhouse and to plunge ourselves over the precipice of the Jacobean staircase and bounce down the stairs, which were wide enough to accommodate at least two of us abreast. As we tumbled down, creating mayhem in our wake, poor Grandma couldn't hide the look of horror on her face as she screamed, 'The bairns, Brenda! The bairns!' But our Wacky Races on the Space Hoppers that Christmas proved to be short-lived. Later that day, all three were found in the back passageway of the house, entirely deflated.

CHAPTER 21

TV Stars

1979

The Christmas holidays took a turn for the better when Grandma received a letter from school to inform us that there had been a heating malfunction in the school's boiler room and due to the freezing weather, the Christmas break was to be extended by a further two weeks. Naturally, I was ecstatic as any normal eight-year-old would be. With two more weeks of going out to play in the snow, I couldn't believe my luck and as we weren't sent any additional homework to do, it meant that my time was my own.

We'd seen a pretty heavy snowfall in Weardale over the holidays and our days were spent sledging up the Banky Field on the farm or building snowmen. But the novelty of building snowmen soon wore thin and because of the volume of snow that was falling, I decided to be far more adventurous and build an igloo. Over several days, Roger and I toiled in the back garden and the end result was a feat of engineering. We had constructed our very own snow cave and it was large enough for both of us to sit in, not that we got to use it. After trying it out for the first time, Grandma forbade us from going inside it again for fear of the roof collapsing in on us. She was so frightened that anything would happen to Roger and I and frustrating as it was for us at the time, anyone could understand her reasoning.

When the time came for me to go back to school, I was keen to get back and see my friends. I know that Roger was sad to see me go, as we had played together every day for the last six weeks. With my tin trunk and bag loaded into the Land Rover, Richard took me back to school on the longer route via West Auckland, as even the sturdiest of vehicles wouldn't make it over the tops across the fells to Barney. He put the heater on full blast to warm me up, as I was sitting in my school uniform with my tracksuit bottoms over my short school trousers and wellies. We made it there without incident and soon I was in the dorm catching up with my friends, or at least the ones who had managed to make it back through the snow.

As Barney was on a similar altitude to Stanhope, there was as much snow at school as there was back at home. The rugby pitches were buried in thick, deep, crispy white layers and because of this, the only feasible outdoor sporting activity for us to do was cross-country running. Mr Sherbrooke took us out on walks at the weekend and I recall one particular Saturday when a group of us boarders was walking along the lane behind the Prep School in deep snow. I ran up on to a mound of snow and jumped up and down when I had made it to the top. I'd only been up there a few seconds when the noise of metal clanking beneath my feet alerted Mr Sherbrooke. He shouted at me to climb back down and having stepped forward to kick some snow away from the mound with his foot, revealed a car wheel. An entire car had been buried in the snow after its driver had abandoned it. I'd never witnessed snow on that scale before and I haven't since. In fact, that winter of 1978–9 had been the coldest winter for sixteen years and it managed to isolate many parts of northern England.

As the heavy snow ushered us into a new year, the whole of Britain's infrastructure seemed to be coming apart at the seams, with strikes taking place all over the country. It was known as the 'Winter of Discontent'. The impact that this had on an eight-year-old boy was that we couldn't get certain food items at school due to the lorry drivers being on strike. There was no sugar to put on our cornflakes or in our tea, so we had to make do with Sugar Puffs instead. That was about the extent of it. Of course, across the country there were children who were hungry as their striking parents struggled, trying to keep their families afloat, so for a young lad, albeit recently orphaned, I was lucky to be at a good school with plenty of food and warmth. If I'm being honest, I don't really recall being aware of the plight of others in the country, but only seem to remember the grown-ups muttering about rubbish piling up on the streets and the army having to be called in to dig graves as everyone else seemed to be on strike.

One morning at breakfast, Mr Sherbrooke instructed us to go upstairs and put on our tracksuit bottoms or jeans, along with our wellies and winter coats. Once we were back downstairs, he led us down to the cellar to collect our sledges. Sledging on a school day? This didn't seem right, but we didn't question him and kept our fingers crossed that we would manage to blag another day without lessons. Once we were all lined up in the playground with our sledges, the mystery was revealed to us. Because the road along to the school was so blocked with snow, the food delivery trucks couldn't get through and most of our supplies had been left at a small shop in the town. Our mission was to go into town to the shop, load the supplies onto our sledges and drag them back up to the school. Of course, we thought this was the most exciting thing in the world, although getting the heavy sledges back up the hill loaded with supplies was no easy task, especially when you factor twenty-two schoolboys having a snowball fight into the equation.

As the school term progressed, it was agreed that I would not go home for my weekend leave that we got once in every three weeks. Naturally I was upset, but as the weather was so bad I understood the reasoning behind the decision. Of course, I was having fun at school and there was never a dull moment, but I missed my family dearly. I looked forward to the twice-weekly letters, which continued to arrive from Grandma, and I kept each one in my pocket to read again and again until the next one arrived. I was always acutely aware that given Grandma's age and the fact that I had already lost my parents, she and Grandad wouldn't be around forever and so, from the first week away at school, I made a conscious decision to keep every single letter that she wrote to me and even now, I still have them all, safely packed away and treasured. I often watched other boys bin their letters after reading them and I thought that one day, they would probably regret doing it and cease to take their parents for granted.

One morning, I received a letter from Grandma telling me that a television crew from Tyne Tees Television, our local ITV channel, would be coming to the farm. They planned to film a documentary about Richard and the family for the *Farming Outlook* series, which they transmitted every Sunday. As my elder brother, now nineteen, was currently the youngest farmer in Britain and was managing the farm only with the assistance of my grandparents, they thought he would be a perfect subject for the programme. Grandma said that they had been given the filming dates, which would commence in two weeks. The producers were keen to film all the family, so Grandma had written to Mrs Sherbrooke to ask permission if I would be allowed home for two days during that week in order to take part. I read the letter at the breakfast table and was unable to contain my excitement, but sadly, it was to be short-lived. No sooner had I read it than Mrs Sherbrooke came into the dining room holding an opened letter in her hand.

'Mews, I've received a letter from your grandmother, asking if you can go home for two days to take part in a television programme,' she announced at the top of her voice. Now all the other boys were looking at me.

'Well, I don't think you should be taking part in television programmes as you are here to learn so I will be writing to your grandmother and telling her the answer is no,' she said.

I couldn't believe it: two days was all they asked for. We spent half the days that term drawing and colouring in because hardly any of the day boys made it to school due to the snow. I stared back at her silently with tears running down my face. It wasn't the fact that she said 'no' to the request, but the pleasure that she appeared to take in denying the permission. That night, I felt more homesick than ever and as I lay crying in my bed after lights out, Watson, our dorm monitor, came over to me and said I had to go down to see Mrs Sherbrooke. Standing outside her sitting room door, she called me in. The first thing that hit me was the heat in the room. She always kept the heating turned down low around the school, but in her sitting room was an electric fire, all the bars on it blazing red.

'What's all this crying about, Mews?' she asked.

'I'm just homesick, Miss,' I stammered, still snivelling and wiping my eyes.

'Well, you need to snap out of this. I appreciate that you have lost your parents but you need to get over this and start growing up!' she retorted.

At this I felt shell-shocked. *Get over it? Grow up? How could she be so cold?* I wasn't given time to respond as she instructed me to get to bed and stop crying. It took me years to get over the words that she uttered to me that night and I still replay back that moment, years later. I really tried to like her and I went out of my way to gain acceptance from her. In turn I wanted her to like me and approve of me the way that she did with some of the other boys. I knew that she had her favourites, especially the boys who came back from their homes abroad at the start of term bearing gifts for her, such as large bags of pistachios or other delicacies, but I knew that if I was to survive the next three years in this place, I had absolutely no option other than to keep my head down. That meant trying to switch off my emotions.

Two weeks later, the television crew came to Stanhope Hall and from the moment they arrived, Grandma plied them with hot food. They filmed around the farm with Richard as he, like all other sheep farmers, braved the icy temperatures to head up the fields and onto the fells. They filmed scenes in the house with the family, minus myself, sitting around the table, having their tea. The finished programme was finally transmitted when I was at home for the Easter holidays and I was delighted to see my family on the television screen. I was referred to as 'the younger brother who is away at school'. I was still angry with Mrs Sherbrooke for not allowing me home to be filmed, but I was far more bitter because of the pleasure that she took in saying 'no' and denying me this rare opportunity.

The spring term progressed and the snow finally began to melt. By now I was fully submerged into life at Barney and I no longer felt like a new boy. When it came to dealing with Mrs Sherbrooke, I remained polite and courteous as it would do me no favours to be in her bad books. Her husband, on the other hand, was the shining light at the Prep School. Although firm in his discipline, he had a gentle sense of fun and always had time for us. From taking us out on early morning runs to Saturday afternoon swimming sessions, he ensured we were never bored.

In the previous term I had been making models in the school's craft room but I found the idea of using Airfix model kits creatively restricting. I was bored with following instructions and had little interest in making models of battleships or military aeroplanes. I was also aware that Grandma and Grandad didn't have the money to buy such things. It was around this time that I asked the ladies in the school kitchen if I could have any old bleach bottles or jars that they were going to throw out. From this rubbish, I would start to build 'junk models' such as alien spaceships and weird animals using any items that I could find. Each term I would enter these into the modelling competition but without ever winning anything. It didn't matter to me as I'd take my models home to my grandparents, who would shower me with praise, even if it wasn't always clear what these creations were supposed to be.

In addition to the model making we had a collector's club and we were all encouraged to bring our own collections in to school but as yet, I'd never collected anything. Stamps would be a good start and I tore off the first class ones that were attached to Grandma's and presented them. Mrs Sherbrooke scoffed when I showed my collection.

'Call that a collection Mews? I'll show you all a proper collection,' she said, and with that she led us all into her private dining room. When I saw her collection laid out on the dining table for our inspection, I felt sick to the pit of my stomach. Rows of wooden framed cases with glass fronts, each containing rows of dead butterflies, each one pinned down through its body, cut down in its prime. How could she do something so cruel to something so beautiful? She'd collected most of them during her time living in Africa and she grinned with pride as she showed them off. To me, this was no different than killing elephants or lions. I stepped back away from the table and looked at her sadistic smile. Now I had truly taken the measure of her.

On one of the weekends when I did make it home that term, Richard took me back to school on the Sunday evening. Because it had been snowing heavily again in recent days, we had to take the long route back via West Auckland. The Land Rover was in the garage for repair, so he had no option but to drive me back in Grandad's mustard-coloured Maxi car. Not long after the drive through West Auckland, the little car broke down and without a phone box in sight; we were stuck. Richard tried in vain to get the engine to turn over, but the car was having none of it. As the ignition key was turned again and again, the car groaned. After about half an hour, we were getting pretty cold and as the few vehicles that had passed us didn't stop to help, the situation was increasingly serious. But before he had a chance to think of his next move, somebody did stop. A well-dressed man in his fifties pulled over, got out of his Mercedes and approached my brother.

'Anything I can do to help?' he said. Richard then explained to him that he was taking me back to boarding school and the car wouldn't budge.

'Which school are you at?' the man asked, now directing the question at me.

'Barnard Castle School,' I replied.

'Ah, Barney! I know it well. Are you at the Prep School?'

I nodded, conscious my legs were feeling colder by the minute.

'I know John Hay very well. He teaches there, doesn't he?'

'Yes, Sir,' I responded.

'OK, what I suggest we do is that I take this young man in my car to Barney and if you give me the name and number of someone to come and pick you up, I'll call them from the Prep School.'

Richard was visibly torn, questioning whether he should take up this stranger on his kind offer. Even back in 1979, we were warned of 'stranger danger', but at that moment we weren't in a situation that offered up any better alternatives. Seeing the nervous, doubtful look on my brother's face, I quietly pointed out to him that the man knew Mr Hay, one of our teachers, so he must be a good person. As the snow continued to fall,

Richard had to make a decision. Reluctantly, he agreed to allow the man to take me back to Prep School in his car and ring for help. The man wrote his name and telephone number on a piece of paper, handed it to my brother and took the name and number of the person he was to call for assistance. I took my bag and coat and hugged Richard goodbye.

'Promise me you will ask Mrs Sherbrooke if you can phone Grandma when you arrive and let her know that you are safe.' I agreed and climbed into the back of the stranger's car. No sooner had we been travelling in the car for five minutes, the man pulled over, got out of the car and walked over to a red telephone box on the roadside. After several minutes, he returned and said, 'I've just called your brother's friend. There's no sense in him waiting in the cold until we reach Barney so they are heading over to pick him up straight away.'

The remainder of the journey was pleasant enough as the man questioned me all about school and what I enjoyed doing there, what my favourite sports and pastimes were and so on. On reaching the Prep School, I climbed out of the car and the man escorted me to the front door. He explained to Mrs Sherbrooke what had happened and I thanked the stranger for his kindness. Mrs Sherbrooke shut the door and instructed me to go upstairs. When I asked if I could phone Grandma to let her know I was safe, she told me snippily, 'There's no need to fuss, Mews. I'll phone your grandmother. Perhaps your brother should consider buying a car that works.' Again, these comments would lodge themselves in my mind for years to come.

The stranger who helped us was no more than a kind gentleman and although I'm grateful he stopped, over the years Richard has tortured himself that something might have happened to me that night. We've had many a tearful chat about it late at night after several drinks in the years since. Richard did nothing wrong that night and placed his trust in a stranger who in this case turned out to be a good person and we were lucky this stranger happened to be something of a Good Samaritan.

CHAPTER 22

Cemetery Photo Shoot

The late spring brought about a welcome end to the harshest winter in years and I was soon looking forward to coming home for the Easter holidays and seeing my family again. A year had now passed since Mam's death and although I had thrown myself into my new life at boarding school, there wasn't a day when my heart didn't ache for her. Such longing was a tough sentence for a young lad like me and given the opportunity of a quiet moment, my thoughts would veer back to the two people that I had lost. As fate had dealt me an unjust hand, I genuinely thought my parents would be somewhere watching my every move and so I concentrated on making the best out of life at school.

I was aware from Grandma's letters that when I returned home, I would be able to go to the cemetery and see the newly erected headstone marking the resting place of Mam and Dad. Now that I was home from school, Auntie Brenda had arrived with my cousin Gaynor in tow, the pair of them laden with packages. She had a tartan shopping trolley, the type used by old ladies, and in it would be a multitude of surprises, such as colouring books, new pyjamas or, on this occasion, chocolate Easter eggs. On the morning after their arrival, the sun shone and the snowdrops and daffodils burst through the ground after their patient wait under all the snow that had covered them over the long winter. We were going to walk along to the cemetery to see the headstone and already I was dreading it. We climbed the driveway up the hill, Roger and I each clutching a bunch of marguerites from Grandad's garden, wrapped in pages of the *Northern Echo*.

The headstone was huge. At least it seemed so compared to me and as I stood next to it, the top of the black granite slab reached up to my waist. The front of it was designed like an open book – the Bible, to be precise. With a dedication to my dad on one side and Mam on the other, the two pages were united across the top of the stone with the words 'Peace, Perfect Peace'. It was the name of a hymn that Roger and I had learned at school before Dad had died and here it was, providing the most fitting of banners across their final resting place. My eyes read every word on that headstone and it was when they reached the bottom that my heart jumped. Beneath both pages and nestling above the flower vases that sat on either side, it read, 'Dearly loved Father and Mother of Richard, Philip and Roger'. I felt like I had been punched, seeing our own names on the headstone right in front of me; I couldn't take it in.

I walked off to the small spring next to the fence under the guise of getting some water for the flowers, leaving the rest of my family standing over the grave. As I stared down into the water, I cried silently, frightened of making a noise or letting anyone see me upset. The last thing I wanted just now was an audience of well-meaning loved ones offering a comforting arm. I hadn't cried for Mam and Dad in ages and I felt guilty because of it. Poor Grandma cried every single day and who could blame her? But I no longer did. I felt afraid. Afraid of the day coming when I would stop crying for them altogether. I needn't have worried – that day never came.

I attempted to cast my mind back to happier times. When I shut my eyes, I remembered Mam standing at the kitchen sink, peeling vegetables. I could recall her smile and her manner, but I could no longer remember her voice. I think that memory slipped away within a few months after their deaths. It broke my heart because I knew even then that I would never be able to recall it again. As I heard my name called, I opened my eyes and found myself back in the present. I wiped away my tears and rejoined the others around the grave; I expected to have to stand around while some prayers were said and flowers were arranged. Nothing could have prepared me for Auntie Brenda whipping out her camera on Grandma's instruction. I couldn't believe it. As Gaynor, Roger and myself were moved into position behind the headstone, Auntie Brenda took the picture. As the shutter clicked, I stood there with very mixed emotions. There was no way that I could be expected to smile as I stood over the spot where my parents lay buried, yet I was encouraged to do so. Different arrangements of people were moved into place for more photos and finally, the last one of Roger and I stood either side of the headstone was taken. They eventually managed to get us to smile. The grown-ups weren't being insensitive, it was normal to them. The family seemed to have this bizarre tradition of taking photos at graves and so we went along with it.

Once the photo shoot was over, we headed back down the hill, Roger and I racing each other and rolling down the grassy bank, only to be told off by Grandma for showing a lack of respect in this sacred place. In reality, we were desperate to laugh, desperate to smile. I felt that I'd had enough tears for a lifetime, never mind a childhood, and I'm sure Roger felt the same.

Richard didn't come to the cemetery and I couldn't blame him. He was dealing with his grief in his own private way and that certainly meant avoiding standing with a group of relations around a grave. As he carried on with his duties of running the farm, there could be no doubt that he was aware of the scrutiny he was under, not only from family but also members of the farming and local communities. It was almost as if that was the heavier burden for him rather than having Dad's watchful eye overseeing his every move.

To give my grandparents a break from coping with two young boys for the entire four-week Easter holiday, I went to stay with my Auntie Brenda at her house in Seaburn. When we were together, Roger and I could be quite a handful. We were a pair of boisterous little boys with so much energy between us and to have us both stay for a week in Auntie Brenda's small house was deemed a bad idea. That's how I started to go to Seaburn on my own.

Back in the 1970s, Seaburn was still in its heyday as a small seaside town that attracted crowds of visitors every summer, with its long, sandy beach looking out across the North Sea. My cousin Gaynor and I built elaborate sandcastles with moats around them, each one an architectural masterpiece and each new one more complex and ambitious than the last. Lazy days on the beach with egg sandwiches and orange squash for our lunch were the best. We didn't have fancy holidays abroad and we never longed to be anywhere else than on this beach. Following a fun day building sandcastles, we occasionally got to go to the funfair. Set just back from the seafront, it was a traditional fairground of the time, where the helter skelter and ghost train were my favourite rides. There was also a small roller coaster and a big wheel that I longed to have a go on but would never stand a chance of being allowed on it.

After a fun day on the beach, we were content to spend our little bit of pocket money on a couple of rides before squandering the last few pennies on the one-armed bandits. With our energy and money spent, we went to the fish and chips kiosk, where Auntie Brenda would buy us a cone of chips each to eat as we walked back up to her house. There was nothing more perfect than a day like this and my aunt was never short of time for us. I used to feel sad to leave the beach as there was something about the sea that drew me back there every time that I visited. I rarely came away from the beach without a small stash of seaweed, which I used to take back to Stanhope, where Grandad would hang it outside the back door of the farmhouse 'to tell the weather'.

Having a cousin who was a girl the same age as myself had other benefits too. Even at the age of eight or nine, I was content joining in with Gaynor as she played with her Sindy and *Charlie's Angels* dolls. Even today, the world still seems obsessed with children playing with gender-specific toys and it was worse back in the seventies. At my cousin's house, I could play to my heart's content and she happily indulged me.

I wasn't really what you would call a sissy boy, but the grown-ups would often refer to me as 'sensitive' and they saw no harm in letting me play with dolls.

A trip to Seaburn at Easter also meant that I would be taken to the shops to buy new clothes. Despite the Masonic lodge kindly paying out for my school fees and school uniform, it was down to Grandma and Grandad to now pay for other clothes to wear outside school. In order to make the budget stretch as far as possible, Auntie Brenda used to take us up Sea Road to go and see the 'Indian man', as she referred to him. The Indian man ran his own shop, selling the latest fashions, and I loved going there. He would always treat me like an adult and asked me directly what clothes I would like to wear rather than ask my aunt. If I felt I was being coerced into wearing something I didn't like, a simple pleading look from me to the ever-patient proprietor would result in him going off into the stockroom and returning with something far more to my taste. More than an hour later, we would leave with bags bulging with enough clothes to last me for the remainder of the year.

My week at the seaside slipped by and just as I was getting into the rhythm of life on the coast, falling asleep at night to the droning of the foghorn, it was time for me to return to the farm and before too long, back to school.

30th April 1979
My Dear Philip
A few lines my dear in answer to your welcome letter. So
pleased that you have arrived safe and well. Richard is
very busy seeing to the field fences as someone is always

leaving the gates open and the sheep get out on the roads and Richard gets into trouble. People don't realise how serious this is. Well, dear, Roger was delighted with his letter – he was so excited he could hardly open it so will you please us all very much if you always address the letters to him.

I hope that your cough is better. You looked quite smart when you left home. I do believe that you are growing up. Roger missed you when he came home from school, running all over shouting, 'Philip!' He is always fighting with you when you come home but he really loves you, like we all do. I missed you, pet, and the house seems empty without you and your trunk. Never mind, it won't be long before you are home again.

Well, my bonny lad, I have to do my washing now. Take care of yourself and be a good boy, do as you are told, say your prayers and always remember your Grandma loves you very dearly. Roger and you are in my thoughts and prayers. May God Bless, Guide and Guard you and keep you safe.

Your loving Grandma, Grandad, Richard and Roger
xxxx

CHAPTER 23

Croquet &
Gooseberries

As the Easter holidays drew to a close, I was now dreading the last day at home. The day that I returned to school would always consist of the same routine: double-checking my trunk to make sure I hadn't forgotten anything and choosing which games or books I would take back with me. Grandma insisted on warming my uniform on the storage heater that stood in the corner of Mam and Dad's bedroom. Although I outwardly protested at such gestures, thinking of them as mollycoddling, I secretly loved the comfort of having warm clothes to put on before getting in the car to leave once again. It was another act of love on her part and it would have been churlish to refuse.

I would usually start to get upset just as I was about to leave and as the car pulled out of the farmyard, I would look out of the back window as the sight of Grandma, Grandad and Roger waving to me disappeared from view. Richard always took pity on me and placated me by calling in at Ronnie Bell's petrol station in the village and buying me a packet of Rolos. I would offer one to my big brother and he would leave me to happily munch my way through the remainder of the packet during the journey to Barney.

In the summer months, we reverted back to driving to Barney across the moors and as the little car struggled to make it up the winding incline of Softly Bank, I knelt on the back seat, looking out of the window at the sun casting the warmest of summer evening glows across our village nestling at the heart of this beautiful dale. Half an hour later, the car was making its way up the leafy winding drive to Westwick Lodge and I looked up at the sun. It was still shining down on this April evening and it was the same sun that was shining over our farm back home. This reassured me and I felt that it was connecting me with my family that I was parted from. Up in the dorm, I quickly unpacked my bag (the trunk would be done the next day) and went back downstairs to join in a game of yard cricket that was underway.

Summer term at Barney was lovely. On hot afternoons sitting in the classroom, I tried my best to pay attention to Miss Willatt while listening to the soothing distant whirr of the lawnmower outside somewhere in the school grounds. The smell of freshly mown grass sifting through the open window only served to tease us boys as we longed to be outside playing rounders or Danish longball. We dreamt of the bell ringing at half past three signalling the end of lessons. Not only were we desperate to go outside and play but we were itching to shed our school uniform and wear our T-shirts and shorts. This might seem rather silly to most people but when you wear a school uniform for seven days a week, months on end, you crave the opportunity to wear something of your own choosing.

It was during one of those promising summer mornings that I received a letter from Auntie Brenda bearing the most wonderful news that I was to join her, my Uncle Ron and cousin Gaynor for a week-long holiday in Scarborough in August. After breakfast I couldn't wait to tell everyone that I was going to go away on holiday. When asked by a couple of the boys where I was going, they laughed at me.

'Scarborough? You're not even going abroad?' was the comment from one snotty-nosed lad, whose parents lived in Bahrain. But I ignored him and anyway, I didn't care. I had never been abroad before in my entire life and at eight years old, I wasn't bothered. I couldn't have been more excited about my holiday to Scarborough and as far as anyone else was concerned, I might as well have been told that I was going to Disneyland.

The summer term at Barney was always the best, apart from the exams. As the last hour of the afternoon's lessons approached, we were taken outside by Miss Willatt to sit on the grass in the sun while she read to us. The strict rules on our access to forbidden areas of the grounds were relaxed and we spent the remainder of the afternoons running about in the orchard and gardens. Every weekend in the summer our time would be filled with outdoor activities. The traditional annual gooseberry-picking competition was held in the orchard on a Sunday afternoon every summer term. Split into four teams, our task was to pick as many gooseberries from the copious amount of bushes growing in the orchard. Pairs of tracksuit bottoms with the ankles tied in knots were used to collect the berries and the prize of a double helping of ice cream at tea was enough to fire up the competitive spirit in us all. Each team split itself into two, with one half picking the gooseberries and running up the hill with them before tipping them out on the lawn, while the other half of the team topped and tailed them. After more than two hours, the buckets of gooseberries were weighed and the winning team announced. Mr and Mrs Sherbrooke weren't daft, as they managed to get the entire gooseberry crop picked in one afternoon and although we boys were aware of this, we didn't care as we had such fun doing it.

One of the formal lawns at the front of the Prep School was used for playing croquet. I'd never really seen it being played before, only read about it in *Alice in Wonderland*. Thankfully, mallets and balls were used here instead of flamingos and hedgehogs. To us, croquet was just another game that we had been introduced to, such as Danish longball, and we didn't see it as something posh people did. Only now, all these years later when I try to play down how posh my school was, I come unstuck when I tell people that we played croquet. Even this posh pastime presented the opportunity for mischief. One afternoon, some of the older lads grabbed a small boy and used the metal hoops to pin his arms and legs down onto the ground, while another boy appeared with handfuls of worms and bugs. The creepy crawlies were promptly deposited down the inside of the poor boy's T-shirt and the perpetrators ran away, leaving him wriggling and screaming. It was funny at the time and I was relieved that I was never chosen as a victim.

We still went for many Sunday treks with Mr Sherbrooke in the summer term and it was during one of these that I was introduced to wild swimming, a fashionable pursuit now, for the first time. As I'd only learned to swim properly nine months earlier, I was still nervous about swimming across the river. We were at the Meeting of the Waters, near Greta Bridge, on this baking-hot Sunday afternoon and Mr Sherbrooke challenged each of the boys to swim across the pool of the river to the other side. The confident swimmers went first without any sign of hesitation and it was when the last handful of boys was left that my turn came.

I was shaking with nerves as the group across the other side shouted words of encouragement. After five minutes I eventually plucked up the courage, climbed into the cool water and swam across the other side. My heart was pounding as I thrashed my arms and legs in the water, the muffled cheers of my friends barely audible. Despite getting the odd mouthful of river water, my arms soon came down onto the sandy bank of the river. I caught my breath as I climbed up the other boys cheered and I was elated. I had overcome another fear and made the return trip across the river without hesitation or need of encouragement. I never told Grandma that I had been swimming in the river, as she would have had a fit and certainly wouldn't have allowed me to do it again. It was best to save her from any more worry and not say anything, thereby securing me the freedom to go wild swimming again.

It was still light when we had to go to bed in the evenings during the summer term. The dorms were too stuffy to sleep comfortably and so we kept the large sash windows open all night. It was the early hours of the morning when I woke to hear screaming. A boy in the bed opposite me had woken feeling something near to his face. On switching on his torch, he was horrified to see a bat flying around his bed. By now the rest of us in the dorm were awake and there was quite a commotion. Mr Sherbrooke soon ran through to see what all the noise was and before too long, he was attempting to throw a sheet over the bat to then release it back into the night. After twenty minutes of failed attempts he succeeded, and to the sound of a dozen cheering boys as the occupants of the next dorm had now joined us. We were sent back to our beds and the bat flew off into the night.

The exams at the end of term were all set by Miss Willatt and covered all the subjects in the class. There was even a handwriting exam and by now I was proving myself quite adept at doing joined-up writing with a fountain pen. Geography was a favourite subject, as I longed to travel around the world and see different countries, and I recall that I was almost top of the class in English as writing stories had become my forte. I struggled with maths a little and this, sadly, would not change in the coming years.

With the end-of-term exams out of the way, the summer holidays were soon upon us. Richard came to collect me from school and Mrs Sherbrooke was not best pleased that yet again I was the last to leave. She had little sympathy for my brother trying to run a farm and collect me in the middle of hay-timing and made her frustrations known to me as I sat on my trunk in the hall. I think that she tried to make me feel embarrassed because I was the last person to be picked up, but if that was her aim then she failed. I knew that Richard was up against it with the hay-timing and that he was doing his best. Her attitude only served to develop my dislike of her into what would be a deep-rooted hatred. She was a nasty, vindictive snob and I saw right through her. When Richard did arrive to pick me up, she had dispensed with the pleasant attitude with which she had greeted the other parents and merely showed him the barest civilities. As I walked towards the car, I was glad to see the back of her for the summer. She would spend the summer in the big house with all the staff still coming in to cook, clean and do the gardens while she played at being lady of the manor. In contrast, I would be going home to Stanhope Hall, a house that was filled with warmth and love. There were neither of those things at the school.

Once I was home, Grandma greeted me in the kitchen and I changed out of my stifling uniform. In my T-shirt and shorts, I ran up the yard and across to the fields, where Grandad and Roger were with the other hay-time workers. Grandad wiped the sweat from his bald head and popped his old trilby back on as he greeted me. After catching up with him and Roger, I jumped on the back gate of the hay sledge as it turned another corner of the field. I let out the longest of sighs to go with the largest of grins on my face.

The summer holidays were here and all was well.

Stanhope Hall
Saturday June 2nd, 1979
My Dear Philip,
I am very sorry my bonny lad to be late with a letter to you. I got on with my Spring Cleaning, polishing and rushing around and I forgot to post your letter. Never mind, you know your Grandma loves you very dear and would not hurt you for the world. Roger will be coming home shortly, Grandad has gone down for him.

He has had very bad weather, a lot of rain. It was lovely yesterday, some of the caravan people were sun bathing, the first nice day.

Well my love, it was lovely having you home again. You are such a good boy, no bother. You always seem to be helping me, doing jobs for me.

It pleases me to see you on your bike in the yard. Your mammy and daddy would have been so proud of you. Well dear, I hope that you and the boys at school enjoyed your birthday cakes. I am not so clever as your mammy doing cakes and lovely trifles but I do my best. We will have to have a better time next birthday all being well.

I must close now my dear boy. It is nearly dinner time and it will be busy today. Take care my pet and don't worry, we are all well.

May God Bless you and keep you safe.

Your loving Grandma, Grandad, Richard and Roger

xxxxxx

I had only been home for the summer a couple of weeks when another letter arrived from Mr Humble at the Masonic Lodge.

24th July 1979
Dear Mrs Close,
What a lovely photograph of Philip. I am sure that winsome smile will gain him many friends. With your permission, I will let the Brethren of the Lodge see it when I tell them of his satisfactory report.

I, too went to boarding school but I was eleven, so by

the time Philip is eleven he will be settled in and at an advantage. On my third night, I don't know whether I was tipped out of bed (mattress and all) or shaken out by a bomb dropped from a Zepplin [sic] in World War One.

Next term, if it is agreeable to you, I should like to take you on a visit to see Philip at the school, when maybe, he will show us around the school.

With Kind Regards
Yours Sincerely
Oliver Humble

CHAPTER 24

Buckets & Spades

A couple of weeks after Oliver Humble's letter, Grandma and Grandad took Roger and myself to Seaburn the day before we left for Scarborough. Roger was to remain there with them while I jetted off to the East Yorkshire coast with my cousin Gaynor for a week of fun.

We had to be up early the following morning, as the taxi was booked to take us to the station. Not only was I giddy as a kipper to be going to Scarborough, but the excitement of travelling for four hours by train almost tipped me over the edge! When we arrived at Scarborough, we had a half-hour walk with our cases to Mrs Harris's boarding house. Back in the sixties, Auntie Brenda and Mrs Harris had been neighbours in Scarborough and both of them took in visitors on an informal basis. When Auntie Brenda and Uncle Ron moved to Sunderland, they remained in touch with their old neighbour.

Mrs Harris was a short, friendly, silver-haired lady, who looked as if she had been that age for a lifetime. She showed me to my room and in broadest Yorkshire accent she explained that although there was a wash basin in my bedroom, the only toilet for guests was outside in the backyard. Downstairs, she pointed out the parlour, where there was a television – 'If you want to watch *Coronation Street*'. After a year at boarding school, I was pretty much weaned off the telly so spending a week without one didn't bother me at all.

As the rest of the family were seasoned guests at Mrs Harris's, I soon fell into their holiday routine and tagged along as we headed to the supermarket to buy the groceries. Although the boarding house wasn't self-catering, there was a loose arrangement whereby the guests bought the groceries and Mrs Harris cooked the meals for you. The reality was that this was the only affordable way for our family to go away without Auntie Brenda having to do all the cooking. Eating out was expensive so we restricted that to a bag of chips on the way home each evening after a night out. By having Mrs Harris cook our meals, it meant that there was money freed up to go and see shows.

Any major British seaside town in the seventies was still enjoying their heyday of the 'end of the pier' variety shows. Auntie Brenda led the way down to the promenade, which was bustling with stalls and shops selling candy floss, sticks of rock and locally caught shellfish. Before the days of the internet and online ticket purchasing, the buying of tickets for the best shows in town involved walking from one theatre box office to the next and getting the best deal possible. The two major shows in Scarborough during that summer of 1979 were *Larry Grayson's Generation Game* and *The Marti Caine Show*. On the first evening we went to see Larry Grayson's show. At around this time he presented *The Generation Game* on a Saturday night on BBC1, which would easily attract 17 million viewers every week. During the performance, which involved lots of camp innuendo that completely passed me by, they cut to a stage version of *The Generation Game* and asked for couples to come up on stage. Immediately, I stood up and grabbed my cousin's hand and as she sat there, mortified, I realised she wasn't willing to volunteer as it was obvious to everyone but me that they were looking for adults. I was intoxicated by the bright lights and longed to be on the stage and that night as Larry and his Scottish co-host Isla St Clair did a brilliant job of embarrassing the poor volunteers on stage, I fell in love with the theatre.

During the day we idly wandered along the seafront and pitched ourselves on the beach. It was on one carefree afternoon that Gaynor and I, having already taken it in turns to bury each other in the sand, decided to embark on building a mammoth sandcastle. As we took it in turns to dig or collect water from the shore in our little buckets, we became acquainted with another boy and girl roughly the same age as us. After inviting them to join in with our sand construction project, we asked them their names.

'Philip and Gaynor,' they replied.

We laughed amongst ourselves at the coincidence. What were the chances of that? We made friends instantly the way that kids do and parted at the end of the day without ever keeping in touch. Children tend to live in the present and it never occurred to us to continue the friendship beyond that one single blissful afternoon. Other days were spent exploring Peasholm Park with its model ship battles on the lake and winding paths that led up to the Zoo World. This area of the park was dotted with gigantic fibreglass volcanoes and dinosaurs for us children to clamber on. At the age of nine, I was right in the middle of my dinosaur obsession so for me this place was like a dream come true. Like any family, these moments were caught on camera and I still have a series of photos that Auntie Brenda took of me sitting astride a Stegosaurus or underneath the huge T-Rex.

After one particularly fun afternoon at Peasholm Park, on the way back to the boarding house my aunt and uncle said that they had a surprise for me. I followed them along a back lane, unable to focus for trying to second-guess what the surprise could be that they had in store. Eventually they stopped and told me to shut my eyes and as I stood there, in the cobbled back lane behind the houses, Auntie Brenda gently placed her hands on my shoulders and turned me around forty-five degrees to my left.

'Open your eyes,' she said.

In front of me was a large green wooden gate. Along the top of the wooden gate was a sign that read 'Alma Mews Cottage'. Gobsmacked, I immediately did a double take: here was a house that bore the same name as my mother. I was thrilled to see this and so taken that my aunt and uncle had been so thoughtful as to show me this as a surprise. It was testament to the kind of people they were, so kind and generous. Naturally, the camera had come out and after Auntie Brenda knocked on the door and asked the owners for permission to have our picture taken outside the cottage, I posed for a snap to show the rest of the family back home.

Auntie Brenda didn't drink, so the evening was the perfect opportunity to go to the cinema. She took us to see *The Water*

Babies and *The Smurfs* one rainy day earlier in the week, and later took us to see *Lord of the Rings* while Uncle Ron visited his old local for a few pints. The film was not the Peter Jackson epic of course, but the animated feature, and as the horses bounded across the screen with their menacing red eyes glaring at us, I was terrified. Not as much as Gaynor, who was sat right back in her seat barely able to move and gripping onto her mother's arm in fear. Eventually Auntie Brenda decided we ought to leave as Gaynor was petrified although, all these years later, my cousin still maintains that it was me who was scared and that was the reason we left early. We have had to agree to disagree and seeing as this is my book, it's my version of events that goes down as historical fact. Sorry, Gaynor!

The week-long holiday eventually drew to a close and I was sad to return home. Between the zoo, the dinosaurs, the beach, the theatre shows and the cinema trips, I had had the most amazing time. Auntie Brenda certainly knew how to have a good holiday and I would be eternally grateful to her and my uncle and cousin for sharing their week away with me. On the train back to Sunderland, I read through the holiday diary that I had kept during the week, reliving particular moments over and over again in my mind while secretly wishing that I could stay for another seven days.

CHAPTER 25

Dumpling

Following the thrill of the summer holidays, I came back down to earth with a bump. On that first afternoon back at school after Richard had dropped me off, I carried my bag up to D Dorm, which was the larger dorm for the older boys down the other end of the school house. There were twelve beds in the dorm, with six down each side of the room. The two monitors were always allocated the two beds nearest the far wall, the two beds next to the electric radiator, which was clearly a perk of the job.

Keith, my friend from my old primary school back home in Wolsingham, had started at the Prep School that day and I felt so reassured to have him join me as a boarder. He had been my friend at the time when I had lost my parents. To have that connection, that continuity, meant the world to me and for the first time since I went away to school a year earlier, I didn't feel alone. But I couldn't hang about in the dorm for long, as a message came through that all boys were to change into their windcheaters and head out onto Prep Pitch for a game of rounders. The group of us descended on to the pitch, where we were greeted by a new face.

'Good afternoon, boys. I'm Mrs Mockford and I will be taking Middle Division this year,' she said.

Mrs Mockford was in her mid-twenties, slim with shoulder length black hair parted in the centre and flicked out to the sides in the Farrah Fawcett-Majors style, which was still very popular at the time.

There was a moment's silence that was starting to look uncomfortable until one of the newly appointed monitors replied, 'Good afternoon, Mrs Mockford,' with the rest of us trailing behind with varying degrees of enthusiasm.

During that evening's game of rounders, three of us managed to get off on the wrong foot with her and received a stern telling-off in front of the other lads. My old pal Keith was one of the others and following our run-in with her, it took all our concentration not to burst out laughing and receive a further, more serious punishment, such as the slipper from Mr Sherbrooke. I felt sorry for this new teacher – her first day in her new job and already she had us cheeky buggers to deal with.

Mr Sherbrooke kept his punishment slipper in a desk drawer in his study. It wasn't an actual slipper but a white size-ten sandshoe. Scrawled across it were little stick men, each of which, he reliably informed us, represented ten strokes that he had done on misbehaved pupils. There were some boys who 'courted' the slipper and seemed to be on the receiving end of it on a regular basis, but up until now, I had kept a fairly low profile and managed to avoid it. Having said that, with my old friend Keith in tow, I wasn't sure just how much longer my clean record would last.

Classes with Mrs Mockford were efficiently run and she didn't stand for any mucking about. As a recently qualified primary school teacher, she was quick to assert herself as a no-nonsense, straight-talking woman who had no time for silliness in or outside the classroom. As there wasn't a dedicated classroom in the main Prep School for our class, we moved into the ground floor of Longfield House, an old Victorian building used to house a number of sixth formers. Inside, it reeked of aftershave and 'hippy juice', the cheap patchouli aftershave still popular in the seventies. Mrs Mockford would regularly have to go stomping up the stairs to shout at one of the residents for playing their David Bowie albums too loud, much to the amusement of those of us in her class.

I will give Mrs Mockford the credit of being a good teacher, she just took some getting used to after a year with the friendly, cosy approach of Miss Willatt, who only taught the Lower Division. She is the woman to whom I have to give credit for getting me into reading books in a big way. Each term she had a class book and if there was time towards the end of the day, she would sit and read to us. Thanks largely to her brilliant choices, she had the entire class transfixed from the moment that she opened the book. She started us off on *The Silver Sword* by Ian Serraillier, set in Nazi-occupied Warsaw, which I loved, before moving on to Eve Garnett's *The Family From One End Street* and J.R.R. Tolkien's classic *The Hobbit*. She challenged us to make ambitious reading choices and as she read to us each afternoon, the entire class hung on to her every word.

Although the Prep School was a private school, in those first two years that I was away we still played football instead of rugby. One of the star players was Tony Underwood, who would go on to become one of the England rugby team's most iconic players. In my first year, he was one of the many boarders at the school whose parents lived abroad but by the time that I had returned for my second year at Barney, Mr and Mrs Underwood had moved to the UK and were regulars on the side of the pitch, no matter what the sport was. Some of the loveliest people you could meet, they cheered every Barney boy loudly as they played, with Mrs Underwood already showing us the energetic supporting style that, in later years, would cause the British public to fall in love with her. They could not have been prouder of their three boys at the school and we were all incredibly saddened to hear of Mr Underwood's sudden passing only a year or so later. I really felt for the boys, and in particular Tony, as having lost my own parents, I knew what it was like to have that cloud of bereavement hanging over you as you mourned a parent. Despite being widowed, Mrs Underwood remained a loyal supporter of the Barney teams for many years to come and always had a kind encouraging word for all the boys.

Now that I was quite settled into life at Barney, Grandma kindly suggested that on some weekends when I came home, perhaps I might like to bring home a friend, particularly one who lived oversees and didn't have the chance to visit home so often. That year, two Nigerian brothers, Tunde and Yemi, arrived at our school and were immediately the subject of fascination for many of the boys because they were black. I think poor Yemi was puzzled by our interest in the texture of his Afro hair and skin colour as most of us, including myself, had never met a black person before.

The brothers immediately settled into Prep School life and I'll never forget their faces on the first winter day when snow fell and they went outside. Yemi stood there open-mouthed, his hand outstretched, as the snowflakes fluttered down and settled momentarily on his warm palm before melting. There we were, the rest of the boys, gobsmacked that somebody hadn't seen or felt snow before. Funnily enough, snow is not so abundant in Nigeria as it is in the north of England.

One weekend, Yemi came to Stanhope Hall with me and met the family, who gave him the warmest of welcomes, as they did any of the boys who came to stay at our farm. I felt so lucky to be at school with boys who were from all over the world and as they shared stories of their home life, I was fascinated at the thought of travelling to countries such as Fiji, Tanzania and Cyprus, to name a few.

Over the winter, Mr Sherbrooke kept up the tradition of the early-morning run to keep himself fit. At supper the night before, he offered to take anyone mad enough to want to get out of their bed at six-thirty in the morning along with him. There were one or two weekends where I went along, as by now it had been pointed out to me on several occasions, particularly by Mrs Sherbrooke, that I was perhaps putting on more weight than I ought to. One cold spring morning that year, I got up and instead of us doing the Junior Barney, a local three-mile course, a handful of us jumped into Mr Sherbrooke's car and we drove up to the moors. As we got out in the middle of a thick fog, we could barely see before us, so thick was the pea soup blocking our view. Despite this, we started to run and at one point I noticed a wire fence running along the line we were running and seeing that there appeared to be a bit of a dip on the other side, I ran across to peer over, only to stop dead in my tracks: about two feet over the other side of the fence the ground dropped away into an abyss and it soon became clear that I was stood right on the edge of a deep quarry. I've never been great with heights and I almost filled my shorts there and then! I managed to run the rest of the route far quicker than my usual plodding pace, my heart still beating ten to the dozen as I thought back to how close I was to the quarry edge.

It was around this time that I started to become far more self-conscious about my body and as I've already mentioned, people had started remarking, most of them very directly, how I had put weight on. Of course, if you want to motivate a fat kid to lose some weight, the best method is to ridicule them in public about it. At least, I think that must have been Mrs Sherbrooke's theory. One lunchtime when we were in the dining room, she decided to broach the subject in her usual caring, tactful manner as she sat on a small table at the side of the dining room, legs dangling over the side and holding a lit cigarette in her hand.

'Mews, you're getting fat. I'm going to have to start calling you "Dumpling". Yes, I'll call you "Dumpling" from now on,' she announced callously.

I'm normally a very forgiving person but I cannot find it in myself to pardon Mrs Sherbrooke for the way she behaved all those years ago. I have attempted to reason it in my head, but I have drawn the conclusion that she was simply a nasty, cruel individual. I know she wasn't consistently like this, but the way in which she treated certain boys was calculated. There is no other explanation.

Despite there being a degree of solidarity amongst the boarders, it was inevitable that one or two boys would pick up on her jibes and run with it. It wasn't very long at all before I became afraid to take my top off in front of other people and swimming classes soon changed from something I had enjoyed to being an event that I dreaded. This would stay with me right into adulthood. Sadly, it was something that defined my childhood and I have never forgiven Mrs Sherbrooke for the major part she played in that. Kids can be cruel, as we all know, but adults should know better.

Stanhope Hall
June 8th 1980
My Dear Philip,
Hulloa my love, here is Grandma with her few lines
hoping that they find you safe and well as this leaves us
all fine here at home. Well dear, we have had a severe
storm since I last wrote to you. Lightning, thunder and
rain for about four hours. I was worried wondering if you
were safe inside or not.

I forgot to take poor Sammy the goldfish out of the
window and then it was too late, poor Sammy died.
We were all really upset because Roger loved it so much,
it was his friend. Grandad and Roger buried it in the
garden amongst the pansies.

Roger can ride your Chopper bike now, he is very good
so he does not want his old one. We have two boys from
Wales staying here and they go to school every morning
and they go off and visit all kinds of different places and
then come home for six o'clock. They go home tomorrow.

I must be closing now as they will be wanting tea and

I must get washed and changed. Take care of yourself and remember Grandma loves you dearly and always thinks of you. Say your prayers and clean your teeth my bonny lad. May God bless you and keep you safe.

Your loving Grandma, Grandad, Richard and Roger
xxxxxx

CHAPTER 26

Getting a Good Look

1980

The summer of 1980 began with my returning home to Stanhope Hall for the holidays and even though I had over eight weeks before I went back to school, Roger was already looking forward to joining me at Barney in September, as the Masonic charity had been generous enough to pay for his education, too. For the past two years, he had lived on the farm with Grandma and Grandad while I was away. He was excited at the thought of wearing his school uniform, which Grandma had already bought at Swinbanks. There was no way she could have managed all this sewing and altering single-handed, so as usual, Auntie Brenda was drafted in. A skilled seamstress, there was nothing she couldn't make out of some thread and material. Having her up to the farm on regular weekends not only gave my grandparents more practical help, it also gave them the opportunity to emotionally support each other.

The summer holidays really got going once the state schools

broke up and our great friends, the Devitt family, came up from Sunderland to spend the summer in their caravan. A number of the families that had caravans on the farm had moved to other sites in the area with shower blocks, hot water and flushing toilets and these included our good friends Estelle and Lyndsey. By comparison, the site at Stanhope Hall was very basic but it made up for it in character and things to do. None of the other caravan sites were part of working farms with dogs, hens and horses roaming about and I suppose that was our unique selling point.

Now that the Devitts were up at the farm, Jimmy and Theresa Devitt kindly offered, without a second thought, to take Roger and I out for the day, as they had done for many previous summers. One afternoon, we had gone in the car to Killhope and up towards the Lake District, a favourite haunt of Jimmy's. On our return to the farm that evening, Theresa noticed as the car trundled into the caravan site that there appeared to be someone in their caravan. Jimmy sped up, fearing intruders, but a familiar face appeared at the window, pulling the net curtains to one side. Theresa's Auntie Ruth, more affectionately known as 'Ticker', waved enthusiastically from the window.

'It's Ruthie! How the hell has she managed to get in the van, Jimmy? She doesn't have a key,' Theresa said. Jimmy couldn't help but laugh, and nor could the rest of us.

Once we were in the van, the answer to the mystery was revealed to all. Ruthie, tired of sitting in the house back home in Sunderland, had decided to have a few days up at the caravan so she jumped on a series of buses and made the four-hour journey up to Stanhope. Assuming her family would be in, she went straight to the caravan only to find it locked and empty. Being the resourceful woman that she was, she found one of the caravan windows ajar and by stacking a chair on top of a bin, she clambered up the precariously assembled tower and climbed in through the window, whereupon she popped the kettle on and made herself a cup of tea. Not bad for a woman fast approaching seventy! We all fell about laughing as she recounted the story to us with the straightest of faces.

A week later, on a sunny July morning, the cases were packed for Roger and I to go to Auntie Brenda's house at Seaburn for a week. Richard was to take us in the car, so we would thankfully avoid the multitude of buses that it took to get there. In recent months, Grandad had not been his usual self. A kind, quiet man, he found it increasingly difficult to smile. He had been through the most dreadful time during the war when he served out in Burma and had come home looking forward to a more settled life. Mam's death had knocked him for six and as they were particularly close, he never got over the loss. He was devoted to his family but it seemed two years of putting on a brave face for everyone was taking its toll.

Downstairs in the kitchen, Grandad was sitting in the armchair, looking more and more visibly upset, but he said nothing. I tried asking him what was wrong, but he ignored me as his eyes filled with tears. Suddenly, in one movement, he jumped out of his chair and went upstairs, emerging ten minutes later, fully dressed in his best suit, his trilby hat and carrying his small weekend suitcase. He still had tears in his eyes and seeing him in this state shocked me to the core. I asked him where he was going and all he could respond was, 'Home, away from here.' Now hysterical in floods of tears, I grabbed on to his jacket, pleading with him to stay.

'Please don't go, Grandad! Please…' I said and then I sobbed uncontrollably. But he just pushed past me and walked out the front door. And so I ran down the path after him, now screeching, 'Grandad, please!' But all he could do was turn around.

'Get back in the house,' he said.

I looked into his eyes for a split second before he turned and walked away down the path. Everyone was shocked at Grandad's outburst. Richard had gone to feed the animals while our bags were brought downstairs. I have no recollection as to what happened next, other than we went in the car to Seaburn to stay with my aunt.

Over the next week, Auntie Brenda and Uncle Ron had to go and 'visit relatives' so Roger, Gaynor and myself were left in the care of their neighbour June for the two days. On the night that they returned home late, they came to collect us and we went straight to our beds. That same night I had the strangest of dreams, where I dreamt that I was playing football in the front driveway of my aunt's house with Grandma and Grandad. As we kicked the ball to each other, Grandma clutched herself and collapsed to the ground. Looking at her, I could see that she was dead and as I started to scream, Grandad took hold of my hand.

'Philip, things aren't what they seem, bonny lad. Be a good lad and look after your Grandma,' he said, and before anything else happened I woke up. I'd barely had chance to get dressed before breakfast when Auntie Brenda came in and asked Roger and I to come into the sitting room. As she sat us down on the settee I knew what was coming – I'd been there before.

'Now, boys, I have some very sad news,' she said. She was struggling to hold back the tears. 'Grandad has died.'

She gave us both the tightest of hugs, as all three of us were sitting in shock and crying.

'He was a lovely grandad and you must always remember him that way,' she added as I sat back, trying to take it all in. I needed some air straight away and Auntie Brenda reluctantly allowed me go out into the street to have some time on my own. I walked across the road and called for my friend Gavin to see if he fancied coming out. His dad had died the previous year and as we walked together along the path, I talked about Grandad. To be honest, I was numb and I couldn't really take it in. No explanation was offered to us kids as to the cause of Grandad's death and when we enquired, we were simply told that he had passed away in hospital.

It would be another ten years before I would learn the truth.

It turned out that following his outburst at the farm, Grandad had decided to go home to Brandon village and as he was clearly in no fit state to drive, he must have travelled by bus. Concerned at the circumstances under which he had left, Richard wanted to speak to him. As they had no telephone at the house in Brandon, the following day Richard drove down there. He rang the doorbell and at first there was no answer. He could see smoke coming from the chimney so he knew that Grandad must be home so he tried ringing the doorbell a second time. Eventually, Grandad came to the door but didn't open it. He refused to let Richard in and seemed to be still very much upset. Reluctantly, my brother eventually walked back to the car and returned to Stanhope.

The following day, Grandma left Auntie Brenda's and went

back home to Brandon to make her peace with her husband. When she tried to unlock the front door, the lock had the snip on so the key wouldn't turn. She walked around the back door to see if it was open, but again it was locked. Concerned that there was no response from the house, she went to Mr Evans the neighbour to ask him for help. Mr Evans was a large, well-built man and soon he was in Grandma's backyard. After several mighty shoves, he managed to get the back door open. As he tumbled into the hallway of the house, his eyes caught sight of the pair of feet dangling above him from the banister and his immediate response was to rush back to the door to prevent my grandmother from going in.

Poor Grandad, he was the loveliest, funniest and most gentle man I ever knew. Having bravely served in Burma during the World War II, he witnessed first-hand the horrors that the Japanese Army inflicted out there and he had looked forward to a happy and peaceful retirement. Just as he was about to realise this modest dream, he was robbed of his eldest daughter, his beloved Alma, and he never got over it. I cannot write about his passing without thinking there was something that I could have done to persuade him not to take that decision. Having gone through what we did with losing Mam and Dad, I will always be eternally grateful to the family for protecting Gaynor, Roger and myself from the true reality of Grandad's death and for me personally, it meant that it would not be yet another thing to haunt me in those years. He had decided that he simply could not carry on and he chose to leave us on his own terms.

While us kids whiled away the summer holidays that week in Seaburn, the rest of the family was left with the grim task of arranging a funeral. Brandon was a close-knit community that grew out of the coal mining industry. The local colliery was the biggest employer in a town dominated by the huge cast-iron structure of the headstock with its wheel on top, visible for miles around. As a result, most of Grandma's family still lived in the town. Like Weardale, Brandon's people came together in times of crisis but sadly, on this occasion, it wasn't so much a coming together in support of my grandmother. News soon spread around the town of Grandad's death, but this was closely followed by the mention of suicide. Because the family had to await a formal inquest, it meant that there was a delay before Grandad's body could be released to the family and funeral arrangements made.

It's sad that despite Grandma's unwavering support for all her family over the years, some of her own family were not wholly supportive in return. These were tough working-class women and what they viewed as plain speaking, many others including myself would see as being rude and lacking tact. As they congregated at Grandma's house, one by one they hobbled into the dining room, muttering about this ailment and that.

'You shouldn't be burying him in the cemetery, Maggie, not if he's killed himself,' one of them piped up before she even had a chance to get her coat off. Another went upstairs to the toilet and on her way she shouted, 'Here,' and on the staircase they looked up and pointed to the banister on the landing, 'he must have done it from there.'

As they sat crammed into the back room next to the scullery, Grandma waited on them with cups of tea and cakes as they prepared themselves for the main event. Right on cue the front doorbell rang and Grandma spoke to her daughter.

'Brenda, that will be the undertakers. Will you get them to take your dad into the front room, pet?' she said.

As Auntie Brenda went through to the front door, there was a hushed silence in the room. It was unheard of for these particular women to stop talking but, as they sat there, the excitement on their faces couldn't be hidden. Hitching themselves forward on their seats, they put down their tea cups and waited for the starting pistol. They could hear the funeral directors carrying the coffin through the front door and negotiating the turn into the front room. Back in the dining room, they could barely contain their curiosity and their excitement. The funeral directors unscrewed the coffin lid and placed it against the wall. Auntie Brenda made her way back through to the scullery to her waiting mother and was almost bowled over by the stampede of old women as the entire group of them barged past her, pushing the others out of the way, desperate to get a look.

'I've never seen a suicide before,' Auntie Ivy muttered as she dashed through, moving quicker than her stumpy legs had allowed her to do in the past twenty years. Grandma, still standing in the dining room, tears rolling down her face, looked at her daughter as the sound of 'oohs' and 'ahhs' and muttering could be heard from the front room. Taking her daughter's hand, she went through to the throng leaning over the open coffin that had been positioned in the centre of the room.

'I think you should leave,' Grandma said as she addressed the group of ladies, who were shocked at her forthright manner. Reluctantly, they filed out of the room, one or two glancing behind them to get one last look, passing the undertakers in the hall.

'Mrs Close, I will leave you with your husband, and we will be back tomorrow morning,' the funeral director said to her.

'If you could please wait five minutes,' she said.

Shutting the door behind them, Grandma spent those moments with the man that she had been married to for almost fifty years, with their daughter by her side. After a short while, the door opened and she emerged into the hall.

'Please could you put the lid back on and screw it shut? Thank you.'

The undertaker nodded solemnly in agreement and with his colleague, he carried out her wishes. Grandma returned to the dining room, where the group of women once again fell silent, having heard her instructions regarding the coffin lid.

'Other people will want to come and see him,' remarked Auntie Mary, Grandma's bossy older sister.

Grandma looked her in the eye. 'Nobody else is getting to see him, Mary,' she said sternly.

Now that the show was over the women hurried to put their coats on and leave, not that they didn't want to be there but having witnessed my grandad's homecoming first-hand and the added salaciousness of it being a suicide, this news was too good to keep to themselves. To be able to tell people at the funeral 'I was there when they brought him home, I saw him' was an opportunity they weren't prepared to miss. Meanwhile, Grandma and Auntie Brenda remained in the house, steeped in grief and wondering how they were going to get through the next twenty-four hours.

Grandma told me the bulk of this story many years later, still upset and bitter at the way some, but not all, members of her family had behaved towards her at that time. After his tragic death, my poor grandad deserved compassion, not judgement, and his widow needed support instead of scrutiny and gossip.

It was a busy funeral the following day and Grandad was laid to rest in the cemetery at Meadowfield on the road leading into Durham, his grave sitting in a shaded spot just a stone's throw from the children's plot, where his eldest granddaughter was buried.

Back at the farm, Grandma got on with life without her husband. But she didn't have time to stop and grieve properly or even make some sense of his decision to depart this world on his own terms. She had her two boys to see to and with Roger leaving home to join me at boarding school, time was ticking by. As far as her boys were concerned, she still had a job to do and she was determined to see it through to completion.

CHAPTER 27

Big Mews, Little Mews

September approached and life at Stanhope Hall was busy. The hay-timing was done in the most difficult of circumstances during the weeks surrounding Grandad's death and Stanhope Show would be coming up soon. All this time, my little brother was counting down the days to putting on his Prep School uniform and leaving home. As Roger was only seven years old when he was due to go to Barney, he was very young for the school year. Now he was going to start a new chapter of his life as the youngest pupil at Barnard Castle School. He was a small, thin boy back then and losing his parents and now his grandfather had left him particularly vulnerable. This was something that we, his family, were only too aware of. Grandma was a worrier at the best of times but despite her strength, even she was unprepared for the further emotional wrench of sending away her youngest lad. It was a huge responsibility that she now had to bear on her shoulders without Grandad at her side.

It had been Grandad's job to paint Roger's name on his battered tin trunk and mark up the other items that he had to take away with him and now that he was no longer with us, I stepped in to give a hand, although I wasn't as neat at painting. It was also Grandad who had taught me how to tie my school tie, polish my shoes and tie my shoelaces and he had planned to do the same for Roger. Richard was so busy with the farm, as he couldn't really afford to pay anyone to help him full-time so it was down to me. This was where Grandad was also a big miss, as he was great at helping out with many of the tasks around the byres and stables, such as mucking out and keeping the place tidy.

As the day approached for us to head off to school, I did my best to talk Roger through tying his laces and doing his blue-and-brown-striped school tie. The laces he managed no problem, although the tie proved to be trickier, but he practised in that last week to try and get it right.

Auntie Brenda had done a marvellous job in sewing the mounds of name tags that had to be attached to every last sock, handkerchief and flannel. On the day that we were leaving, Auntie Olive called in to Stanhope Hall to wish Roger luck and having brought her camera with her, she seized the opportunity to take some pictures of us both outside the front of the house. We posed in our smart, clean uniforms complete with knee-length woollen socks, short grey trousers and peaked school caps. Grandma had managed to find a blue Adidas sports bag that matched my own so that Roger could be just like his big brother. With the bags placed at our feet, we posed for photos on the flagstone path at the front of Stanhope Hall. Roger's face was beaming with pride to be joining me at boarding school and Grandma stood behind us, a protective arm around each of our shoulders. Looking back at these pictures, it's easy to see the anxiety on her face as she prepared to see us off but, despite feeling this, she was still so proud of her boys. In her heart, she knew that the both of us had been handed the opportunity of a lifetime to be able to attend such a prestigious school as Barney. She'd never had the education that we were receiving and she made sure the two of us knew how fortunate we were and that we never once took it for granted.

With the trunks packed in the car, Roger and I squeezed into the back seat to allow room in the front for Grandma. She had dressed up in her smart two-piece navy suit that had become her trademark in recent years of mourning. Always immaculately turned out, she never left the house without her smart hat, dress gloves and handbag. She might have been a tough, working-class woman from a coal mining family, but she couldn't bear the thought of going out of the front door dressed in a headscarf, tabard or with rollers in her hair as many women did.

Once more the car pulled up the driveway of Westwick Lodge and Mrs Sherbrooke greeted us with a cheery smile, the same one that she saved for parents at the front door.

'Ah, come in, Mews,' she said, looking down at Roger, with his thin legs standing in his little grey shorts. She didn't use his first name. 'I'll have to call you Big Mews and Little Mews,' she announced. 'Well, your brother knows his way around, so there's no need for Grandma to go upstairs and see your dorm,' she continued, while doing her best to usher Grandma out of the door. Thankfully, Grandma stood her ground and replied quietly yet assertively, 'I'll just take a moment to say goodbye to the boys, if you don't mind, Mrs Sherbrooke.' She hugged and kissed me while whispering in my ear, 'Please take care of him, Philip, you're the only one he has.'

I didn't shed tears, as I was determined to play the role of the brave big brother as best I could. Turning to Roger, who by now was crying quietly, his legs trembling, she hugged him so tight. Knowing he was so young and vulnerable made it all the harder for her to say goodbye. Eventually she stepped back, aware that Mrs Sherbrooke was holding the door open, waiting for her to leave. With goodbyes done, she closed the door behind Grandma.

'I'll show Roger up to his dorm, Mrs Sherbrooke,' I said.

'He has his own minder to look after him, Mews. Stop fussing over him,' she said.

As another boy now stood waiting in the wings to take my little brother upstairs, Mrs Sherbrooke called me over.

'You've been appointed a monitor this term, Big Mews. It's quite a responsibility, you know.'

'Yes, Mrs Sherbrooke, thank you.'

'Well, don't stand around here, hadn't you better go up and unpack?'

I had been placed in the larger D Dorm while Roger was in A Dorm, along with a handful of other new boys and their minders. Once I had unpacked, I went along to see how he was getting on and along the way, I ran into Antony, Mrs Sherbrooke's son, who was the year above me and had now progressed to the Main School.

'Hello, Mews, how was your summer holiday?' he enquired.

'Pretty rubbish really, my grandad died,' was all I could offer as a response.

Sherbrooke kindly said that he was sorry for my loss and did his best to continue the conversation in a more upbeat manner. He was a decent lad, with an outgoing, optimistic personality. Eventually, I made my excuses and left him on the landing as I headed into A Dorm to see how Roger was getting on.

He was still slowly unpacking his bag, not quite sure as to what to do or where to put his things, his minder nowhere in sight. On seeing me walk through the door, he shot me a look of relief that I was there to help him. With his belongings eventually put away, I walked downstairs with him and started to show him around. He carried his handful of toy cars and a game down with him and in the large playroom, we found the locker that had been assigned to him. We walked up into the craft room, where I explained that that was where we made models and did art, before showing him the Lower Division classroom. Miss Willatt was already in there, getting the room ready for her new students, and she greeted Roger in her usual warm, kindly manner and soon relaxed him and made him feel at ease.

That evening at supper in the kitchen, despite having already met one or two other new boys, Roger naturally gravitated towards me and this did not go unnoticed by Mrs Sherbrooke. I had somehow expected her to show a more kind and caring attitude towards us this term, not only because Roger was a new boy but also because it was only a few weeks ago that we had lost Grandad. I knew that she had been told of his death, as Grandma made a point of phoning her up in the summer holidays to let her know. Looking over the top of her glasses at us, she caught me whispering something to Roger.

'Big Mews, your brother has his own minder and doesn't need you fussing over him,' she said in a loud voice.

Poor Roger, everyone was now looking at him and he didn't know where to put himself. It was hard enough for him with this being his first night away from home but to have to cope with being singled out publicly was more than he needed.

The following morning, at breakfast, Roger met Mr Sherbrooke. As the new boys lined up, each one with their 'minder' guiding them through the rituals of life as a boarder, Mr Sherbrooke checked their hands and faces to ensure they were washed correctly and pointed out to certain boys, including Roger, that maybe they had better have another try in doing their school tie. I would always keep a watchful eye on him, I had promised Grandma that much. As I sat in my monitor's seat at the head of North Table, I looked to the South Table on the other side of the room at Roger slowly making his way through a bowl of cornflakes. In that first week, he, like many of the new boys, had difficulty adjusting to the new way of life that had been so suddenly thrust upon him. Naturally, he would look to me for reassurance and guidance but Mrs Sherbrooke often intervened. This trembling thin, blond seven-year-old desperately needed love and tenderness and the 1970s tough boarding school approach did him no favours.

At lunchtime one day in that first week, Roger, along with the rest of his class, had just returned from their first swimming lesson and as usual, they had to get quickly changed in time for lunch. As the boarders lined up for the daily hand inspection, Mrs Sherbrooke caught sight of his dishevelled tie.

'Little Mews, stand here a moment,' she said, pulling him out of the queue. Once the rest of the boys had sat down, she turned Roger to face us all.

'Little Mews, how long have you been here?' she said.

Roger, now shaking and his eyes showing the signs of welling up with tears, answered timidly, 'Four days.'

'Four days, *Mrs Sherbrooke*,' she cut back to him. 'You've been here four days and you still can't do your tie properly, Mews. The other boys seem to have managed, yet you can't.'

Tears were pouring down his cheeks now and as I sat there helplessly, the tears were welling up in my own eyes.

'Take your tie off and do it properly!' she snapped.

The rumble of a trolley signalled the arrival of the dinner ladies with dishes of hot food at the door. Mrs Sherbrooke instructed them to wait until Roger had done his tie. Now physically shaking, he nervously undid his tie and wiped the tears and snot from his face. He tried to focus on doing his tie as she stood over him. Not knowing where to start under such pressure, he looked over at me.

'Philip…' he pleaded, but as I stood up, she interjected.

'Big Mews, sit down.' Turning back to Roger, she said, 'Your brother can't help you now.'

As everyone stared at him, most in sympathy, Roger took the next two minutes to do his tie, shaking and trembling throughout. He eventually made it and as he went over to his seat, silently sobbing, Mrs Sherbrooke turned to the dinner ladies and signalled to them that they could come in and start serving lunch. But she didn't take the pressure off Roger and just when I thought she couldn't possibly be any more vindictive, she tackled him again one lunchtime while he was in the middle of eating.

'Little Mews, why are you holding your cutlery in that manner?' she said.

At this Roger stopped in his tracks and looked up at her, then glancing back down at the knife and fork he was holding, he tried to figure out what she was referring to. Impatient for an answer, she tried again.

'Why are you holding your cutlery in the wrong hands?' she said.

'He's left-handed, Mrs Sherbrooke,' I offered.

Oh dear, I was in for it now! She turned her head and behind those thick glasses, her eyes bore into me.

'I wasn't asking you, Big Mews,' she said.

Turning back to Roger, she challenged him once more: 'At this school we eat properly, so swap your cutlery around.'

He knew that he had no choice but, since he had been eating left-handed all his life, he struggled to adapt to this new technique as anyone would. A painfully slow eater at the best of times, he had been eating even more slowly ever since Mam died. Now that he held his knife and fork the other way around, his pace slowed even further. This annoyed Mrs Sherbrooke. She had a house rule that if you didn't eat your main course, then you weren't allowed any pudding. As she wasn't prepared for him to take so long to eat, she made him clear his plate away every lunchtime with half of his food left and she would then forbid him to have any pudding.

Poor Roger was a skinny little thing to start with, but it wouldn't be long before our eagle-eyed grandma would discover that his weight had dropped. As she had been desperate to get his weight up over the four-stone mark, she monitored it religiously and during that first weekend home, seeing that he had lost several pounds, she took me to one side and asked what was going on. I told Grandma everything. She cried and held us both so tightly. On the next day, when Richard picked us up, Grandma climbed into the front seat, all dressed up.

'I didn't know you were coming,' Richard said to her.

'Oh yes, I need to have a quiet word with Mrs Sherbrooke.'

On arrival at school, when the door opened, Mrs Sherbrooke's smile soon disappeared when she saw my grandmother not smiling at her. Grandma turned to us and kissed and hugged us both.

'You boys, go and take your bags upstairs. Grandma needs to have a word with Mrs Sherbrooke,' she said.

I don't know what was said but, from that day on, Roger was allowed to eat holding his cutlery left-handed and soon he was queuing for his pudding with the rest of the boys.

Brandon Village
Durham
22nd September 1980
My Dear Philip
Here is your Grandma again with the news. We are all well hoping that you and our Roger are keeping well and happy. Well my bonny lad, I hope that you are still keeping an eye on our Roger. I know that you are not his minder but love him because we just have you and Roger and we have to love each other.

Auntie Brenda has made a lovely birthday cake for Roger. I am still at Brandon but will be going back to Stanhope on Thursday. I don't think that Auntie Brenda will be home for Roger's party as they have a friend coming to stay. Roger will be excited for his first weekend home and I am longing to see you both. Be a good boy my darling Philip. Grandma loves you both very dearly. Say your prayers, it is alright saying them quietly to yourself. God doesn't mind as long as you say them. God Bless my son. I love you. Clean your teeth and play the game.

Your loving Grandma xxxxxx

CHAPTER 28

The Terrapin &
a Pickled Snake

A new school academic year meant that it was a new class for me too. I had spent the last two years dreading entering the Upper Division, which was taught by the infamously frightening Mr Hay. Everyone referred to him as 'Old Hay', always behind his back but never to his face. Having already taught at the Prep School for more than twenty-five years, Old Hay had been there longer than even some of the classrooms. He had the reputation in Barnard Castle and the school for being one of life's eccentrics, with a passion for mathematics and origami harmoniously entwined with his love of beer and fags. Every day, once he had eaten his lunch, he would sit in his classroom and puff his way through as many Marlboros as it was possible to do so in thirty minutes. By the time that we came in from the playground after lunch, the Upper Division classroom was thick with smog and God help the boy who dared ask if he could crack open a window. By the end of a year being taught by Old Hay, it's a wonder every boy in the class didn't leave with a craving nicotine addiction, let alone buggered lungs!

The first thing that any of us in the class learned about Old Hay was the loud, booming voice that shouted across the room was not his angry voice. On the occasions that he got really angry he would stand close to you, look you right in the eye and speak to you in a quiet, calm manner, his breath permeating your nostrils and droplets of spittle hanging on his lips. If you found yourself faced with that, then you were definitely in trouble.

Maths was Old Hay's speciality and he didn't have a lot of time for boys who couldn't master it. He had an obsession with the binary code and seemed to spend more time teaching us that than anything else. He didn't have much time for subjects such as History, Geography and English Literature, though – he simply ticked the boxes on the curriculum by doling out textbooks and giving us a chapter to read for prep before half-heartedly testing us on it the following morning, eager to get it out of the way and on to more Maths. It would only be two months before I would have to sit the entrance exam for the Main School and every day, we had Maths and English drummed into us by him.

Although Maths was not my forte at school, there were several boys in my class who found it more of a challenge than I did. Sadly for those poor lads, Old Hay had little time or patience for those who couldn't grasp the subject and he had devised a series of punishments of varying degrees, which ranged from basic verbal humiliation to standing a boy with his back to the wall and grasping their hair tightly, he would proceed to bash the back of their skull against the wall repeatedly. Clearly, he took the phrase 'drumming it into you' a tad too literally. He would then end up even more angry and frustrated when the concept of algebra continued to be as confusing to the crying, wretched boy stood before him.

Of the varying degrees of punishment doled out by him, the worst was the terrapin. Amongst junk in his classroom was a small aquarium that sat in front of the window and contained one occupant, a terrapin. Old Hay would sit at his desk, chewing small lumps of raw meat in his mouth, and would then take it out, covered in tobacco saliva, and feed it to his reptile friend. Should he be in a particularly bad mood, he picked on an unfortunate individual who had given an incorrect answer to a sum and he made the trembling boy stand next to the tank. Lifting the terrapin out with more care than he ever showed to any of his pupils, he took the terrapin and held it against the boy's earlobe. Rooted to the spot in fear, my classmate, afraid to move an inch, would start to feel the pain once the terrapin began to nibble on his earlobe. As the searing pain would sting him from the red-raw ear down to his toes, the boy would endure this torture and Mr Hay would only remove his reptile pal once the victim's ear was bleeding.

I must point out that this punishment was rarely given out and over the years, Roger and I laughed it off, putting it down to the style of teaching back then. Obviously, as I have grown older, I'm horrified at the memory and can't believe it actually occurred. I'm sure that Mr Sherbrooke never found out about it, as he would certainly have put a stop to it.

Thankfully, I was never on the receiving end of the hungry reptile, but I did have one encounter in that classroom that scared the life out of me. Old Hay collected all sorts of stuff and had piles of old newspapers and magazines which sat underneath the large window. One lunchtime, myself and another boy had been selected by him to tidy up the cupboards that ran along underneath. On my knees, I opened up a cupboard and started lifting out papers, boxes and passing them to my classmate to put on the side. I couldn't see clearly what I was lifting out and as my hands grabbed a large glass jar, I gently lifted it off the shelf and as I passed it up to go on the side, the light from the window illuminated the contents. What I saw gave me such a start that I almost dropped it: curled up in the jar was a snake, its head staring at me. My reaction came with a yelp and this alerted Old Hay, who was puffing on his fourth Marlboro in a row and engrossed in a book at his desk. He looked up and squinted through the fog of cigarette smoke over the top of his gold-rimmed, half-moon glasses.

'It's only a dead adder, Mews, it's hardly going to bite you,' he laughed before returning to his book.

Despite the nature of the punishments that he doled out to unfortunate boys, Old Hay commanded a tremendous amount of respect amongst the boys at Barney, who laughed off his methods and temper as eccentric. On many an occasion, you would hear a boy reel off the old doctrine of 'Old Hay might be scary but he will get you through your entrance exam.' I listened attentively in each class that he took and was determined to do well in my entrance exam that I needed to pass in order to progress into the Main School.

At the end of term, I was called into Mr Sherbrooke's office to be informed that I had passed the entrance exam and that in the September I would be in Durham House. Grandma and

Richard were delighted when they received my letter to tell them the news. Roger was pleased for me but he did confide in me that he would miss me once I left the Prep School and would no longer see him on a daily basis. But he was now settling into life at school and was making friends, which seemed to help him stay out of the glare of our house mother.

CHAPTER 29

A New Normal

It was in November during that same academic year that Roger and I were allowed home for the weekend for a very special family celebration. Richard was celebrating his twenty-first birthday and all the family, along with Mam and Dad's friends, would be there. When we arrived home at Stanhope Hall, the house was busy. Auntie Brenda, Uncle Ron and our cousin Gaynor were already there and as soon as we arrived, Gaynor excitedly greeted us and took us into the dining room. The long dining table was now covered in an array of gifts, ranging from ornaments of sheep and silver tankards to boxes of crystal glasses. The idea of these presents would be that he would put them aside for his 'bottom drawer' and use them to make a home of his own one day.

On the sideboard was the most magnificent birthday cake in the shape of a book, which was the result of Auntie Brenda's hard work. I would like to say that it was because of Richard's interest in reading that she made it into the shape of a book but that was more of a coincidence as she had recently completed a course of cake decorating night classes and the book-shaped cake was the fanciest design she had learned. It did the trick and the cake was a real showstopper.

Visitors came and went that afternoon and cars were loaded up with food to take to Stanhope Town Hall, which was the venue for the party. As everyone took it in turns to use the one bathroom in the house, us kids sat downstairs watching *The Generation Game* on the telly (yes, my memory is *that* good!) while Grandma and Auntie Brenda were putting the finishing touches to their hair and make-up. Roger and I were, as usual, wearing matching outfits, this time consisting of blue cords and beige sweatshirts. All ready to go out, Grandma was so proud of how smart we looked. Naturally, all eyes would be on our family and it was important that everyone saw that it was business as usual.

On our arrival at the Town Hall, some ladies were busying themselves laying huge plates of food on a long buffet table. A group of Mam's closest friends had approached Grandma, generously offering to help put together the food for the party, and given the large number of friends and family that were due to attend, she graciously accepted. Along with the enormous platters of beef and ham were bowls of homemade coleslaw, potato salad, pies and countless dishes of pease pudding.

Once all the guests had arrived and the food had been served, the dancing got underway. In place of our dad, Uncle Alec gave a speech to the gathered guests and I am reliably informed that he paid tribute to my brother, parents, grandmother, etc. But I wasn't in the room at that point as I had been told that Roger and I would be expected to stand up next to Richard during the speech. I was petrified at the thought of standing up in front of a large group of people and painfully shy to the point where being the centre of attention in front of people I didn't know well would send me running into hiding, so that is how I happened to spend the speeches hiding in the toilets. As much as Grandma tried to coax me out, I refused to budge and only when I was sure that the speeches and photo calls were over, did I dare to slide the lock open on the inside of the toilet door. I know that Richard had a great birthday party and for me, getting to stay up until 2 a.m. was the biggest treat of the night. However, it seemed like no time at all before Roger and I returned to the daily routine of boarding school life for the final weeks of the winter term.

Soon, December was upon us and this was to be our first Christmas without Grandad. Despite that, Roger and I were excited as ever at the thought of the approaching festivities. Grandma, as always, made a tremendous effort to make our Christmas as special as she could. We went to stay at Auntie Brenda's for a couple of days when we came home from school, to ensure that we were there in time for Gaynor's birthday. My cousin was allowed to invite some friends over and Auntie Brenda made hot dogs and coke floats for everyone. As they had recently bought a video recorder, Gaynor got to choose a video from the limited selection at the new video shop up the road. Stuffed from hot dogs, we all crammed into the living room with our fizzy drinks to watch *Gregory's Girl* on the gigantic Betamax video recorder.

The following day, Auntie Brenda took us all into Sunderland town centre so that we could see the Christmas decorations in the shops. Along the main shopping street outside the department stores the brightly coloured lights stretched across the road, the double-decker buses only just clearing them as they passed underneath. Every Christmas Grandma always bought a tin of Quality Street to take back to Stanhope Hall and she bought Auntie Brenda's family a tin of Roses. You were either a 'Roses house' or a 'Quality Street house' and we were always the latter, particularly as Roger loved the penny toffees in their bright yellow foil wrappers. We picked up a *Radio Times* and a *TV Times* so that we could select the best films to watch over the Christmas holidays. Back then the two magazines were big treats for us and we flicked through the pages in the bus on the way back to our aunt's house. Roger and I both loved the atmosphere in town at this time of year. The place was crowded with people and buzzing with colour as the shops piped out the Christmas music. It was such a contrast from the relative quiet of our village back home.

Back at the farm, we now had the tree up and Grandma did her best to fill the huge gap left in our lives as we faced our third Christmas without both our parents and our first without Grandad. She enlisted Roger and I to help her prepare the festive food and drink. We stood at the sink and made ginger wine to Grandad's recipe as he had always done for years. Grandma made batches of mince pies and a large Christmas cake, which Roger and I helped to decorate with icing and small plastic snowmen.

By the time I was ten, I knew that there was no Santa Claus but like many kids of that age, I didn't let on to the grown-ups as I tried to hang on to that last little bit of the Christmas magic for as long as I could. I didn't like to ask for much from

'Santa' as I was well aware that Grandma paid for these gifts out of her own pension and savings. On Christmas morning, as I followed an over-excited Roger downstairs into the sitting room, I was truly floored by the sight before me. In front of the piano was a large bike for Roger, while over at the other side of the room was a pile of presents topped by a camera, the type that took the 110 film cartridges. On the sofa was a long box, all wrapped up and addressed to the two of us. As we ripped the paper away in a fit of frenzied excitement, I couldn't believe it when the wrapping revealed a metal detector. I didn't understand how Grandma could afford this and although we had always been treated incredibly generously at Christmas, I wasn't prepared for this. Standing at the sitting room door, she had been watching us for the last five minutes. Almost as if she could read my mind, she said, 'Grandma asked Richard for a little money from the farm's account to give to Santa for one or two special presents. Happy Christmas.' All I could do was burst into tears as I hugged her.

The rest of the day was spent playing games and eating the wonderful Christmas lunch that Grandma had made for us, each and every morsel prepared and cooked with an abundance of love. Later in the afternoon, my cousin Nicholas came to collect Grandma, Roger and myself to take us to Auntie Olive's for Christmas Day tea. Christmas at their farm was a lively affair and along with my little cousin Adam, Roger and I were the only kids there, the rest of my cousins now having grown up. Uncle Alec's brother dressed up as Father Christmas and handed out gifts from his sack for everyone.

Before too long we all joined in an array of party games while Grandma took the opportunity to sit back and relax for once.

Auntie Olive was an excellent cook and had made a huge spread and as we sat at the table, my uncle would encourage us to 'reach up' and get plenty to eat. By nine o'clock, we were in the car on the short drive back to Stanhope Hall. We had had such a lovely evening with our family and I know that it helped us all through that first Christmas without Grandad.

CHAPTER 30

Always On Edge

1981

Before we knew it, the Christmas holidays were over and Roger and I were once again standing on the steps of the Prep School in our uniforms, teeth chattering against the cold, with the trunks unloaded and ready for another term away from home. But it was good to catch up with our friends, talking about Christmas and showing each other the presents that we had received.

It was a regular Saturday afternoon a couple of weeks into term and all the boarders were out playing in the yard when Mrs Sherbrooke appeared.

'Big Mews, can you find your brother and can both of you wash your hands and go straight over to the school chapel to see the Reverend Moore, please?' She didn't give a clue as to why we had been summoned to see the school chaplain.

'What does he want to see us for, Miss?' I asked.

'He will tell you when you get there, Mews,' was her only

response and with that she walked back through the walled garden and into the house. My mind was racing. What on earth could the chaplain want with Roger and I? Then it dawned on me: something was wrong at home. Something had happened to Grandma. It must be serious if we needed to go to the chapel. As I ran up onto the mound to find Roger, all the while my head was spinning with a variety of possible scenarios and none of them good. I grabbed my brother out of a makeshift den and disarmed him of the stick that he was using as a machine gun; we washed our hands and ran straight to the chapel. By the time we reached the steps, I felt sick in my stomach and could already feel my legs trembling as we raced up to the entrance. Stopping at the huge oak door, we took a moment to get our breath back. I had not uttered a word of my fears to Roger. As I stood there, I cast my mind back to the morning when Richard sat us both down to break the news that Mam had died. Tentatively, I turned the handle and pushed the heavy chapel door slowly open.

Before we had even stepped into the antechapel, the Reverend Moore greeted us.

'Ah, the Mews brothers! Come in, come in,' he said, as he beckoned us in a cheery voice. Now I was really confused. How could he be so upbeat if he was to break the news to us that Grandma had died? Of course, there was little rationale in my thinking, but I lived each day of my life with the fear that she would die imminently and that Roger and I would be left with no one.

'Right, boys, I'd like you to help me out at Holy Communion tomorrow morning!' he announced.

I found that now my legs were shaking more than ever, as

I realised there was nothing wrong with Grandma. But the lurching feeling in my stomach didn't go away and in truth, all I wanted to do was cry with relief. He actually wanted Roger and I to go to the antechapel during the offertory hymn the following day and collect the bread and wine. We were then to walk up the aisle to the altar at the far end, all of this in front of three hundred boarders and a dozen masters. Normally, such a task would have had me frozen to the spot but in light of the realisation that Grandma was OK, I readily agreed and followed the Chaplain's instructions for a short rehearsal. Meanwhile Roger didn't seem at all bothered by it and was more than happy to follow my lead. How I envied him his innocence. He had been protected from so many things in the past few years and due to his incredibly young age, many other dreadful aspects of our lives had passed him by unnoticed.

The following day, we performed the task without a hitch and later that week, Grandma would be delighted to hear that her two lads had been chosen to carry the bread and wine, although she did admit to being disappointed that she couldn't have been there in person to witness it for herself.

As the term wore on, Roger became more self-assured and I saw his confidence increase a little as the weeks progressed. Mrs Sherbrooke had stopped singling him out from the crowd and in return, he learned to keep a low profile. I don't recall any specific memories of Roger getting picked on, but as the youngest boy in the school, he was a vulnerable little lad. Grandma constantly fretted over the both of us, but particularly Roger as she knew I was better equipped to take care of myself. I did love the fact that my little brother was at school with me and we used to meet up in the playground and talk to each other about Mam and Dad. If either of us was feeling down, we would seek out the other. It wasn't just Roger relying on me as his big brother, I very much relied on him too.

In the Easter holidays, apart from spending a week at Auntie Brenda's, we stayed at Grandma's house in Brandon. We knew that Grandma's elder sister, Auntie Tamar, was poorly, so each day we walked down to her little bungalow to see her in an attempt to cheer her up. Many years ago, Auntie Tamar was particularly close to Mam and had been like a second mother to her. She was, like most women from the colliery villages, very plain speaking, but you didn't have to scratch far beneath that tough exterior to find a huge depth of kindness in her. She lay in her bed and Grandma cut up fresh pineapple in the kitchen and brought it through to the bedroom in an attempt to get her ailing sister to eat something. Everyone else knew it was cancer. Although Auntie Tamar knew that she was dying, her smile remained bright as she encouraged Roger and I to tell her all about being away at school while we sat on her bed. Before we left her on the last day, she asked us both for a big cuddle and then she reached over for her handbag.

'Here's a pound note for each of you. Now promise me you won't spend it on anything sensible. Here's another pound for your Richard to get himself some cigarettes,' she said, and with that, we said our goodbyes.

At school several weeks later, I received a letter from Grandma telling us that Auntie Tamar had died. Grandma had nursed her pretty much to the end. I read and re-read that letter as I cried in the dorm. Then I found Roger, who was up in the dorm making his bed, and sat him down to break the news. I felt selfish because the truth was that I was only partly crying for Auntie Tamar. I couldn't help but think that this was yet another death in the family, the fourth death in as many years and irrational as it might seem, I genuinely started to believe that someone in my family would die each and every year. I don't know how I had become so paranoid, but it was always there in the back of my mind, every single day.

The highlight of the last term at the Prep School was undoubtedly the Leavers Camp. Mr Sherbrooke booked the school minibus and took the nine leavers from the boarders up to Lunedale, along with two sixth formers to assist him. There was a rundown old shepherd's cottage on the hill, where we would sleep on the floor in our sleeping bags. Each boy had to take a letter of consent from home in order to be allowed to go on the camp and to start with, Grandma was having none of it, so I had to draft in Richard for support. Eventually she relented and I was allowed to go.

For the three days of the camp, we went running around the Bronze Age burial mound known as Kirkcarrion, on the other side of the field, as well as going on hikes and swimming in the river. We stayed up late while Mr Sherbrooke fed us his legendary corned beef curry and told us ghost stories, including one about an old shepherd who haunted the place. That ensured none of us got to sleep at a decent hour! The old cottage had an outside toilet and on that first night, I was so scared to go out to use it that I thought I would wet myself. Eventually, my impatient bladder told me that I had no choice but to brave it and as I stepped outside, the wind blew, making a creepy, howling noise.

'Don't let the old shepherd get you,' Mr Sherbrooke said dryly as a word of caution.

As I crept along the path in the dark to the outside toilet, I wished that I hadn't forgotten my torch. Somehow I managed to find the door to the outhouse and as I reached for the light switch, I remembered there was no electricity. I stood trembling and started to pee into the toilet. Just as I was in full flow, a voice behind me gave out an almighty scream. I jumped out of my skin and now I was peeing on my legs and on the floor as I screamed and turned around to see one of the sixth formers with a torch lighting his face, laughing uproariously.

'Ha, ha, Mews! Did I make you jump?'

It's a wonder I didn't empty my bowels there and then. By the time I emerged from the toilet, wearing my piss-soaked pyjama bottoms, Mr Sherbrooke said that I had no choice but to remove them and go and wash my legs in the water trough that sat under the dry-stone wall alongside the cottage. Reluctantly, I complied and within a minute I was scooping freezing cold water from the trough and over my legs, with my pyjama bottoms dunked in the trough in an effort to wash them as they were the only ones that I had brought with me.

Back in the cottage, I got dried off and as a reward for being the victim of the prank, I was allowed to move my sleeping bag to a spot closer to the log fire that had been stoked up. With more ghost stories to follow, none of us got much sleep that night!

The following morning, we were lined up and informed of our initiation as leavers. The task was to climb into the large metal water trough that was straddled over the top by a dry-stone wall – the same one that I had washed my legs in the previous night. Once we had climbed in, we were to duck under the water and the wall and get out on the other side. It was a cold blustery day for June so none of us fancied doing this.

Mr Sherbrooke gave us further instructions: 'You only have to go in the trough, if Villiers and Graham [the sixth formers] catch you. If you manage to outsmart them, you can escape the initiation. You have a five-minute head start.'

With that, we legged it down the hill as fast as we could, looking back to see if there was a sign of Villiers and Graham. It was only when we reached the gate at the bottom that we would see them behind us on the hill, looking down towards us. Standing to catch my breath, I tried to work out my next move. I thought that we had a good head start until I saw them bounding down the grassy slope towards us. The adrenaline was pumping around my body as I jumped over the gate and made for the shelter of the trees on the Bronze Age burial mound. Over the next half an hour I heard shouts and yelling as several of my friends were captured and taken back up the hill to the trough. I lasted about another half an hour before Villiers caught me and dragged me back up. Though I did manage to wriggle loose and escape, my freedom lasted less than a mere thirty seconds and before long, I too was dunked in the cold water and under the wall.

After another half an hour, there were eight of us drying off from our soaking and only one lad, Winford, evading capture. As the two sixth formers searched the surrounding area in an attempt to find him, we started to worry as to where he might be. It was only when Mr Sherbrooke went to use the loo that he found that Winford had locked himself in the outside toilet the whole time. He was marched over to the trough as the rest of us cheered and applauded his cunning and tenacity. As an extra punishment for being a 'clever dick' and outsmarting them, they made him go through the trough twice, accompanied by much laughing and whooping from everyone else.

I really enjoyed the Leavers Camp and was even sad to be leaving the Prep School. It was the genuine people like Mr Sherbrooke who gave us the good memories, along with the other lads there.

On my last day at Prep School, Roger and I sat waiting in the front hallway. We were the last two boys to be picked up for the summer holidays. I stared at the sideboard outside the dining room at the model making and boarder trophies, neither of which I had ever managed to win. I make no secret of my disappointment, despite trying so hard to win them. It wasn't winning that I wanted, just recognition, I realised. I knew that as I left this short chapter of my life behind, there would be greater opportunities and freedom afforded me in the coming years.

As I said my goodbyes to Mrs Sherbrooke, pretending to be sorry to be leaving her, I felt such a hypocrite. I thanked her for the last three years, and for looking after me so well. Naturally, I was playing the game, as I knew if I had been anything other than overly grateful to her, she would have taken it out on Roger and he had another two years still to go in that place. I'd never felt so relieved as I was to walk out of that door for the last time.

I asked Richard to go slowly down the drive so that I could look across at the orchard and in that moment, I imagined the ghosts of the boys I had made friends with in the past three years, frantically picking gooseberries, lighting camp fires, watching fireworks and playing British Bulldogs, laughing and yelling to each other. The voices and images trailed off as we pulled out of the entrance and on to the road home for the summer and I couldn't wait for the welcome that was waiting for us at the other end.

Brandon Village
Durham
19th May 1981
My Dear Philip
Hulloa darling, here is Grandma again to let you know
I am thinking of you and our Roger and loving you both.
I'm sorry darling I am unable to come to your sports
day. Auntie Tamar died in hospital on Monday and the
funeral is on Thursday. Richard will be coming and I
have given him a £5 donation to give Mrs Sherbrooke
from you both. I can't do any baking or help in any other
way. I will be thinking of you and our Roger all day on
Thursday so stick in and do your best. Richard is going to
take you to Auntie Brenda's Friday morning so when we
have seen to Auntie Tamar's house and everything, I will
come to Sunderland on Saturday and we will all go to the
leisure centre and I will see you both swim.

I am so sorry that this had to happen but comfort our
Roger as he will get so upset if I am not there. I looked
forward to coming so much. I must close now darling.
Take care of yourselves. Our Roger is always getting hurt
– some of the boys must be very cruel. I can't understand
why they pick on him because our family never hurt
anyone.

God Bless my bonny lad
Your loving Grandma xxxxxx

CHAPTER 31

Ending on the Right Foot

Daunted. There was no other word to describe how I felt about going into the Main School at Barney. By comparison, the Prep School had been a small, cosy and gentle environment, even with the likes of Mrs Sherbrooke and Old Hay. In contrast, going to the big old building, where I would be one of the youngest of six hundred boys, initially filled me with dread.

The dorms were great big long rooms with vaulted ceilings that were propped up by long metal bars stretching across the ceiling. L Dorm was managed by two monitors, sixth formers, who were known as 'Feds', and they kept us in check at night. Our chief 'Fed' was known as 'Fatty Graham', who actually wasn't really fat but was a friendly guy who seemed to spend all his spare time playing squash and blasting out his Meat Loaf records. His sidekick, whose name I can't remember, was obsessed with David Bowie and he played Bowie albums in the dorm from morning till night. Out of the seven new first-years in Durham House, three of us had come from the Prep School so it was a relief to have people that I knew to chat to, as well as making new friends.

There was one word on all the boarders' lips that first week at the Main School: 'De-bagging'. This was the tradition of older lads grabbing unsuspecting first-years from some place in the school and carrying them to their dorm before stripping them naked and tying their clothes at the top of the beam on the ceiling out of reach. It was nothing more than playful and as the end of the first week approached, being one of the only first-year boarders not yet de-bagged, I began to think that I had escaped this initiation. How wrong could I have been? One afternoon when I was walking along the north corridor lined with trunks, four of the lads from the dorm jumped out and grabbed me and although I put up a respectable amount of resistance, they soon had me de-bagged in L Dorm and I was forced to shimmy up the beam to retrieve my uniform.

The biggest shock of joining the ranks of the older lads in the Main School was the freedom. Having come from the Prep School, where almost every minute of every day was timetabled for you, I found myself with a glut of spare time, particularly over the weekend and trying to find something to do. Frank McNamara had only taken over as headmaster at Barney the previous September and the school that he inherited was rather down at heel, to say the least. With the support of the governors, he soon implemented numerous ambitious plans to drag the school kicking and screaming into the 1980s, but during that first year we would have no choice but to make do with what there was. We had no TV room for the first-years and we weren't allowed in the ones dedicated to the older boys so we had to be more imaginative when it came to finding something to do. As we weren't allowed in the dorms until bedtime and there being no common room, all we had was a tatty old Victorian classroom with wooden flip-lid desks that also seemed to be from the same era.

As I'd never been a particularly sporty person, I only ever did games when it was absolutely compulsory and within my first weeks at the Main School, I discovered that I could fake a sore tummy or sickness in order to get a note from the Sister in the school sanatorium. This would get me excused from games and it worked every time. But it didn't take long for her to see the pattern of my appearances at 'the San' every Monday and Wednesday morning, and from then on, she sent me off packing. On some days, I really couldn't be bothered to go to games, particularly if it was cross-country running, and I found it harder to hide away in the main building.

I started to spend a lot of time in the school library, not doing my homework but just looking through books. I'd never seen so many books in one place before and the building soon became my refuge. I would read books on History and Art, but Geography was my favourite subject.

Mr Fender was a Barney institution. He'd been a teacher there longer than anyone cared to remember and was one of the kindest and most talented people I have ever met. Not only was he my form teacher that first year, he also taught us French and Music. He was able to speak five languages fluently and played numerous musical instruments. Having no immediate family of his own, he made Barney and its pupils the centre of his life. He had a sitting room on the top floor, which was crammed with chairs and an old battered sofa whose suspension had seen far better days. The walls were lined with bookcases that were full of books, annuals and piles of comics. Any boy was welcome to knock on the door and go in and watch television or read comics. Mr Fender allowed us to make toast by sitting with a slice of bread on the end of a toasting fork against the old gas fire. On some afternoons, it wouldn't be unusual for there to be almost twenty boys crammed in there watching TV, with the fire going at full pelt. On Sundays, he would take a car full of boys on a short hike in the Dales, making lunches of instant mashed potato, baked beans and hot dogs on his little gas stove by a stream before piling back to his house for a slap-up tea. Once we had eaten him out of house and home, he delivered us safely back to school in time for prep.

Those were wonderfully innocent days and nobody could have been kinder to us than Nelly Fender. He truly understood what it was like for us to be away at school without our families and showed all the boys such kindness and generosity. When he retired from teaching in 1983, he left a huge void at Barney. I was saddened to hear of his passing years later, but smiled in the knowledge that he had led a long, full life and achieved so much in it.

Boys in Durham House, like me, were also made welcome at the home of our house tutor and his wife, the Reverend and Mrs Moore. They lived in a small cottage on the school grounds and made the young Durham House boys welcome after school each day. Their small dining room would be crammed full of boys crowding around the black-and-white portable TV, watching *Dangermouse* and *Grange Hill*, while Mrs Moore fed us with orange squash and freshly baked biscuits. It was acts of kindness such as these that really made a difference to boarding school life, especially in those early years.

Next door to the Main School sat the majestic Bowes Museum, which is even more imposing than Barney school. The museum was built in the style of a French chateau and housed thousands of items originally collected by its founder, John Bowes. I had been there once before, back in 1977, with Mam and Roger on a school trip and on my first return visit, I was immediately reunited with the Silver Swan.

The star exhibit of the museum, it was an eighteenth-century clockwork swan made out of silver. Twice a day, a uniformed man with an air of importance would turn the key to wind it up. Against the background of haunting tinkly music, the swan would move its neck and head from left to right, then up and down, before finally reaching down to pick up one of the tiny fish in its beak, which had sat on a glass base designed to look like flowing water. Crowds of visitors would gather round, emitting gasps of wonder at this truly magnificent piece of craftsmanship.

On my first visit since starting the Main School, I went to pay my child's entrance fee and saw that I could join as a Friend of the Bowes Museum for only a pound for the year. Grandma had sent me a letter that very morning with a crisp green one pound note in it so rather than blow it in the school tuck shop, I handed it over to the woman at the cash desk and she duly filled out my small blue membership card.

Over the next twelve months, I lost count of the number of times that I visited the Bowes Museum or the number of hours that I spent in there, not only looking at the exhibits but whiling away the time quietly by myself. I always ended up in the lower ground floor, which contained local exhibits underneath its stone vaulted ceilings, including a pair of stuffed Siamese calves. It remains to this day one of the creepiest things that I have ever seen and although I was really quite afraid of it, I couldn't help but go back time and time again to see it, fascinated by the sight.

The school had a tuck shop in the grounds which opened in the afternoons for boys to buy chocolate, crisps and fizzy drinks. Grandma always sent me a pound note every week and I would buy two chocolate bars every Wednesday afternoon. Once games had finished, I would walk across the school grounds to the back gates of the Prep School to see Roger. It was usual for elder brothers to meet with their younger brothers at the gates and I looked forward to catching up with him and reassuring myself that he was OK. At the gates, I would secretly hand him one of the chocolate bars. If there were too many people watching, I would discreetly remove the wrapper and hand him the chocolate to hide in his pocket and when I left him, I gave him instructions to go to the toilet and lock himself in a cubicle to eat it. It sounds grim but it wasn't worth getting found out by Mrs Sherbrooke and if he didn't have the wrapper, there was no incriminating evidence. In return, Roger would pass me letters that he had written to Grandma for me to post. He wasn't saying anything bad in the letters but he felt more comfortable if Mrs Sherbrooke didn't read them.

Due to the lack of television in the school, they would have the occasional cinema night at weekends, where they would erect a large screen in the auditorium known as Big School. One evening, as the seats filled with rowdy boarders, Mr King, an old stalwart of the school, walked up to the front to speak to us all. He was a quietly spoken man and on this particular evening, he had difficulty in making himself heard as he attempted to speak over the chatter. What he lacked in volume, he more than made up for when he gave you a look, though. A strict disciplinarian who carried a graceful air of authority about him, he could give you a look that would clearly say, 'Don't even think about it'. As the room eventually fell quiet, only then did he begin to speak again. He announced that the screening would be *Walkabout*, the 1971 film starring Jenny Agutter.

'Now, erm.. this film contains… um… scenes of nakedness… um… of the… um… female form…' he said. But he couldn't continue under the sudden burst of whoops and whistling that broke out and reverberated around the hall. He tried to quieten us all down, holding his arms up, outstretched.

'Now, settle down… I erm… expect you all to behave like proper public school gentlemen… um… and behave accordingly,' he said, as he walked back down the aisle, no doubt aware that his words had fallen on deaf ears.

Film nights soon became a regular part of school life and on another evening that year, towards the end of term, they showed the François Truffaut film *Fahrenheit 451* (1966), set in a futuristic utopia. It tells the story of a Britain of the future, where printed books are banned and in an age of fireproof houses, the sole purpose of firemen was to seek out books and publicly burn them. I was fascinated and enthralled and it is still my favourite film today. The film nights were fun, but as the school's facilities were upgraded and TV rooms provided for each house, film nights, like some of the other school traditions, were consigned to the past.

After school each day, we were encouraged to take part in activities to stimulate the mind and the body. Barney offered an excellent range of things to do, from horse riding and dry-slope skiing through to pottery and fencing. Each term, the school put on a play to be performed at the end of term in front of the pupils and parents. Every day after lessons, I would head over to Big School and sit in on rehearsals, even though I wasn't a member of the cast. That first autumn term they were performing *The Matchmaker* by Thornton Wilder and as Mr Wilkinson directed the actors through their performances, I watched in awe.

I had already fallen in love with the theatre several years before and longed to be part of a school production, but sadly there were few parts for an eleven-year-old lad whose voice was yet to break. Week after week, I could see the production coming together and as the days counted down to the first dress rehearsal when lighting desks were installed, props started appearing, I volunteered to help Mr Gorman, the school's eccentric art teacher, to paint the flats of the stage set.

It was during this first year in the Main School that something rather odd started to manifest within me. Since the death of my parents, when Grandma took over bringing me up, I was introduced to superstition on a huge scale. Having lost Mam, Dad and Grandad and then Auntie Tamar, I was of the firm belief that some higher being, be it God or just fate, had decided that I would lose a family member each year from then on. I know it sounds as if I was mad, but that was the way my brain was wired at the time as I lived with this perpetual fear each and every day.

Grandma had never got over losing her daughter. What

parent would? During the long days and nights that followed Mam and Dad's deaths, she cried. She could be stirring up a cake mixture in the kitchen or polishing the brasses, but you could guarantee she would be doing this through a veil of tears. Unable to make any sense of her daughter's untimely death, she searched for reasons as to why her Alma was taken away from her at such a young age. There were all the logical reasons, such as the fact that Mam was a smoker and that there were other underlying conditions. None of these sound explanations provided any comfort to Grandma. In her head, when she and Grandad handed Mam to my dad on her wedding day, nineteen years earlier, she was in excellent health.

I soon learned that Grandma was superstitious about everything and as such, every aspect of our lives was governed by it. There was the belief that walking under a ladder, crossing on the stairs or mixing red and white flowers together would somehow bring upon the family more bad luck than we had already had to endure. I soon fell into a habit of living my life adhering to each and every superstition that Grandma had taught me and by the time that I was in the Main School, I had somehow managed to develop several of my own.

When climbing the stairs, I always had to finish on my right foot. With the many staircases that were dotted around the school, I developed a system where I learned the number of steps on each staircase and taught myself how to climb them so that when I reached the top or bottom of any staircase, I would always land on my right foot. I know, it's crazy! Should I become distracted and land on my left foot, I had no choice but to go back to the other end of the staircase and start again.

I really believed in my head that by doing this, I would fend off death in the coming years for any member of my family.

There came a time when the thing on the staircases wasn't enough. I started counting the steps I took before I would reach a door, making sure that the end number was never seven, my logic being that seven was the age that I was when I lost my parents so it was unlucky.

Naturally, having my life dictated each day by these silly beliefs made me increasingly anxious. Of course, there was no way that I could tell a single soul about this. As the years progressed, I managed to keep my superstitions to a manageable level, but even to this day, when I am at home, I feel happier if I finish on my right foot when climbing the stairs, knowing full well that it doesn't make one jot of difference!

CHAPTER 32

Boarding School Antics

Life was never dull at Barney and if we ourselves weren't up to mischief, there was always someone else who was up to no good. As we weren't allowed in the dorms during the day, we had to find somewhere else to hang out. At the very top of the school was a set of music rooms, where people took lessons for piano amongst other instruments. I had been learning the piano since Prep School, albeit under duress, and we were sent up to this creepy set of rooms to practise in our spare time. One of the lads in the year above came up with the ingenious idea of making a homemade ouija board so that we could hold our own séances. With a glass pinched from the dining room, five of us sat in a circle and attempted to contact someone from the other side. Although I was uneasy with this, considering my mates were treating it as a laugh, there was a part of me that genuinely hoped we might get through to a member of my family. We sat and concentrated.

'Is there anyone there? Show us a sign,' I said. Each of us had a finger on the glass and I know mine was shaking. With eyes tight shut, I felt the glass move towards me. Not daring to open my eyes, I spoke again, 'Give us a sign.'

Bang! The internal windows looking out on to the staircase shuddered as we all jumped back from our seats and looked out. The lights were now off and it was almost pitch-black. My heart was pounding and before we had a chance to open the door, the windows started banging again. One of us knocked the table and the homemade board over in the panic so the glass smashed on the floor. The lights went on and the ghosts were revealed… three fourth-year lads were standing outside on the landing, laughing hysterically at us. Bastards! I almost filled my pants and after that I never went near the ouija board again.

If we were ill at school we went to the sanatorium, known to everyone at Barney as 'The San'. Sister MacKenzie ran the place when I first started at the Main School and she kept it in tip-top condition. Downstairs was a large ward containing ten beds, although it was rare that there were ever more than two boys staying overnight at any one time.

In my early years at Barney, a sickness bug swept the school and the San was full to capacity on both floors. We had one black-and-white telly to entertain us, but it was inevitable with so many boys confined that mischief would occur. One evening, a couple of the older lads crept into the surgery and pinched handfuls of the discarded plastic syringes from the disposal unit. After they had been washed out, the syringes proved to be effective water pistols and what started off as a handful of lads having them soon snowballed into nearly every boy staying there. Sister MacKenzie came back from the main building one evening and on opening the door to the downstairs ward, she found about twenty of us jumping around, squirting water at each other and having a riot. We were soaked through, as were the beds, while the floor looked as if the roof had been raining in. The headmaster was called for and we were lined up, awaiting his arrival. I was petrified we would get suspended but as it was, he banned us from having access to the TV, made us mop the place up and each of us had to write a letter of apology to Sister.

Having so many teenage boys living in such close quarters, chaos could erupt at any time. Food fights were rare, but hymn book fights far more prevalent. At morning Assembly in chapel one day, as we were seated one lad threw his small hymn book at another boy across the other side of the chapel. Within seconds, a volley of hymn books flew in all directions across the pews. I was in the choir at the time and our hymn books were larger. Much larger and far heavier. Not wanting to be left out, I picked mine up and lobbed it across the chapel, where it hit some poor first year smack in the face, sending his black-rimmed National Health specs spinning to the floor. It only took a few seconds for everyone to spot that the headmaster had walked in and his face was puce with rage.

At night in the dorms, the Feds who were in charge used to sell toast at a cost of ten pence a slice. If you didn't have the cash, they would let you have a slice if you paid them fifteen pence at the end of the week. As the years went on, post-lights out catering grew more sophisticated. By the time that I was in the fourth year, some of the lads would volunteer to do a 'Takeaway Run'. It was actually referred to as something else but thankfully, times have changed and we don't use those words any more. They would take your order and cash, along with a fifty-pence delivery charge, and phone the order in from the sixth-form phone.

Years later, Roger took on the mantle of doing the Takeaway Run to make extra money. They would tie sheets together and shimmy out of the dorm window and on to the corridor roof before climbing down the fire escape and legging it into town down behind the Bowes Museum. One night, one of the masters, emerging from the pub, had seen Roger and his sidekick going into the Chinese takeaway. Rather than challenge them there and then, this particular master popped back into the pub and made a quick phone call. When the boys arrived back at school and were sneaking in through the back door, they were greeted by the waiting master on duty.

'Good evening, gentlemen. Allow me to relieve you both of these carrier bags while you two go straight up to your dorms,' he said in a cool, calm manner. As he walked behind Roger and his mate carrying the Chinese food, Roger spotted one of the housemasters emerge from the dining room with six plates and a handful of cutlery as the master on duty followed him into the Masters Common Room. Of course they had been tipped off. Roger didn't have to pay back the money to those who had ordered as that was the risk you took. But it didn't put him off and in the coming years he undertook many successful missions after lights out.

In addition to the masters at the school, there were many other charismatic staff who worked there. I remember a local lad who worked in the kitchens, who hated every single one of the pupils in the school. He was a skinhead, with homemade tattoos and a pockmarked face on which he wore a scowling expression every day. I got a feeling that he wasn't the sharpest knife in the drawer, so they put him in charge of the bread at teatime. Small baskets of white sliced bread would be placed on tables in the dining hall and when they ran out, you had to take them back into the servery to be refilled. We nicknamed him 'the Bread Bouncer' due to his ability to put his thick, nicotine-stained fingers through almost every slice of bread as he grabbed half a loaf out of the bag. He would push the bread into your basket, each slice carrying a helping of his disdain, as well as the damage left by his grubby fingers.

Mr Gaffney was the janitor, although everyone, including the teachers, knew him as 'Bilko' (lead character in an iconic fifties TV show). He was the most wonderful and friendly character, who used to rattle his false teeth at the younger lads whenever they went past. If you needed anything at the school, then Bilko was your man. He had the respect of every single person in the school and after decades of service, eventually announced his retirement. The school was accustomed to presenting members of staff with a gift at the end of term in the central hall. They collected money from the staff and boys and because there was so much money collected for him, Bilko was presented with a portable TV and a silver foil-covered mop on his retirement. With the pupils crammed around the balconies and in the hall, the head boy shouted, 'Three cheers for Bilko,' and I have to say he received the loudest cheers of anyone during my time at Barney.

At the end of each term, our trunks were brought up from the cellars or the north corridor and placed at the end of our beds for us to pack up our stuff. One of the favourite tricks some of the older lads used to like to play in Durham House was to persuade a small first-year to climb inside their empty trunk as a dare and allow them to close the lid over. Little did the poor unsuspecting boy know was that once the trunk lid was shut, the clasps were closed over and the trunk was then carried to the back staircase. Remember, this was the eighties and no one yet cared about Health and Safety. The trunk was then sent tumbling down the back stairs with the poor boy screaming inside. We laughed at the time and I even laugh about it now, but the poor lads must have been terrified. I'd hate to think now that any of them were claustrophobic or traumatised by this. You don't think of these things when you are children. It wasn't that the boys were particularly cruel to each other, it was just young lads messing about and having fun.

Some tricks were much worse than being pushed down the back stairs in a trunk and a couple of them spring to mind. In the summer months, it was usual for us to sunbathe on the school fields at weekends. With the intention of revising for exams, we would take our towels up to the top rugby pitch and lie for hours in the sun, usually without sunscreen. We just weren't aware of the dangers of UV rays or skin cancer in those days. It was common on Sunday evenings at the Evensong service in chapel to see dozens of boys with crisp red faces walking stiffly in their abrasive woollen Sunday suits, having spent too long in the sun. On one particular sunny afternoon, a load of us were lying out on the field and one of the lads had fallen asleep on his back. Two other boys had gone for a sneaky fag in the trees and on their way back had come across a large dead crow. They picked up the carcass with sticks and, standing over our sleeping friend, dropped the dead crow onto his chest. He woke up immediately and gave a blood-curdling scream that echoed across the fields and off the school buildings. The poor lad must have almost filled his pants as he jumped up in horror and ran down the field towards the school, still screaming every step of the way!

Another trick was done by one of the Feds in charge of our dorm, who was a brilliant actor and captivating storyteller. One night, while listening to his radio, he heard on the news that a major accident had occurred at the Chernobyl Nuclear Power Plant in what was then the Soviet Union. He pretended to rush over to see the headmaster and returned a short while later with an announcement that the school was in a lock-down situation and that a cloud of radioactive material would reach the UK within the hour. Indeed he was so convincing that some of the boys believed every word that he said and were lying in their beds petrified, awaiting the nuclear Armageddon. As it was, I had sneaked out to go to the toilet and over the central balcony, I saw my housemaster wandering casually out of the Masters Common Room. I took the whole thing to be a practical joke although I was surprised to see the newspaper headlines the following morning, telling the world of the dreadful incident at Chernobyl.

CHAPTER 33

Running Away

1983

I managed a year or two at Barney without being bullied on a major scale but, come the third year, I would have to confront the bullies head-on. Ned started in the Main School on the same day as me and being a good-looking, confident character, with his cheeky Geordie personality he soon made himself popular. As a bully, he was hardly innovative. He acquired a sidekick so that he was rarely alone and used his popularity to create a group of people to back him up in his words and actions.

I'll start off by saying that Ned, like the rest of the lads in my house, knew my story. At least, he knew in so much that I had lost my mam and dad and that I was being brought up by my grandmother. But he did not allow this knowledge to cloud his judgement when it came to selecting me as his victim. It began with all the usual things – the names, the being pushed around, isolating the victim so that made me easier prey. The other lads in my year were too frightened to be my friend for fear of receiving the same punishment, so their survival instinct kicked in. I couldn't, and didn't blame them. During meals, I wasn't allowed to sit with the others and I soon became excluded from all activities, such as watching TV and going into the town. I was fast developing into a cracking little rugby player, but as Ned also played for the house team, I stopped trying during matches so that I wouldn't be selected for the squad. Soon I started to isolate myself and took to spending hours in the school's large central hall that housed polished wooden newspaper reading racks. Many an evening before or after prep I could be found scouring the papers rather than being in the house common room. The teachers thought I simply had a keen interest in current affairs. Also, I had to lock everything from my desk in my locker to prevent it being destroyed, defaced or stolen.

Over the years, people have asked me what life was like at boarding school and I've always said the same thing: when it was good, it was great but when it was bad, it was sheer hell.

Ned was not only in the same house and dorm as me, but his bed was two along from mine. I could hear his taunts and jibes from the moment I woke up in the morning to when I sometimes cried myself to sleep at night.

Being a chubby kid, with a quiet, nervous demeanour, I was easy prey. Sadly, events would give him even more ammunition and none more so than on that fateful November night in 1983. My bed was in the far corner of the dorm and I was on the top bunk. Sleeping on the bunk beneath me was Winford and my old pal, Keith, was in the next bed along. I woke up at about 3 a.m. and felt the most awful pain in my stomach and guts. Knowing I needed to get to the toilet, I pulled back my duvet and using the ceiling support bar that ran alongside my top bunk, I swung down from my bed. At the very same moment that my feet hit the floor, my bowels involuntarily emptied themselves. I stood there horrified, aware my legs were caked in diarrhoea and it was soaking through my pyjama bottoms. With that, I reached into my locker for a spare towel. I'm not sure why Keith chose the top shelf of my locker to store the large jar of his mum's homemade pickled cabbage, but he did. I'm still not sure to this day why he only had a scrap of clingfilm on the jar instead of a lid, but he did. In the darkness of the dorm, with the other lads all asleep, I reached into the locker and pulled out a clean towel from the top shelf, tipping the jar over onto the floor, where it mingled with the pool of diarrhoea that I had already deposited there. In an effort to relieve myself of my shit-soaked pyjama bottoms, I must have covered my hands in…. well, you can imagine!

Still in need of the toilet, I made my way to the back staircase from the dorm and down into the sixth-form house, known simply as 'OSH'. I was completely unaware that I was leaving a trail on the floor and on the door handles as I went. Once I had returned from the toilet, I woke up one of the Feds in charge of the dorm and told him that I was in pain and needed to go to the San. Sister MacKenzie admitted me that night and the following morning I was discharged and allowed to go back to classes. I was excused from swimming, but as I sat on the sidelines, I was already well aware of the sniggering that was directed at me. Mr White, our swimming teacher, came into the pool area and walked over to me.

'Mews, I've been informed that you need to go up to your dorm and the sixth-form house to er... clean some door handles?' he said, barely able to supress his laughter – and who could blame him? I got up and left as a chorus of fart noises echoed round the pool behind me.

Oh Christ, I'm NEVER going to live this one down, I thought to myself.

As the bullying continued, I became distracted. I found it increasingly difficult to concentrate, particularly in classes when I always had Ned sitting behind me, either kicking the back of my chair or taunting me with names. I can't see how my teachers weren't aware of this going on at the time. Bullying was rife, as it is at any school, but you were just expected to grin and bear it. You were expected to toughen up. Ned played on the school rugby team as well as swimming for the school. If you were good at sport back then, you ranked higher in the eyes of the staff than if you shone academically. There were plenty of boys who struggled to get decent academic results, but the school was keen to retain them because of their prowess on the sporting field. Sport was everything. It didn't matter that I was interested in the arts, acted in the school plays, painted scenery, sang in the choir and played in the piano. That counted for nothing.

In retrospect, I know that I should have informed my house tutor, himself an Old Barnardian, but I suspected from previous dealings that he wouldn't have a sympathetic ear for my complaint. That term my grades plummeted and I went from being tenth in a class of twenty-two to bottom of the class pretty much across the board in every subject. Not one of my teachers asked if anything was wrong and most of them sadly presumed that it was laziness. It was the early eighties and many schools, particularly public fee-paying ones, did not take a touchy-feely approach to pastoral care of their pupils. As the Christmas term drew to a close, I was informed that I was to drop down a class to the 'C' set, which was the bottom set. However, I was beyond caring as it meant that I would finally be in a different class to my tormentor. In hindsight, it was one of the more positive changes in my life, as I would now be taught by the wonderful Mr Wilkinson.

Alan Wilkinson was an English teacher and a man the likes of whom I had never encountered before in my life. Previously, my only dealings with him had been when he kindly allowed me to sit in on the rehearsals of *The Matchmaker* in my first year as he directed the actors on stage. I never came across a more exuberant and engaging teacher than Mr Wilkinson, such was his incredible energy and deep-rooted passion for teaching. In the subsequent years that he taught me at Barney, he introduced me to the joys of Charles Dickens and Oscar Wilde, who became two of my favourite writers. In studying Dickens's novel *Hard Times*, Mr Wilkinson brought the world of industrial Victorian England to life and his knowledge on the subject was both enviable and inspiring. I so looked forward to his lessons and the break that they would give me from the bullies. As for the rest of the teachers that I had in the 'C' set, they were all great and I had hit lucky. Once again, I was motivated and could focus, at least during lessons anyway.

But once again the tormenting started back in the common room, and everywhere else for that matter. Being in different classes, Ned found it difficult to maintain the momentum of torturing of me. It was a Wednesday afternoon in the summer term and there had been no let-up. Running out of verbal abuse to direct at me and failing to get much of a reaction, he decided to step it up a gear. He drafted in another boy who had started at Barney the previous September and not being the smartest lad, his new sidekick was always more than ready to get handy with his fists. At lunchtime that day he had tripped me up, sending me and my tray of shepherd's pie flying across the floor of the dining room to howls of laughter. Back in the common room, they made a beeline for me, desperate to get that longed-for reaction. In the end, they kept it simple – Ned's sidekick punched me on the ear. I spun around in my seat and lashed out at him. Within seconds he had me on the ground and a circle had formed around us as he sat across me and punched me as I pathetically flailed my arms.

Eventually he got up and as the tears streamed from my eyes, I heaved myself off the floor, aware that I still had an audience standing around me. I grabbed the books and pens that were scattered across my desk and flung them in the face of this Neanderthal. Before Ned and his cohort had a chance to react, I barged through them and ran out of the room. I ran to the back porch of the school and out in the open air, I continued to run. This time I had had enough and I couldn't cope anymore. I had two choices: either I ran up the staircase and threw myself off the top balcony to end this misery now, or I ran home to Stanhope to plead with my family to let me change schools. At that moment I was so desperately unhappy and I felt that I could have chosen either option.

As I ran out of the school grounds along the road behind the Bowes Museum my face was soaked with tears, my ear still ringing from the coward's punch and my head so fuzzy I could barely think, let alone see in front of me. Breathless, I slowed to a walk. I walked along the back roads into Barnard Castle's small town centre and at one point passed a teacher's wife, who recognised me from the Musical Society. On seeing me crying, she asked me if I was OK. But I ignored her for fear that if I told her what was wrong she would try and take me back to school and nothing would change.

The road to Stanhope, passing the greens and bunkers of the golf course, took me out of the town. All I wanted was to be home with Grandma and to know that I was safe. I was so tired. Tired of trying to survive the onslaught from this bully and his pals, day after day after day. I was tired of crying for my dead parents. Tired of fearing that every time Grandma shut her eyes for an afternoon nap she wouldn't wake up. Tired of worrying who was going to look after Roger and I if Grandma died. So, so tired. I wanted my childhood back.

I must have been wandering for hours along the road to Middleton-in-Teesdale as the light was starting to fade and the sun had gone down. A small red hatchback car slowed down and pulled up alongside me. It was Mr Stevens, my housemaster.

'Come on, Philip, get in,' he said.

Surprised at being called by my Christian name, I relented and got in the car, shivering with cold now. He gave me a sympathetic smile and asked me what the trouble was. I didn't say anything. Back at school, he took me straight to see Sister in the San. Of course I didn't tell them the truth as to what had happened, as I feared the repercussions too much, but it didn't matter as they already knew who was responsible.

I was allowed to go home alone that weekend to try and clear my head. Grandma and I spent the weekend together at the farm, although I had now decided not to tell her the truth as I was aware that she already had so much on her plate. And I couldn't tell Richard, as he had enough on his plate with running the farm and what else could I do? I couldn't change schools. Roger was doing his best to get through school life and as he was still at the Prep School, he still had Mrs Sherbrooke to contend with. There was nobody I could talk to. I was alone, completely alone.

Returning to school on the Sunday evening, once again I had to face Ned and his mate. They didn't apologise; I didn't want them to. As much as I hated them and what they did to me, I didn't want to be near them. So I kept my head down and to save losing face, Ned now only made the occasional remark. But it didn't matter anymore as they had ground me down so far, the best that I could do was to keep a low profile and keep out of their way.

My final reprieve came the following term when Ned announced that he was to leave the school because his parents could no longer afford the fees. In the closing weeks of that term he managed to treat me in a more civil manner and for me the nightmare would hopefully be over. With me and my tormentor parting ways, I could once again look forward to the future at school and beyond.

CHAPTER 34

Comfort Food

1984

There were long drawn-out periods of immense loneliness at Barney. I wasn't very good at joining in and I found the harsher aspects of school life difficult to cope with. Wintry afternoons spent on cross-country runs in the Teesdale countryside, slipping and sliding in the snow, the icy wind blowing against my bare, reddened, chubby legs. Playing rugby in the driving rain that was almost horizontal at times, my fingers so numb with the cold that I couldn't hold the ball. This was all done under the guise of toughening us up, to make us proper men. Men who wouldn't cry, men who wouldn't feel, men who would grow up believing all was well in the world as long as we won at rugby. Failure to fall in line with this would make a boy appear as weak and as a result, he would become a target for the bored, sadistic characters in the school. Inevitably, I became one such target.

By the time that I was thirteen, I was mentally exhausted. I had been through so much in the last five or six years and I had no energy. No energy to try. No energy to jostle for position. No energy to fight back alone against Ned and his bullying cohorts. In truth, I was done. All I could do was stay out of the way as much as possible. It was easier than confrontation. There was little point in saying anything, as the situation could not be improved or changed. It would take decades of social change to come about to make a difference but, sadly, not in time for me. In my later years at Barney a little respite came, but as one set of bullies left, so another set took their place, keen to assert their authority, no matter how small. So, with the absence of my family (albeit a little contact with Roger), I found my comfort in food.

The transition from the Prep School into the Main School was marked by a sharp downturn in the quality of the school meals. I understand now that it is far easier to cook lunch at a high standard for thirty boys than it is for hundreds. The lunches at Prep School had always been tasty and I soon developed the habit of having second helpings of pudding. When Mrs Sherbrooke picked her moment to publicly name me 'Dumpling', it made me ever more self-conscious but no less willing to eat when tasty food was on offer.

In my final year at the Prep School, Mrs Sherbrooke had been ill for about six weeks and her role was taken up by the kindly Mrs McNamara, wife of the Main School's headmaster. Recognising that I had a bit of a weight issue, she quietly took me into her study one afternoon and brought up the matter. At first I was upset, but realising she had gone out of her way to be sensitive and discreet, I agreed with her that I would knock any second helpings on the head and none of the other boys would be any the wiser. I really appreciated her kindness and was sorry to see her go when Mrs Sherbrooke finally recovered and returned to work.

In the Main School, Grandma had continued to write to me twice a week as she had done for the past three years. Every Wednesday and Saturday I received a letter from her telling me her news and her mid-week correspondence always contained a small green one-pound note. It was against the school rules for pupils to go into town on Wednesdays – apparently, something to do with it being market day, but it was never quite clarified – but this didn't matter as there was the school tuck shop, which sat at the far end of the grounds overlooking the cricket pitch. It was run by a kind Irishwoman and I'm not sure that any of us actually knew her name as we always referred to her as the 'Tuck Shop Lady'. I always went there with my pound note on a Wednesday afternoon, taking care to make sure that it was quiet – the last thing a fat kid wants is for others to see him buying three bars of chocolate and a can of Coke. She never judged me or made comment as to what I was spending my money on, but she always had a few kind words for me.

I always gravitated towards women for conversation back then and I found that they exuded more warmth and humanity than men. Other than the wonderful Mrs Moore, who was the school chaplain's wife, Tuck Shop Lady was the only other really comforting voice that I heard in those long days away from home. Having bought my small haul of goodies, I took myself off to one of the music rooms up in the attic floor of the school, where I was sure of peace and quiet. It was there that I would sit and eat two of the chocolate bars and wash them down with Coke. The immediate taste would remind me of home, bringing back memories of my last weekend visit and sitting in front of the TV under Grandma's smiling gaze. I always saved the third bar of chocolate to smuggle across to the Prep School for Roger, but after eating my own sweets, I inevitably felt sick. Yet week after week I went through this ritual, in later years replacing the music rooms with my own bedroom cubicle in the dormitories that housed the older boys.

Meanwhile, at her home in Brandon, Grandma had her own ritual. Thursday was pension day, so she would get dressed in her navy two-piece suit and would complete the look with a matching hat, gloves and handbag before setting off on foot down to the shops. She carried a large black leather shopping bag that zipped across the top and steadfastly refused to possess a tartan shopping trolley on wheels, despite the fact that it would have made her life easier. The Post Office would always be her first stop and everyone knew her by name. The postmaster would always enquire as to how Roger and I were getting on at school, as Gran bought her weekly supply of stamps, the stamps for her TV licence and any bits of stationery that she thought we might need for school.

Once she had bought her bread at Greggs, she went into the Co-op for her groceries. While picking up her weekly food shop, she would buy packets of biscuits, such as coconut marshmallow fingers, gypsy creams and Jaffa Cakes. There was always a packet of fig rolls that she insisted on buying every time: 'They'll keep you regular,' she would always say. Grandma was obsessed that we were 'regular' and she took no shame to enquire as to the status of our most recent bowel movements whenever she saw us. Added to this would be a box of Cup-a -Soups, teabags and other goodies to take to Stanhope for our tuck boxes. Once her shopping was done, she got the Number 49 bus back up the hill to the village and on unpacking, she took the items intended for her boys through to the front room, where they would await her next journey to Stanhope. We knew that day by day she was thinking about Roger and I, and in this unplanned chapter of her life, her two boys were her primary concern. She loved Richard and the rest of the family dearly but she always felt that they could fend for themselves. When it came to Roger and myself, she was all too aware of our vulnerability and she saw it as her role to be our guardian and protector.

At Barney, we had one 'Exeat' weekend for each half term although it was never a full weekend. Back then rugby was always the top priority at the school, over and above everything else. The school felt it was more important that our Saturday afternoons on Exeat weekend were spent out on the rugby pitches supporting the school teams rather than being at home with our families. I always looked forward to phoning home on the Thursday night prior to our weekend home, knowing that Grandma would have travelled up to Stanhope that day and would have spent the afternoon cleaning and airing the house ready for our visit. She would get emotional on hearing my voice for the first time in weeks and depending on if I had one or two ten pence pieces for the payphone, we had to talk quickly.

'What kind of cake would you like, bonny lad?' she would ask. 'Three colours or would you prefer a spider cake?'

Grandma knew that her chocolate 'spider cake' was my favourite. She covered one of her homemade chocolate cakes in glazed icing and drizzled rings of a different colour in concentric circles across the top and then, using a skewer, dragged it backwards and forwards across the cake to create a spider web pattern.

Come Sunday afternoon, we were finally released into our family's care at four o'clock and Richard was always waiting in the car to take us away back to Stanhope. I can always recall that feeling of getting into the warm car, his Neil Diamond tape playing and the smell of his Embassy Regal cigarettes. I know it's now not the done thing to smoke in the car with children, but this was the eighties and the smell had a cosy familiarity to it that I rather liked. Thankfully, it was only an eighteen-mile journey home for us and I pitied some of the other lads who travelled as far as Manchester and who were also not allowed to leave the school until four.

The journey home was filled with excitement, with Roger and myself always having a fresh batch of rude jokes to tell Richard. We would never have dared to tell them to Grandma, so for the journey across the moors to Weardale our big brother was our captive and very appreciative audience.

By the time the car pulled up in the yard at Stanhope Hall, Grandma would usually be waiting in the kitchen busying herself, with the tea already on the go. She always gave each of us the biggest of cuddles, each one accompanied by her tears of joy. This is what she was now living for, seeing her boys and spending some precious time with us. Our favourite tea on a Saturday afternoon on Exeat weekends was Findus fish portions, chips and frozen peas served with bread and butter, all washed down with a mug of hot, sweet tea. As a one-off treat for our first meal back home, we were allowed to eat it off trays in the sitting room in front of the TV and a roaring log fire.

The house was gleaming from top to toe and it was clear that Grandma had been working tirelessly over the past two days to get our home ready for us coming back from school. That feeling of being back at home, with the cosiest of food and the love of those we treasured most, this is where I wanted to be.

Until I was almost fourteen, I shared a large bedroom with Roger and Grandma at Stanhope Hall. It had been Mam and Dad's bedroom and we had never moved out after Dad had died. Their double bed was where Grandma and Roger slept and I had an old wooden single bed in the corner of the room. It was an intimate set-up and only served to give Roger and I that added reassurance that was needed in those early years after the loss of our parents. The windowsills of the house were almost two feet deep and on the one in our bedroom would sit two cardboard boxes, each with our names written across the front in Grandma's recognisable hand. Inside each box was an array of goodies that she had bought, all ready for us to take back to school. Orange squash, biscuits, chocolate bars, packets of Trebor soft mints (a favourite of Roger) all crammed in together. Next to each of the boxes was a Quality Street tin with our names taped onto the lids, each one containing a cake that had been lovingly baked and iced by Grandma.

Back downstairs, Grandma had more treats for after we had finished our tea in the form of chocolate, which we would eat together sat watching Saturday night TV. We were allowed to stay up and watch *The Professionals* but anything after that was off-limits and we certainly weren't allowed to watch any of the Hammer Horror films that were often shown on Saturday nights.

The rest of the weekend was spent hanging about on the

farm and we always called in to see Auntie Mary and Uncle Dryden next door or Uncle Harold and Auntie Ethel down on Rose Terrace. The rest of the time, it was just Roger and me as we didn't really have any friends in the village, certainly none our own age. Having been away for several years, I'd lost touch with most of the friends that I'd known at primary school and although it was frustrating at times, Roger and I were fairly content with each other for company.

There's never an adequate enough way to explain how it feels to get in a car and leave your family behind, especially as a small child. I know that if I were to ask some of the boys who went to school with me back then, they too would admit that even as middle-aged men, they still occasionally get that sinking feeling in the pit of their stomachs on a Sunday afternoon. The feeling that doesn't allow you to relax or settle because in the back of your mind you know that you will need to change out of your own clothes and put on your school uniform. The weekend was no barrier to the school uniform – we wore it seven days a week. Richard would arrive at the house sometime after four o'clock and we knew it was time to go upstairs and get changed back into our grey outfits, complete with brown-and-blue striped ties. This time, Grandma had our clothes warming on the large storage heater that sat in the corner of the bedroom. Putting on warm clothes again felt so reassuring and it sweetened the pill a little that it was our school uniforms we were putting on. Grandma was determined to wrap us in love and home comforts until the last minute. If the weather wasn't bad, she would accompany us in the car to school but, on other occasions Richard took us himself.

People have asked me over the last twenty to thirty years how

I felt about going away to school and within a few minutes, I always find myself rambling somewhat incoherently in trying to explain myself. The truth was that even at my happiest times at boarding school, there wasn't one moment when I wouldn't have wished to be back at home in the kitchen on the farm with Grandma.

Back at school I unpacked my tuck box into the wooden locker that sat underneath my desk in the house common room. I was more than happy to share my goodies with my friends, especially the boys whose parents lived abroad and had remained at school over the Exeat weekend. I would usually make my tuck last a week but it didn't take long for me to eat my way through it. Every time that I felt homesick or lonely, I unlocked the padlock and helped myself to a treat, finding comfort in the cold atmosphere of school and using food as my blanket. At the end of the day, school could never compete with the warmth and cosiness of home. Apart from the moments when I saw Roger, there was no love at school. The day boys could go home each night and see their parents and receive that love in person, I received my love through the letters from Grandma and her wonderful homemade cakes. Between this and the affection that we received at home, this is what got me through and thankfully, that love was in abundance.

CHAPTER 35

The Strength of
a Woman

Now that she was on her own, Grandma was determined in the course of the remainder of her life. Her task was to give her two youngest boys the love and comfort that they needed to get them through this chapter and hopefully into adulthood. I say 'hopefully' because she never once took it for granted that she would be there in two months' time, let alone two years. I remember that whenever Roger or myself talked about future plans, such as what we would like to do in the summer holidays, Grandma was always sure to follow our comment up with the assertive line 'all being well'. When talking about herself, she would inevitably add the words 'if God spares me', because by uttering that phrase, she saw it as offering up a prayer in passing. Her faith was central to her being and I know that she loved God and feared him at the same time. I once asked her if she was angry with God and she was astounded by my question.

'Angry with *Him*?' she asked me. 'Why would I be angry?

He's given me you two boys to look after.' To her, it was simple. Despite the fact that she never found herself able to comprehend why her daughter was taken away from her at such a young age, she understood the nature of the job that lay before her.

In 1915, when her father went off to France to fight on the battlefields of the Somme, Margaret Freeman was only five years old, the second youngest of nine children. Her eldest brother Bill had joined the Machine Gun Corps two years later and within several months, Maggie, as she was known to her family, had lost both her father and her brother. By the time that the Armistice was called, on 11 November 1918, almost every family in the country had lost someone on those battlefields.

With the different mix of personalities amongst her siblings, Maggie was content to blend more in the background and was happy to let her elder sister Mary take centre stage. Growing into a young woman, she watched her older siblings get married while she remained at home and helped her mother. She left school at fourteen, which was the norm in 1924, and within a couple of years, she went into service at a stately home in Lancashire. Unable to settle, months later she returned home and resumed working in Durham. She was the last girl in her family to marry and she told me that her big day garnered little support from them. It wasn't that anyone disapproved of her choice of husband but she once told me that she thought some of her siblings were disappointed that if Maggie married and moved out, they would have to lend a hand with their mother. For years, Grandma wouldn't really talk about her wedding day and I never understood why and then one day it came out.

'Your Grandad and I got dressed up and we went into

Durham on the bus, we got married and we came back home on the bus,' she said.

'Was it the Cathedral? Did you get married in Durham Cathedral?' I asked her. She looked at me and tears had formed. I was mortified that I had perhaps upset her.

'No…' she paused, taking a deep breath, 'it was the Registry Office.' To her, this was a huge revelation and only then did I understand how heavily it had weighed on her all those years. She had wanted to be married in the eyes of God, so strong was her faith and yet somehow she felt that she had been short-changed. When they returned to her mother's house after getting married that afternoon, she put the kettle on herself and popped out to the baker's van to buy cakes for everyone, serving them on her mother's best china. Within seven years, they had two daughters and another World War had been declared, with Grandad going off to France within a month of the announcement by Prime Minister Neville Chamberlain.

Fast forward to 1982… Grandma was now well into her seventies, a widow not only grieving the death of her husband but that of her eldest daughter. Sitting alone in her house at Brandon village, she could settle in the tranquility of her little home. She never really liked being at Stanhope Hall any more as the pain of her loss was all around her in everything she saw, like constantly sprinkling salt onto a raw open wound. She wasn't deterred from hard physical work but instead she found herself embracing it as she used it to distract herself from her memories. She worked incredibly hard and never once complained, no matter how tired she became or strenuous she found it. To her, work was an expression of love. Every task she undertook, she did it with love.

Every January, she returned home after spending the Christmas break with her boys at the farm. Unlocking the door on a cold winter afternoon, she put her suitcase down and scooped up the small pile of brown envelopes, junk mail and last-minute Christmas cards that had gathered on the hall carpet in her four-week absence, the cold, stale air of the house meeting the crisp frost outside and little difference in temperature between the two. She was home, this was her place – she wouldn't take her coat off, there was little point. No sooner had she closed the front door behind her than she would make a start on setting the fire in the back room and getting the house warmed up. There was always a danger that the pipes had frozen and the ensuing heat would cause them to burst. She prayed to God, literally, as she set the fire in the hope that He was listening and would ensure the pipes remained intact and her house stayed dry. He wasn't always listening, apparently, for one year she was confronted by sodden carpets that had formed a layer of ice across the top. Such a scene of devastation never deterred her from her faith and she always believed that her God was there for her. Although she always boiled her water in the little charred kettle that sat on the coal fire, she had an electric one that was reserved for rare occasions, allowing her time to get the fire lit. With the fire lit and burning up a treat in the grate, she would finally sit back in Grandad's rocking chair with a cup of tea, still wearing her coat.

Grandma and Grandad had bought the house in 1967 when the colliery closed and the pit houses were vacated ahead of their impending demolition. Brandon village sits on the hill above the town and on a clear day there are clear views not only of the imposing structure of Durham Cathedral but of Penshaw Monument, out towards Sunderland. Her home stood second from the end of a solitary row of six terraced houses, each fronted by a small garden with garden paths that climbed up to the front doors. On the other side of the main road was Mr Harle's farm with its rolling fields of galloping horses and grazing sheep, the skyline topped off with a long row of trees that allowed sunlight to dance through them on warm summer evenings.

Grandma and Grandad had taken great pride in their home and made the best of what they had. Grandad made picture frames out of old pieces of wood and framed the lids of chocolate boxes to create attractive pictures to hang on the walls and on the stairwell hung a framed drawing of 'The Praying Hands' done especially for Grandma by Eleanor Makepeace, a talented cousin on my dad's side of the family. The little back kitchen of the house was known as the scullery and consisted of a series of mismatched freestanding wooden kitchen cupboards which were interspersed with a fridge, an electric cooker, a sink and an old electric washing machine that was topped with a hand-powered mangle. Any spare wall space provided a gallery for the numerous pictures drawn by Roger, myself and our cousin Gaynor. As Grandma didn't really use her front room (that was kept for best), the single coal fire in the back sitting room next to the scullery was the single source of heating for the house. One of the few perks of Grandad having spent years down the pit was that Grandma received free coal for as long as she required it.

Unfazed by carrying buckets of coal from the little coal house on the other side of the back lane, Grandma eventually got her home warmed up and settled back into her Brandon routine. Although she knew all of her neighbours in the little row of houses, they weren't in and out of each other's back doors on a daily basis. I knew them all by name and can still remember some of them all these years later. Mr Graham, Mrs Hutchinson and Mr and Mrs Evans... names that bring memories flooding back, all of them now long gone. She wasn't one for watching the television or listening to the radio, so the crackling of the coal fire and the ticking of clocks provided the background soundtrack to everyday life at 48 Brandon Village. Grandma's days here were now spent in quiet contemplation while she went about her jobs. She would always find herself something to be keeping busy with, be it cleaning, polishing the brasses or writing letters to Roger and myself, but there were several incidents at the house over those few years that broke the peace.

In 1981, one summer evening while filling the metal bucket in the small coal house across the back lane, a gust of wind came across the hill and caught behind the coal house door, causing it to swing swiftly shut and in the process knocking poor Grandma off the steep set of steps and into the lane below. She later told me that she had lay there for about half an hour trying to raise the alarm before Mr Evans, who lived three doors down, had found her. She was taken to hospital and thankfully had only suffered minor cuts and bruising to her face. She wasn't about to let the incident deter her from living independently, and once home she went about her usual business. Auntie Brenda had tried suggesting that she move into one of the more manageable retirement bungalows further into the town, but Grandma was having none of it and the subject was laid to rest.

A couple of years later, one morning Grandma received a knock at the door. A local builder had been doing some work in the area and had noticed that there were some loose slates on the scullery roof at the back of the house. I was never sure how he had managed to see them as the scullery had been part of a single storey section of the house and was hidden from view by the large rear wall at the back of the yard. Grandma, who had no reason to be suspicious, allowed him through with his ladders to take a look at the roof. Once he had clattered about on the roof with a hammer in his hand (God only knows why he needed the hammer), he informed her that the whole thing required replacing and that he could do it at the cost of several thousand pounds. The full amount would be required in cash ahead of commencement of any work done on the property. Having made several trips to the Post Office over the coming days, Grandma withdrew the money, which had amounted to three quarters of her life savings. Satisfied that she had left enough in the account for her funeral one day, she handed over the envelope of cash to the builder when he called. On asking him if he would be starting work that week, he assured her that he would, but today he had to go and finish another job. Ever observant, Grandma noticed that he was wearing beige chinos and a sweater with polished shoes and as he drove away in his big car, she spied a set of golf clubs in the back seat.

Two weeks passed and no sign of the builder. After two days of heavy rain, the scullery roof had started to leak, in several places, something that had never occurred before the builder had been on the roof with his hammer. With several pots and dishes strategically placed around the scullery to catch the water,

Grandma walked up the hill to the payphone to call him for the umpteenth time that week. She was informed on this occasion that he was playing golf, despite the downpour outside.

Another two weeks passed by and aware that the work needed to be completed before she came up to Stanhope for the school holidays, Grandma made one more attempt to contact the man who had taken her money. He promised to come the following day but sadly, never showed up. She decided to take matters into her own hands and dragged Grandad's old wooden ladder out of the garden shed, propped it up in the yard and climbed up onto the scullery roof to assess the damage for herself. A neighbour, not quite believing what he saw, ran around to the yard and coaxed Grandma down from the roof.

Once the situation had become clear to the family and attempts were made – sadly, without success – to track the rogue builder, a replacement tradesman of good reputation was engaged and he fixed the damaged roof for a modest fee. Grandma told me that she wasn't angry with the dishonest builder, but believed that he would get his just desserts one day in the form of divine retribution. I was angry on her behalf – I still am to this day.

Sunday evenings were always reserved for going to chapel. At one time, there had been several Methodist chapels in Brandon, all of them housing healthy weekly congregations, but as the years wore on, attendances fell and the smaller chapels closed. It was decided in the early 1980s that the best way for the Methodist church to survive in Brandon was for all the chapels to merge into one. Rather than one building winning out over the other, all the old chapels were closed and a brand-new one was built in the centre of Brandon.

Grandma loved going to chapel on Sundays although not so much from the social aspect as she wasn't one for polite chit-chat. She told us that she genuinely felt closer to God in the surrounds of the chapel and she loved the inner peace that she gained from attending and taking communion each week. It was one Sunday evening in 1983 when the Minister announced, 'I'm going to keep the sermon very short over the next few weeks as I know you ladies are keen to get home and watch *The Thorn Birds*.' The announcement was met with a mixture of appreciation and knowing looks amongst the female members of the congregation. *The Thorn Birds* was an ever-so-slightly racy drama series set in Australia and involved a priest, played by Richard Chamberlain, and his relationship with a beautiful young woman. It was a pretty scandalous storyline for Sunday night drama back in the early eighties and Grandma found the whole scenario very amusing indeed, never failing to find the story hilarious on the countless retellings in subsequent years.

During the school holidays, Roger and I would always go to stay at Brandon village for a week, especially in summer, and Grandma went to great lengths to keep us both entertained. There were the inevitable trips into Brandon to visit her many relatives and let them all see how the two of us were growing up. Our favourite would always be to visit Auntie Elsie and Uncle Bill. Auntie Elsie was Mam's favourite of her many cousins and she made great efforts to keep in touch with us after Mam and Dad died. Eight years older than Mam, Auntie Elsie was the warmest, kindest lady you could meet and both Roger and I held her in great affection. Her husband, Uncle Bill, was witty and intelligent and he would always take us on the most fascinating walks. He had a boundless energy and could make the most mundane countryside walk into an adventure, telling Roger and me stories every step of the way. He and Auntie Elsie were regular visitors to Stanhope Hall over the years and they made a special effort to keep in touch with us.

With her tall slim figure, blonde hair and quiet, kind nature, Auntie Elsie bore a striking resemblance to Mam and she was the image of her as she walked from the car down the farmyard to Stanhope Hall on her frequent visits. She was now in her nineties, and I still enjoy my rare visits to see her and was overjoyed that she had read and given this book her seal of approval. It was people like Auntie Elsie and Uncle Bill that made a real difference to our lives and gave Grandma that extra support.

It was around the mid-eighties when another January dawned and with Roger and myself once more safely back to school, Grandma prepared to return to Brandon village. Susan, one of Grandma's nieces, also lived in in the village and had been kindly helping out Grandma in recent months. Rather than returning to a cold, empty house after the school holidays, Susan would pop in and set the fire to get the house warmed up and the rooms aired. She bought milk, bread and other things for the scullery so that Grandma wouldn't have to go straight to the shops in the first day or so. On this cold January morning, Susan had gone to the house, as arranged, to open it up only to discover that there had been a break-in.

Burglars, seeing the house in darkness for weeks on end, had broken in and almost emptied the place, leaving little more than the furniture. Poor Grandma wasn't wealthy, she had no real jewellery to speak of, but they still found plenty to help themselves to. Susan went back up to her house to call the police and then called Stanhope, but Grandma had already set off on her journey down to Brandon. When that she arrived, unaware of what had happened, the police were still there and the fingerprint person was packing up their equipment. Grandma broke down at the news and was found on her knees in the front room, sobbing and pointing to the empty mantlepiece.

'My photos, they've taken my photos!' she cried. The empty space on the tiled mantle had once proudly been home to two small brass photo frames, one containing a picture of Grandma Freeman, our grandma's mother, and the other of Grandad's parents. She was devastated: it was the only photo of her mother that she had and now it was gone. The frames wouldn't have been worth anything and stealing the photos was about as callous as you could get. That was until Susan emerged from the scullery.

'They've almost emptied the kitchen cupboards,' she said.

Grandma tentatively went through to see for herself with a police officer following close behind her. Her face confirmed her fears as she stood staring at the empty drawer that once housed her cutlery. They had even stolen the mugs from the cupboard. Poor Grandma, as if she hadn't been through enough already, this had happened. She waited six months to tell Roger and I about it – she hadn't wanted to upset me and distract me during my O level exams.

For Grandma, the burglary was pretty much the final straw and she started to fall out of love with her lovely cosy home. Susan brought her cups and other things for the kitchen, while Auntie Brenda arrived the following day with bags of bits and pieces to put in the house. Grandma was grateful for the kindness, but nothing could fill the gap left by the stolen items of sentimental value, nor eradicate the thought of strangers having been in her home and invading the space that for years had been her sanctuary. She remained in that house for several more years before moving into a small retirement bungalow. In the meantime, life carried on and she counted down the days to when Roger and I would be home from school again and reunited at Stanhope Hall.

CHAPTER 36

Not Suitable for Younger Viewers

The summer of 1984 was memorable. Richard was busy on the farm winding down the business having decided that he no longer wanted to run it. He was exhausted and had had enough. He decided to sell off the livestock and the farming equipment and lease out the land and the farm buildings to continue to bring in an income for the family. Farming on a small scale and changes in farming meant that margins were squeezed and it was no longer profitable to farm on such a small scale. We kept Dad's beloved horse Robin and the two sheep dogs and we continued to live as a family at Stanhope Hall. Change was coming and at some point we knew that we may have to sell the farm but for the time being, these interim measures would keep things ticking over.

Grandma, Roger and I went on holiday to Pontins holiday camp in Blackpool for a week with Auntie Brenda and Gaynor. By now I was fourteen, my voice had broken and I was experimenting with trying to bleach my hair using neat hydrogen peroxide. If John Taylor from Duran Duran looked good with his bleached patch of hair sweeping across his eyes, then so could I. Grandma was not impressed. She was in the car when Richard picked us up for the summer holidays. She mentioned something about me 'spoiling myself' and then she let the matter drop. She wasn't so forgiving when I had my ear pierced the following year. That was a short-lived experiment that resulted in my having to remove it two hours after having had it done.

Roger was eleven and had finally left the Prep School. He'd had a tough time there with Mrs Sherbrooke and it wasn't helped that they had kept him back a year, with him being so young, so the poor lad had to spend four years at the Prep School instead of the usual three. He was so relieved to be out of there and away on holiday with his family. We were dragged up on to the dance floor by the Bluecoats, who were there to entertain us all, and forced to learn a dance routine to Wham!'s 'Wake Me Up Before You Go-Go'. I would have been mortified if anyone from school had seen me but, over thirty years later, I don't care if it's public knowledge.

It was around this time that I was starting to become aware of my sexuality but, with the Sunday papers running front-page stories about a gay plague, I buried my true feelings in the hope that they would never resurface. I couldn't talk to a soul about this, I felt, and to be honest, I couldn't even get my own head around those feelings. I was so scared and I felt even more isolated than I had done in the past.

So, this was the summer of 1984. I'd bleached the front of my hair, as was the fashion, I had the T-shirt with the Chinese letters down the front and I was socially awkward. Two out of three ain't bad! Going to an all-boys school (Barney only had girls in the sixth form at this time) meant that aside from my cousin Gaynor and my friends, Julie and Louise Devitt, I had no experience talking to girls. I didn't know how to strike up a conversation with anyone new, let alone girls. If I wasn't hanging out with Roger or Gaynor, I was spending time with Grandma. I used to help her out with the housework and talk to her about so many different things that I came to learn so much more about her. She loved Wham! and hated Mrs Thatcher. She would get so upset when watching news reports of the Miners' Strike of 1984–5 and would curse both Mrs Thatcher and Arthur Scargill of the National Union of Mineworkers (NUM), as she didn't like him either. Grandma had her opinions too. She would comment whenever she saw a couple walking down the street if the man was far taller than the woman.

'It doesn't look right, him bending right down to give that short girl a kiss. He should have gone for someone his own height. Promise me you won't bring a short girl home,' she said.

She had no need to worry.

It was now more than six years since Mam and Dad had died. Life carried on as normal when we were home for the holidays. We would spend time at Seaburn at Auntie Brenda's and also at Brandon in Grandma's house. After Grandad died, a lady from the village called Mrs Carter befriended Grandma and had begun to visit her when Roger and I were away at school. Mrs Carter always addressed Grandma as 'Maggie' whereas Grandma continued to call her friend 'Mrs Carter'.

They were a funny pair. Grandma used to complain that Mrs Carter would come to visit and outstay her welcome.

'I mean, she sat there until long after *Coronation Street* and in the end, I had to ask her to leave. She doesn't use her own electric, you know.'

Mrs Carter would always call in when she knew that we were staying with Grandma. She would insist on giving us a kiss each as we winced. Roger would remark, 'She's got more stubble than George Michael,' and Grandma would throw him a look. One Saturday afternoon, we were watching *CHiPs*, a family-friendly show about two motorbike cops in California. It was during this particular episode that we were watching with Mrs Carter that a character went into labour in the back of a car. As the grunting and heavy breathing started, Grandma and Mrs Carter jumped up from their seats and sent Roger and I into the next room.

'This isn't suitable for two young boys to be watching,' Grandma said. They could have turned the channel over to BBC1 but Mrs Carter said that she didn't want to miss the story as she'd been watching it. Poor Grandma! I hadn't the heart to tell her that we had had sex education at school at the age of eleven and that, with the help of a solitary two-dimensional diagram in a textbook, I knew all there was to know about the birds and the bees.

The incident with the television reminds me of another scenario. At Christmas that year, Auntie Brenda gave me some money to buy myself a handful of paperbacks as a present from her and my uncle. Amongst the books that I had chosen were the novels from the first two *Omen* films. I'd never been allowed to watch the films and although I was interested in reading the books, I thought that they would bring me some much-needed kudos when I returned to school with them. But it wasn't to be. On Boxing Day, Sister Di Pazzi called round to see us, as she did every Christmas. At one point in the afternoon I was showing our favourite nun my Christmas gifts while Grandma was in the kitchen preparing turkey sandwiches. Sister's enthusiastic expression changed suddenly when she saw the two *Omen* books. She picked them up and scanned the blurb written on the back of them.

'Philip, who bought you these?'

'I did, Sister, with money that Auntie Brenda gave me,' I replied.

'Does your grandma know you have these?'

I hung my head in admission that I had purposely concealed the books from my grandmother, who at that moment entered the room. Sister showed the two books to Grandma and, in a nutshell, explained the subject matter.

Grandma went ballistic. 'What have you done? Why have you brought these things into the house?' she screeched. 'Haven't we had enough bad luck with losing your mam and dad?' she continued.

Suddenly the big light was switched on. Grandma spoke to Sister in the kitchen before going upstairs. She returned with a bottle of holy water in the shape of the Virgin Mary in her hand. As she clutched it, she called Roger and I over to stand in front of the fireplace. She removed the metal fire guard and told us to hold hands in a circle. Sister Di Pazzi was clutching the two offending books in one hand and her rosary beads in the other as she started reciting the 'Hail Mary'. She instructed my grandmother to remove the top of the bottle of holy water. My eyes were fixed as she slowly twisted the neck of the bottle and removed the head, which formed the cap. Holy water was now liberally splashed over the books and then over Roger and I. It was then splashed over the carpet and the fireplace before the books got another dose. Sister was now reciting some prayer, asking evil to be banished from this house and she promptly threw the books onto the fire. As the books burned, Grandma was sobbing, her hands shaking, as she tried to put the Virgin's head back on the bottle. Meanwhile Roger and I were just standing there, looking at each other, thinking, *What the fuck just happened?* I know that it was an overreaction, but it shows just how afraid she was.

Due to a fluctuation in the school calendar, Roger and I didn't go back to school until the middle of September that year, which meant that I got to go to Stanhope Show for the first time since Mam and Dad had died. The Devitts came up for the long weekend and we had a barbeque up on the caravan site. Because the showpeople had been staying on one of our fields, they kindly gave Richard a bundle of free tickets for us to use on the dodgems and the waltzer. Roger, myself and Louise Devitt had such a laugh that weekend at the show but it wouldn't be long before school beckoned.

On the last evening of the holidays, Roger and I persuaded Grandma to go for a walk down Stanhope Dene after tea as the sun was still shining and the air was still. We walked down the grassy path that led down from the front of Stanhope Hall and meandered along the track towards the old mill. Auntie Mary, our next-door neighbour, appeared, having fed her cats, and greeted us all, delighted to see us happy and smiling as we headed out for our summer evening walk. As we followed the well-worn path through the Dene, the last of the evening sun shone through the trees as the river flowed in the shadows alongside us. Taking the steady incline up into the woods, we came across the bluebells.

'This is where we used to come with Mammy,' Roger said, evoking a rare memory and sharing it with us. We picked handfuls of wild flowers in the wood – a practice that was perfectly acceptable back then – and held them as we each took one of Grandma's careworn hands and led her along the path. Holding her hand, my thumb rubbed across her wedding ring. Looking down at us both, she smiled with a tear in her eye.

'This is where I want to be, just walking here, with my two lads,' she said and as I looked up at her and smiled, for the first time in years I had the feeling that all would be well. I was content; we all were.

CHAPTER 37

A Fresh Start

1986

Another two years rolled by, in which there had been some major changes at Stanhope Hall. Richard was no longer farming, we had sold the livestock and were now leasing out the land to generate a modest income for the family until a decision could be made about what to do with the farm in the long term. My older brother was keen to move on with his life and start a new chapter, as were the rest of us. I definitely knew that I didn't want to be a farmer and I wanted to leave Stanhope Hall. At this point in my life, the happy memories were overshadowed by the unhappy ones and the house had long ceased to be a place where I felt comfortable. I was still haunted by the bad dreams, which hadn't really eased off in the last eight years, and I was keen to leave them behind me. I was also aware that at seventy-eight years old, Grandma found managing the house to be more of a challenge and we needed to move to a smaller and more manageable place. Roger didn't seem to be too bothered either way and was happy to go with the flow. He loved living on the farm, but even he admitted that it didn't feel the same now that our animals were reduced to one horse and four dogs. It was time to move on and sell the farm, along with Stanhope Hall itself.

Having discussed the matter in great detail for a number of months, we jointly came to a decision. Mr Vickers the auctioneer was instructed and on 28 May 1986, Stanhope Hall Farm was sold at auction. It wasn't an easy decision to make, but in life such major decisions never are. We all needed to move on. The auction was held at a local hotel and afterwards Grandma returned to an empty house, Roger and I having gone back to school that afternoon. It was years later, shortly before her death, that Grandma told me something about that night.

'After Richard brought me back, I filled myself a hot water bottle to take to bed and as I went to switch off the kitchen light, I looked in the mirror on the hall stand and could see into the passage leading up to the back door. Standing at the bottom of the stairs was your Dad, wearing his coat and cap. He looked at me and removed his wellies and then looked back up, with a sadness in his eyes,' she said.

'What did you say?' I enquired.

'Oh, I just said, "That's me off to bed now, Harry, it's been a long day," and I turned to switch the kitchen light off and when I looked back into the passage, it was empty,' she said.

That summer was a turning point for us all. With my O level exams over, I looked forward to going back to school as a sixth former, Richard embarked on a new chapter in his life and we looked for a new home to start over again. Finding a new place to live proved tricky once we had made a start. Grandma thought that we would be better off moving to Seaburn to be closer to Auntie Brenda and for a short time, I reluctantly went along with the idea. Roger had friends in Seaburn and that sold the idea to him. I seemed to be the only one thinking practically: how would we get to and from Barney? I still had two more years to go and Roger another five. Richard couldn't be expected to travel from Stanhope to Barney, on to Sunderland and then back to Stanhope in one day. The 130-mile trip was too much and I wouldn't expect that of Richard, especially when we were travelling home for a short weekend stay. So I stuck my neck out and refused point blank to move to Seaburn, which didn't make Grandma very happy. When I explained my reasons, she understood. For the time being we needed to remain in Stanhope.

We eventually settled on a small terraced house in the centre of the village and we packed up our stuff at Stanhope Hall. Downsizing meant that we needed to sell most of our furniture and we used the cash to kit out the new house. I think that I was more excited to be moving to a house with central heating than anything else.

On the day that we left Stanhope Hall, we couldn't have been more aware that it was the end of an era. Several generations of the Mews family had lived there and that was all going to end that day. I went next door to see Uncle Dryden, who, at seventy-three, was now unable to speak after a recent stroke. But he knew why we were there and he was well aware of what day it was. He held my hand so tightly as he sobbed. He'd lived there all his life and lived next door to the Mews family all his life too. As I sat there with him, I could sense that he had never wanted to see this day come and had things turned out differently, he would have departed this world with the Mews family still in place at Stanhope Hall.

Uncle Harold came up to see us as the removal men loaded up the truck. Auntie Olive came for one last walk around the house – the house where her father, sister and brother had all been born. The house where she herself had been born. The house that had seen so much happiness and laughter, sadness and tears, but as Auntie Olive came to us as we packed the last few items away, she said to me, 'It doesn't do to dwell on the past, Philip. Don't go back, just forward, and you live your life.'

And that's exactly what we did.

Epilogue

2018

Many years have passed since the events depicted in this book. Our loving grandma passed away in June 1997 at the grand old age of eighty-seven, with myself, Roger, Richard and Auntie Brenda all by her bedside. As she took her last breath, she opened her eyes, smiled and said, 'Ah, my Alma,' before going to sleep forever. She died knowing that she had completed her task: she had brought up her lads.

Following the sale of the farm, Richard started up a successful plastics company, where he met his wife, Jackie. He has since sold it and now runs a successful property business, in Stanhope, where he and Jackie live with their teenage daughter Rachel. He has recently retired from serving on the parish council after thirty-four years, although he's still an active member of the Stanhope Show Committee. His main role in life now is being a devoted father.

Auntie Brenda, despite now being widowed for fifteen years,

has travelled the world and continues to have adventures, such as recently crossing the Arctic Circle at the age of seventy-eight. Her love and energy are as boundless now as they were some forty years ago. Her hair and her winning smile have not changed either. Her daughter Gaynor, like her mother, embraces life every day and although she still spends time in Sunderland, she, like me, fell in love with a Scotsman and with the beautiful city of Glasgow.

I left Stanhope in the early nineties to go to college and then on to university in Newcastle, where I studied for a performing arts degree. It was around this time that I nervously came out to my family. They could not have been more supportive. After spending time in Australia, India and Israel, I moved to Hong Kong. In 1997, following Grandma's death, I moved to London and began working in television production. It was here, in 2001, that I met my husband, Martin. We had to wait several years for the law to catch up and we were married in Scotland in 2007 with my family there. Auntie Brenda took Mam's place at top table and Roger was my best man. It was the happiest day of my life, so far. Glasgow is now home, where Martin and I live with a sock-stealing Jack Russell called Archie. I still return to Stanhope every year to see those I love and try not to dwell on the past. Only rarely do I go to cemeteries, as I've discovered that it's more fun visiting the living than the dead.

Roger spent his happiest adult years in Mallorca. He could often be found looking out to the Mediterranean from Mambos beach bar with a microphone in his hand and entertaining thousands of people every summer. In 2016, he fulfilled one of his lifetime ambitions as he graced the airwaves of Radio One Mallorca with his own show, which achieved fantastic audiences both in Mallorca and in the UK. Sadly, his dream was short-lived. On 5 November 2016, we received the devastating news that our little brother had passed away, suddenly, from a brain haemorrhage. He was only forty-four years old. A week later, myself, Richard, Auntie Brenda, Gaynor and the rest of our family arrived in Mallorca and gathered together to say goodbye to our bonny lad.

On the day of Roger's funeral, a community came together, family and friends, to say farewell to our brother, nephew, cousin and friend. Roger brought so much love and joy into our lives and add that to a soundtrack of music and laughter and we are left with countless unforgettable memories that make us laugh and cry. Roger may have once been an orphan boy, but he lived his life with a loving family around him. Mallorca was his home and he was at his happiest there, so his ashes were scattered at his favourite place, where he watched the sun setting over the Mediterranean. The remainder of his ashes were brought home to Weardale and laid to rest amongst the bluebells in the Dene, with Stanhope Hall watching over in the distance.

Acknowledgements

This book has been quite a journey and many people have helped me along the way. Paul and Vivienne Adams, Stephen Bennett, Anna Clayton, Sharon Fullarton, Mark Gaze, Ashlyn Gibson, Mavis Gulliver, Victoria Heales, Bill Holden, Pam and Lucy Pearson for your unwavering support and honesty.

Barnard Castle School and The Old Banardians Society. School days are never plain sailing, but I still think of my time at Barney with the utmost affection. The school has grown and changed over the years and I wish it every success in educating brilliant people of the future.

The Masonic Trust for Girls and Boys and the Brethren of the Stanhope Masonic Lodge. You gave Roger and I one of the greatest gifts of all: education. Thank you from the bottom of my heart for your generosity and for enabling our family to stay together. To Alan Farrar, thank you for guiding me during those Barney years, I have never forgotten your kindness.

Ann Cayton. You have been the greatest of friends. Thank you for understanding me when nobody else did.

The Devitt family. Thank you for the memories and the laughter. RIP Jimmy and Theresa x

The Wolsingham Pearts – you were always there for us and have proved that true friendships last more than one lifetime. RIP Ivan and Sheila x

Sandi Toksvig. Thank you for your guidance and friendship.

Trisha Ashley. You write beautiful stories and you inspire me. Thank you for your kindness and for introducing me to the best agent I could have asked for.

Rebecca Winfield, my agent and everyone at David Luxton Associates. You are wonderful and patient. Thank you for believing in me and in the Orphan Boys.

James Hodgkinson and Jane Donovan, my editors, and all the wonderful people at John Blake Books and Bonnier. Thank you for your nurturing and allowing me to tell my story with my own voice.

The people of Magaluf. Thank you for your love, friendship and support in our family's darkest hour. You were Roger's family and now you're mine. All of you x

To Jackie Mews, Auntie Olive and the Peart Family, Aunt Elsie, Pat and Pauline, Dom and Moira, Ewan and Rhona… The Carrigans. You have all been brilliant and didn't doubt me when I said I wanted to tell my story. To Tony, the curator of our memories, you are wonderful. The best family I could ask for. Thank you x

To the younger people in my life. Rachel, Emma, Alistair, Michael, Simon, Clementine, Søren, Esme and Freddie. I may not see you often, but I'm always in the audience cheering you on to dream big and reach for the stars. Be brave and be bold x

Gaynor. You have been a sister more than a cousin. Thank you for being there, for understanding me and above all, for letting me play with your *Charlie's Angels* dolls. Love you x

Auntie Brenda. We would never have managed without my Auntie Brenda, who carried pyjamas, Easter eggs and a goldfish on her weekly bus treks to Stanhope. Words cannot express how grateful I am to you. I love you so dearly. Thank you. For everything x

Richard. Only now do I begin to truly begin to understand the weight that you carried on your shoulders. Big brothers don't come any better than you. Now we must carry on and live our dreams not only for ourselves, but for Roger. Love you, always x

Roger. You took more steps alongside me on this journey than anyone else and you are the only other person who truly experienced much of what happened in this book. We turned out alright in the end, didn't we? Love you and miss you always my bonny lad x

Martin. What would I do without you? You walked into my life and helped turn the nightmares into sweet dreams. I count myself so lucky that you chose to spend your life with this numpty. Love you x

There are many people, both living and dead, who helped our family during our darkest time. I would like to thank each and every one of you from the bottom of my heart for your love, kindness, friendship and support. You know who you are.

Finally, thank you to the good people of Weardale. Despite my having moved away more than twenty-five years ago, you have shown myself and our family the most tremendous warmth and support. You have something really special there in the Dale and I know you will continue to treasure it. Weardale will always have a special place in my heart. It's true what Dorothy said, 'There's no place like home.'

With love,
Philip

Author Note

Stanhope Hall was my home and meant so much to me and my family. It's wonderful to see Diane Carter, the new custodian of the Hall, breathing so much life and warmth into the place. If you ever wish to visit my childhood home, you can book rooms or a meal at the Stanhope Old Hall website and experience the charm of this truly beautiful old house for yourselves.

www.stanhopeoldhall.co.uk

If you would like to see photos from our lives, please go to the Phil Mews – Author page on Facebook. If you have enjoyed reading this book, please take the time to leave a review on Amazon and help to share the story of the Orphan Boys. Thank you.

Phil